A.S. Byatt's Art of Memory

LITERARY AND CULTURAL STUDIES, THEORY AND THE (NEW) MEDIA

Edited by Monika Fludernik and Sieglinde Lemke

VOLUME 5

Mara Cambiaghi

A.S. Byatt's Art of Memory

PETER LANG

Bibliographic Information published by the Deutsche Nationalbibliothek
The Deutsche Nationalbibliothek lists this publication in the Deutsche Nationalbibliografie; detailed bibliographic data is available in the internet at http://dnb.d-nb.de.

Library of Congress Cataloging-in-Publication Data
A CIP catalog record for this book has been applied for at the Library of Congress.

Zugl.: Freiburg, Univ, Diss., 2018

Cover illustration:
Stefania Cecco: 'Helikoeidḗs' (2019)
Courtesy of the artist

Printed by CPI books GmbH, Leck

D 25
ISSN 2191-3293
ISBN 978-3-631-81422-2 (Print)
E-ISBN 978-3-631-82102-2 (E-PDF)
E-ISBN 978-3-631-82103-9 (EPUB)
E-ISBN 978-3-631-82104-6 (MOBI)
DOI 10.3726/b16916

Peter Lang – Berlin · Bern · Bruxelles · New York ·Oxford · Warszawa · Wien

This publication has been peer reviewed.

www.peterlang.com

Acknowledgements

Foremost, I should like to thank Professor Dr. Monika Fludernik for her help with this project. I wish to thank her for her ongoing support, critical readings and careful guidance in bringing this work to completion.

My thanks also goes to PD. Dr. Dorothee Birke for providing further assistance while concluding this dissertation and for her willingness to act as a co-examiner.

This work was supported by the Italian Ministry of Education and the Regional School Office of Lombardy, which I gratefully acknowledge.

I am especially grateful to Dame A.S. Byatt for her generous permission to quote from her works as listed on the following page and in the bibliography. I would like to thank her for her gracious encouragement and generosity with all scholarly queries over the years.

My gratitude extends to Prof. Dr. Greta Olson whose friendship, kindness and generosity have continued to be a source of encouragement and support.

This book is a revised version of my PhD thesis, submitted to the University of Freiburg in 2015. It is the fruit of a long time involvement with the work of A.S. Byatt, which somehow has kept me entwined with all things English since I was a student and employee at Birkbeck College and University College London and an Italian language assistant at Royal Holloway New College. Many people provided guidance, hospitality and encouragement at that time, and I owe them gratitude, especially Professor Martin Swales, Dr. Joyce Crick, Professors Anna Laura and Giulio C. Lepschy, Dr. Prue Shaw and the late Professor Giovanni Aquilecchia. It is impossible to thank them all but UCL provided an intellectual home for many years.

My scholarly interests developed further in Italy and Germany, and I would like to thank all those who have been supportive and shared their ideas on literature and scholarship. My husband Eggert Blum has offered precious help with bibliographical research for the illustrations in this book. I thank him for his patience and unfailing trust in this project. My niece Stefania Cecco has contributed the exquisite drawing on the book cover and I am especially grateful to her.

For his patience and editorial advice, I am also grateful to Michael Rücker who commissioned this book and guided it with exemplary skills into print.

Finally I would like to dedicate this book to my family and friends.

COPYRIGHT ACKNOWLEDGEMENTS

The author and publisher gratefully acknowledge the following for permission to reproduce copyright material, as listed below:

Excerpt(s) from THE VIRGIN IN THE GARDEN: A NOVEL by A. S. Byatt, copyright © 1978 by A. S. Byatt. Used by permission of Random House, an imprint and division of Penguin Random House LLC and Chatto and Windus and Vintage, imprints of The Random House Group Limited. All rights reserved.

Excerpt(s) from STILL LIFE by A.S. Byatt, copyright © 1985. Used by permission of Chatto and Windus and Vintage, imprints of The Random House Group Limited. All rights reserved. Reprinted with the permission of Scribner, a division of Simon & Schuster, Inc. All rights reserved.

Excerpt(s) from POSSESSION: A ROMANCE by A.S. Byatt, copyright © 1991 by A.S. Byatt. Used by permission of Random House, an imprint and division of Penguin Random House LLC and Chatto and Windus and Vintage, imprints of The Random House Group Limited. All rights reserved.

Excerpt(s) from PASSIONS OF THE MIND by A. S. Byatt, copyright © 1991 by A. S. Byatt. Used by permission of Random House, an imprint and division of Penguin Random House LLC and Chatto and Windus and Vintage, imprints of The Random House Group Limited. All rights reserved.

Excerpt(s) from BABEL TOWER by A. S. Byatt, copyright © 1996 by A. S. Byatt. Used by permission of Random House, an imprint and division of Penguin Random House LLC and Chatto and Windus and Vintage, imprints of The Random House Group Limited. All rights reserved.

Excerpt(s) from A WHISTLING WOMAN by A. S. Byatt, copyright © 2002 by A. S. Byatt. Used by permission of Alfred A. Knopf, an imprint of the Knopf Doubleday Publishing Group, a division of Penguin Random House LLC and Chatto and Windus and Vintage, imprints of The Random House Group Limited. All rights reserved.

Excerpt(s) from THE SHADOW OF THE SUN by A.S. Byatt, copyright © 1991. Used by permission of Chatto and Windus and Vintage, imprints of The Random House Group Limited. All rights reserved.

Excerpts from 'Memory and the Making of Fiction' by A.S. Byatt. *Memory* (Darwin College Lectures), edited by Patricia Fara and Karalyn Patterson, published by Cambridge University Press, Copyright © 1998 by Darwin

College. Darwin College Lectures. Reproduced with the permission of Cambridge University Press through PLSclear.

The author and publisher are especially grateful to Dame A.S. Byatt for permission to quote from the following copyright material in print and e-book editions of this work:

The Agreed Upon 1034 Words from *The Virgin in the Garden* by Dame A.S. Byatt. Published by Chatto & Windus, 1978. Copyright © Dame A.S. Byatt. Reproduced by permission of the author c/o Rogers, Coleridge & White Ltd., 20 Powis Mews, London W11 1JN.

The Agreed Upon 1293 Words from *Still Life* by Dame A.S. Byatt. Published by Chatto & Windus, 1985. Copyright © Dame A.S. Byatt. Reproduced by permission of the author c/o Rogers, Coleridge & White Ltd., 20 Powis Mews, London W11 1JN.

The Agreed Upon 994 Words from *Babel Tower* by Dame A.S. Byatt. Published by Chatto & Windus, 1996. Copyright © Dame A.S. Byatt. Reproduced by permission of the author c/o Rogers, Coleridge & White Ltd., 20 Powis Mews, London W11 1JN.

The Agreed Upon 641 Words from *A Whistling Woman* by Dame A.S. Byatt. Published by Chatto & Windus, 2002. Copyright © Dame A.S. Byatt. Reproduced by permission of the author c/o Rogers, Coleridge & White Ltd., 20 Powis Mews, London W11 1JN.

The Agreed Upon 2011 Words from *Possession* by Dame A.S. Byatt. Published by Chatto & Windus, 1991. Copyright © Dame A.S. Byatt. Reproduced by permission of the author c/o Rogers, Coleridge & White Ltd., 20 Powis Mews, London W11 1JN.

The Agreed Upon 12 Words from *The Shadow of the Sun* by Dame A.S. Byatt. Published by Chatto & Windus, 1991. Copyright © Dame A.S. Byatt. Reproduced by permission of the author c/o Rogers, Coleridge & White Ltd., 20 Powis Mews, London W11 1JN.

The Agreed Upon 241 Words from *Passions of the Mind* by Dame A.S. Byatt. Published by Chatto & Windus, 1991. Copyright © Dame A.S. Byatt. Reproduced by permission of the author c/o Rogers, Coleridge & White Ltd., 20 Powis Mews, London W11 1JN.

The Agreed Upon 24 Words from *Wordsworth and Coleridge in Their Time* by Dame A.S. Byatt. Published by Nelson, 1970. Copyright © Dame A.S. Byatt. Reproduced by permission of the author c/o Rogers, Coleridge & White Ltd., 20 Powis Mews, London W11 1JN.

The author also wishes to thank the following publishers for permission to reproduce in a revised form portions of earlier contributions, as listed below:

An earlier version of parts of chapter 3 was published under the title 'The Power of Fiction in A.S. Byatt's *Babel Tower*' in *Symbolism: an International Journal of Critical Aesthethics* 3 (2003). Used by permission of De Gruyter Berlin/AMS Press New York.

Earlier versions, entirely re-written, revised and updated, of the introduction and of chapter 1 were published under the title 'Unraveling the Past: A.S. Byatt's Theaters of Memory and the Spell of Recall' in *Inventing the Past. Memory Work in Culture and History.* Edited by Otto Heim and Caroline Wiedmer. Copyright © 2005 Schwabe. Reproduced by permission of Schwabe AG Basel.

An earlier version of chapter 4, revised and updated, appeared under the title 'The Gendered Memories of Frederica Potter: A.S. Byatt's *A Whistling Woman*' in *Erinnern und Geschlecht: Freiburger FrauenStudien. Zeitschrift für Interdisziplinäre Frauenforschung* 19.

For permission to reproduce the drawing *Helikoeidḗs* (2019) which was especially designed for the cover of this book the author and publisher wish to thank Stefania Cecco.

Every reasonable effort has been made to trace or contact copyright holders and to acknowledge copyright sources accurately. The author and publishers would be pleased to rectify any errors or omissions brought to their notice at the earliest opportunity in subsequent editions of this book.

Contents

Introduction

The primary purpose of my study is to offer a comprehensive reading of the major novels of A.S. Byatt. Byatt is a prolific and acclaimed writer whose creative activity has evolved over a long time, encompassing a wide spectrum of interests and styles and reflecting in her work several social and generational changes that occurred from the early 1950s to the 1990s and beyond. The present book aims at building on the existing analyses of Byatt's major novels, retaining some of the critical terms which constitute a useful set of tools in investigating her texts: cultural memory, gender, visual culture, intermediality, intertextuality, mimesis and metafiction. The all-inclusive, encyclopaedic nature of Byatt's writing is in fact ideally suited to a combination of these approaches which can fruitfully interact with each other. However, because of the ever-shifting emphasis in her fiction on different forms of knowledge, which surface in the plot of her novels, one may subsume these primary terms into a larger framework. My own contribution to the study of Byatt's *œuvre*, therefore, will lie in connecting previous approaches to produce a more encompassing account of Byatt's work and in adding, where possible, the perspective of blending theory as a potentially fruitful area of enquiry. This proceeding reflects my own cross-cultural path with its exposure to Italian, British and German theoretical frameworks.

To many critics Byatt has seemed a curiously traditional writer. The fluid sense of identity characterizing contemporary culture and the literary production of postcolonial writers used to be pitted against the outlook of this quintessentially English author, whose scope appeared initially to be anchored solely within the tradition of English realism and Victorian culture. An overall glance at her entire *œuvre* to date indicates, however, the full range of her creative output and the extent of her commitment as an artist and literary critic. Through her characteristic self-reflexive mode, Byatt has continued to investigate and subvert this very tradition, engaging with different schools of thought and intellectual trends. Grappling with literary theory, science and the visual arts, the fairy tale, the fantastic, myth and ancient sagas, she has opened up the space of the novel to infinite possibilities of transmutation in the intersections of past and present.

Her creative writing has also been underpinned by an impressive critical output throughout the years, so much so that her work as a literary critic, commentator and art journalist has further broadened her role as a public intellectual in the media and in open debates. Moreover, her collection of essays *On Histories and Stories* (2000) demonstrate her interest in maintaining a dialogue with European writers, in an attempt to counter the once widespread view that English culture all too easily neglects authors not writing in English.[1] In the past three decades, A.S. Byatt has increasingly become a public figure and one closely linked to academia. For a considerable length of time, she lived the life of a London university lecturer, first as a full-time lecturer in English literature at the Central School of Art and Design, then as an extra-mural lecturer at the University of London and, finally, as a senior lecturer at University College London, a position she left in 1983 in order to devote herself to full-time writing.

Byatt's imaginative world is partly rooted in a specific cultural and geographical location, often evoked in her work through echoes of and allusions to her early years of childhood, which were spent in Southern Yorkshire. Born in 1936 in Sheffield, she attended the Mount, a Quaker school in York, before reading English at Newnham College, Cambridge. Although in those years F.R. Leavis's influence on literary studies and the English novel was dominant, Byatt put on record that at Cambridge she tried to resist his powerful influence and moralizing criticism by concentrating almost exclusively on the study of poetry (cf. Byatt 1993: 72). As a result, her fiction often invokes lyric parameters and absorbs *topoi* current in poetry with her narrative concerns. Language and landscape may emerge as focal points in her novels, offering us a glimpse of the apparently idyllic scenery that much contemporary criticism has taught us to read as the product of nostalgia or as a symbol of national retrenchment in the aftermath of the loss of empire. Yet, it is often the legacy of D.H. Lawrence that shimmers through these intermittent lyrical scenes, and on the subject of her ambivalent attachment to D. H. Lawrence and the Northern provinces, Byatt has this to say:

> I understand so deeply his feelings, both coming from the industrial North of England and nevertheless having both grown up in those pockets of it which were still countryside, which gives you the English feeling. This is where I come from. I write a lot romantically about the far North of Yorkshire, but it isn't my country. But the people in Lawrence, I mean my family and Lawrence's mother, they would have known each other and understood each other. They were the same people.
>
> (Byatt. Personal interview 4 November 1997).

This remark is significant in tracing one strand in the legacy of the author's literary ancestry; yet, as we shall see, Byatt will take issue with other aspects of Lawrence's fiction and, most especially, with the celebrated myth of the perfect

1 Cf. in particular ch. 5 titled 'Old Tales, New Forms' in the collection, in which Byatt relates her response to European literature when presiding over the first presentation of the European Literature prize in 1990.

unity between lovers. In *Babel Tower*, for example, this myth will become the terrain for a polemical attack on a once powerful literary tradition validated by a society which, in the early sixties, was about to change beyond recognition. Significantly, the legacy of F.R. Leavis and his role among the expert witnesses in the notorious trial against Lawrence's *Lady Chatterley's Lover* looms behind the parodic portrayal of this eventful literary and legal case in Byatt's novel.

In general surveys of post-war English literature, Byatt's fiction has frequently been discussed in connection with the historical novel and the postmodern turn, largely focusing on *Possession* as a pivotal example of a late twentieth-century trend (Waugh 1995: 182, 185; Connor 1996: 147–151; Murphet 2004: 722; Keen 2006: 171, 176; Childs 2007: 212–213; Waugh 2007: 80; Wells 2007: 538–549; de Groot 2010: 100, 116). A sense of nostalgia may be endemic to revisiting the cultural past and is, therefore, part and parcel of the above critical surveys. Lynn Wells, for example, acknowledges *Possession* as the 'quintessential contemporary novel' tinged by a 'deep nostalgia for the vibrant world of Ash and LaMotte' (ibid.: 538), while Anne Humpherys addresses this very aspect when discussing the author's use of intertextuality in her contribution to *A Companion to the Victorian Novel* (2007).

At a time when Byatt's published fiction only included her early novels, the *New Pelican Guide to English Literature*, edited by Boris Ford in 1983 and reprinted in 1990, classified the author among a group of women novelists, including Doris Lessing, Penelope Mortimer, Brigid Brophy and Edna O'Brien, who 'have dealt with various aspects of the modern woman's dilemma with insight, honesty, and an unsentimental realism' (Phelps 1990: 441). Representing a substantial strand in Byatt's range of themes, the problematic of the woman writer was taken up again by Patricia Waugh in her survey of feminist fiction in *A Concise Companion to Contemporary British Fiction*, edited by James F. English (2006).

Possession (1990) shifted the debate into a new focus and in his account of *The English Novel* (1996), Steven Connor highlighted its central place in the transition from *historical* to *historicized fiction*, i.e. from 'fiction about history' to 'fiction about its own historically relative construction of history' (143). As we know, dramatising the tension between historical events and their representation, i.e. between the alleged authority the past may assume and the more self-conscious and problematized rendering of it, is part of a general movement characterizing the post-war novel, which Linda Hutcheon has famously labelled *historiographic metafiction*.

In her volume on historical fiction, Mariadele Boccardi continued to muse on the general shift towards self-questioning forms of national narratives and the ensuing retrenchment into 'the literary myth of the garden of England' (Boccardi

2009: 171). A number of contemporary novels, including *Possession*, are seen by her as romanticising the loss of the past, while articulating a desire for national narratives, generally labelled as 'Fictions of the Garden' (169). In this context, Byatt's novel has not escaped Boccardi's criticism that such a mode of national self-imagining 'is dependent on existing ideological and economic conditions' (ibid.: 87). The argument is not new. Indeed, it resonates with general views expressed by Terry Eagleton in his Postscript to *The English Novel* (2005) where he claimed for 'the novel of liberal humanism', a governing influence stemming from 'the official ethical and political doctrine of literary London' (337).

In what follows, I shall first provide a brief summary of Byatt's critical reception through the monographs currently available, discuss a series of theoretical approaches that have been significant in the analysis of her work, as well as introducing and adopting my own theoretical viewpoint (Section i). The following sections will sketch out an overview of the key critical terms informing the present study: Section ii will deal with cultural memory, Section iii with visual culture, Section iv with intertextuality and Section v with blending theory. Finally, Section vi will provide a general outline of the chapters structuring the present study.

i. Critical Responses

While A.S. Byatt's creative output has stimulated an overwhelming amount of research and critical articles, only few full-length studies have attempted a comprehensive analysis of her major novels. For a long time, research has tended to focus either on specific aspects of her short stories, such as the intersection between visual and literary culture or the use of fairy tales, a theme also recurring in her longer fiction, or else to direct its attention onto the acclaimed novel *Possession*, which firmly established the author's reputation at home and abroad on being awarded the prestigious Booker Prize in 1990.

Among the full-length studies which have appeared thus far, the volume by Jane Campbell, *A.S. Byatt and the Heliotropic Imagination* (2004), offers a perceptive reading of each of the author's works up to *A Whistling Woman* (2002), including in its framework the four collections of short stories published till then. This study highlights the novelist's evolving views on the woman question as portrayed in her fiction and builds on previous feminist studies, i.e. the volume by Christien Franken, *A.S. Byatt: Art, Authorship, Creativity* (2001), as well as an earlier contribution in article form by Beate Neumeier on the same issue. A contemporary study by Celia Wallhead addresses the specific use of metaphor as a structuring narrative pattern in Byatt's fiction, aptly drawing on George Lakoff and Mark Johnson's theories on metaphor to highlight the recurring themes that make up the complex fabric of her novels (*The Old, the New and the Metaphor* 1999). Paving the way towards more comprehensive accounts of Byatt's *œuvre*, Kathleen Coyne Kelly's first monographic study of Byatt's work, titled *A.S. Byatt* and published in the Twayne's English Authors series (1996), provides an initial advance. This study discusses the realist and postmodern conventions embedded in both early and later fiction, surveyed in chronological order. It was soon followed by Richard Todd's short monograph *A.S. Byatt* in the series Writers and their Work (1997). Todd fruitfully examines Byatt's novels and novellas thematically, focusing on issues which have continued to pervade Byatt's fiction, such as ancestry, Darwinian science, myth, the fantastic, wonder-tales, the power of language and plot, women and creativity. Todd's book remains a concise and useful study. Meanwhile, A.S. Byatt has continued to produce fiction, both in the form of the novel and the short story, thus challenging authors of new critical studies attempting to offer a systematic analysis of her entire *œuvre*.

In 2010, Alexa Alfer and Amy J. Edwards de Campos authored a comprehensive study titled *A.S. Byatt: Critical Storytelling*, which examines Byatt's whole production up to and including her latest published novel, *The Children's Book* (2010), as well as her work as a critic and literary journalist. The volume skilfully combines a close reading of Byatt's novels and short stories with a gradual assessment of her role as a public intellectual in the U.K. It also includes a thorough critical apparatus and bibliography and is therefore helpful in orienting new readers. Furthermore, this volume was preceded by an earlier collection of *Essays on the Fiction of A.S. Byatt* (2001), also edited by Alexa Alfer together with Michael J. Noble, offering a composite series of contributions by scholars from various countries with different theoretical approaches.

One more study, entitled *The Still Life on the Fiction of A.S. Byatt*, appeared in 2010. This is a monograph by Elizabeth Hicks, who has fruitfully investigated questions of intermediality and ekphrastic description in Byatt's braiding of realist literature with modernist and visual culture. Hicks's study necessarily addresses a select number of short stories and novels relating to this particular aspect of Byatt's writing, but it does explore in depth a significant theme in her fiction, which previously had only been approached in shorter contributions or unpublished dissertations.

At the time of my writing, an insightful and full-length study on *A.S. Byatt* by Mariadele Boccardi (2013) had just appeared for Palgrave MacMillan. Aimed at both the academy and the general readership, this volume offers a well-documented overview of Byatt's literary and critical output, set against the appropriate cultural context and evolving critical reception towards the author.

While being steeped in most relevant theoretical issues, it never loses sight of the primary works and successfully intertwines relevant cultural and textual analyses in a concise and confident manner that is also incisive. If a critical observation can be raised, this relates to the bibliographical apparatus contained in the volume, which omits significant contributions on A.S. Byatt's work, and to the comparatively limited space devoted to Byatt's tetralogy in Chapter 3. Moreover, because Boccardi's work is grounded on the historical novel which informed her previous publication, *The Contemporary British Historical Novel* (2009), her analysis of Byatt's work remains largely couched within the terrain of postmodernism, realism and historical fiction. When approaching the subject of memory, underlying the whole of Byatt's tetralogy as well as some of her shorter fiction, Boccardi relies wholly on the contribution by Lena Steveker on the subject. The present study addresses the same theme, which I also first examined in two early essays (Cambiaghi 2003, 2005a), but aims at revising some of the initial premises on which it was grounded, while also interrelating general observations and textual analysis more closely.

Three studies have appeared which approach Byatt's work in relation to a number of wider conceptual frameworks which have dominated academic discourse in the last few decades, namely memory, identity and gender. In her volume *Die Einheit in der Differenz* (2007), Sarah Heinz explores how Byatt's work foregrounds the process of identity formation along the principles of *unity* and *différance* conceptualized in cultural studies and philosophy, showing how these notions interact with narrative and metaphorical patterns in Byatt's major novels. Drawing on cognitive and linguistic studies of metaphor (above all, Max Black's interactive theory of metaphor) as well as on theories of genres, identity and subjectivity (Adena Rosmarin, Elizabeth D. Erdmath and Wilhelm Schmid), she surveys a broad theoretical array to discuss a selection of Byatt's works (*Babel Tower, A Whistling Woman, The Biographer's Tale and Possession*). Her analysis identifies in these novels the appropriate terrain to illustrate how in the postmodern world new forms of identity and subjectivity may emerge from the interaction of their separate realms:

> Diese Identität ist dann nicht mehr etwas, was man erwerben, finden oder verwirklichen kann. Sie ist vielmehr eine wandelbare Kohärenz, die Widersprüche in sich vereinigt und nur auf der Basis von präformierten subjektiven Anteilen individuell kreativ sein kann […]: eine Identität, die Differenz und Widersprüchlichkeit erträgt und Einheit ermöglicht. (Heinz 2007: 403–404)
>
> This identity is not something which can be acquired, found or realized. On the contrary, it involves changeable coherence, encompassing contradictions and engendering individual creativity only on the basis of pre-formed subjective contributions […]: it is

> a kind of identity which tolerates difference and contradictions and facilitates the production of unity. (My trans.)

Heinz illuminates aspects of Byatt's work with careful precision, bringing significant theoretical reflections to bear on its subject matter. Though a more fruitful combination of theory and textual analysis may have served to present a more coherent statement on Byatt's *œuvre*, the relevance of the issues discussed and the in-depth scholarly endeavour characterizing it make this book a valuable contribution to Byatt scholarship.

Another German study, Katharina Uhsadel's *Antonia Byatts Quartet in der Tradition des englischen Bildungsromans* (2005), aptly explores Byatt's tetralogy through the overarching concept of the female *Bildungsroman*, examined as a genre through a genealogy of pre-texts dating from the nineteenth and early twentieth century. Juxtaposing examples of this literary tradition with Byatt's series of novels in their cultural and social context, Uhsadel uncovers interesting points of convergence in the development of the genre and its themes. Thus, Maggie Tulliver's reflections on her own fate and the limitations imposed on her intelligence by the existing patriarchal conventions in George Eliot's *The Mill on the Floss*, loom behind the changed predicament of a woman scientist in *A Whistling Woman*, Jacqueline Winwar. The fictional conference in Byatt's novel will only articulate these issues further, which Uhsadel reads in the light of wider social and cultural changes affecting the life of individuals and society in England in the late sixties. Theories of identity and subjectivity, which are succinctly discussed in Uhsadel's final chapter, seek to illuminate Byatt's handling of these issues further.

In *Identity and Cultural Memory in the Fiction of A.S. Byatt* (2009), Lena Steveker anchors her reading of A.S. Byatt's fiction within the theoretical discourse of cultural memory and identity, along the lines set by scholars such as Jan and Aleida Assmann. Though this overall framework offers a useful set of references to investigate the general themes on which Byatt's work is grounded, Steveker's theoretical premises position the author's creative writing in a frame which originally served different aims. Nonetheless, her approach investigates with insight theories of identity and cultural memory with regard to British cultural heritage.

As I will attempt to convey in this book, A.S. Byatt was grappling with the theme of memory long before the term became a conceptual tool serving a general theoretical and social discourse at the turn of the millennium.[2] Indeed, a

2 Cf. Kerwin Lee Klein's account of the scholarly boom in memory studies (Klein 2000).

close reading of her novels shows that the author absorbed the work of Frances Yates soon after its publication in 1966. And in her essay on 'Memory and the Making of Fiction', she states having felt inclined to write a long novel which would allow her to accommodate

> a piece of public history *lived through* - the Second World War, the 1950s, the time of the Festival of Britain and the Coronation of Elizabeth II, of the coming of television, which I already knew would change all our apprehensions of our experiences and our world, would form and reform all our memories and methods of memorizing in then unimaginable ways. (Byatt 1998a: 61)

In what follows, I shall introduce the key critical terms which are central to my analysis and will be dealt with further in their specific interrelation with the novels examined in each chapter.

ii. A.S. Byatt and Cultural Memory Studies

On the whole, A.S. Byatt's exploration of the past in her fiction can be said to integrate both the cognitive and cultural aspects that cluster around the representation of the past, demonstrating a profound awareness of the workings of memory. This interest can be traced back to earlier writings, such as the autobiographical *Sugar* in the homonymous collection *Sugar and Other Stories* (1987) and, as we shall see, *The Virgin in the Garden* (1978). A recent anthology entitled *Memory* (2008) and edited by both A.S. Byatt and Harriet Harvey Wood testifies to the novelist's in-depth grappling with the more theoretical concerns on the subject of memory. These are 'philosophical, aesthetic, scientific, psychological, personal, social' concerns relating to the history of a founding principle which has become the object of intense scrutiny in the last three decades (Byatt 2008: xiii).

While it is virtually impossibile to cover the full range of arguments which scholarship has produced in the field without superimposing on her *œuvre* an excessively cumbersome theoretical framework which may obscure, more than facilitate, the critical appreciation of the novels under discussion, I shall attempt to map out in summary a survey of the concepts which are current in memory studies, highlighting those aspects which are pertinent to my analysis.

Drawing on a primary classification of mnemonic functions derived from cognitive psychology and the neurosciences, we can broadly identify different types of memory operating in the mind. Although the terminology used in this field is not consistent and also features a greater number of technical terms to describe the various phenomena relating to memory (see Manier and Hirst 2008: 254; Markowitsch 2008: 277–279; Longoni 2000: 15–17), the following categories constitute a primary classification of mnemonic functions in the human brain. *Recollective* and *episodic* memories are self-referential because they directly concern the person who is remembering: they are prominent in autobiographical texts and essential to a sense of identity (see Brewer 1996: 54–55; Manier and Hirst ibid.: 256). Episodic memories refer to events with specific temporal and spatial contexts, often entailing a mental image of the event recalled in the mind's eye (see Longoni ibid.: 15). *Semantic memory*, on the other hand, 'handles conceptual and factual knowledge' (Schacter 1995: 20), including language and abstract thought, without necessarily relating to the personal circumstances in which this knowledge was acquired.

Semantic memory is especially evident in Byatt's elaborate reconstruction of intellectual history in her tetralogy portraying social and cultural life in England in the fifties and sixties and in *The Children's Book*. Elsewhere in her fiction, however, the author uses fictional biography as a means to capture the hazy divide separating the authenticity of real-life events from the fiction of reconstruction and the accuracy of factual representation from the elusiveness of mnemonic processes. This subtle interplay can best be observed in *Sugar* and in *The Biographer's Tale* (2000), a skilfully layered parody of the art of biography probing its own limits in the age of deconstruction and postmodernism. In this novel, a relentless process of subversion undermines the protagonist's faith in his subject and the reader's ability to find her or his way out of a labyrinth of fictional invention and false memories. Both the short story and the novel, which I have discussed elsewhere (Cambiaghi 2005a), allow us to identify a thematic thread that connects real-life memories with the ambivalent quality of imaginative storytelling.

Leaving aside the terrain of cognitive psychology and the neurosciences, we encounter the social, cultural and political dimension of memory science and a concomitant proliferation of terms in use. Both the cognitive processes of memory and the persistent reference to cultural memory in its ongoing dialogue with tradition and intertextuality inform Byatt's fictional work. Indeed, the all-inclusive nature of her writing and the way in which broad intellectual and social concerns are accommodated into her fiction seem to characterize her novels as actual 'textual locations' or 'cabinets of the mind'.[3] It is therefore all the more significant that in an essay entitled 'Memory and the Making of Fiction' (Byatt 1998), the novelist has explicitly referred to a kind of museological approach in describing her creative process, drawing on the *art of memory*

3 Here, I am drawing on an essay by Carmen Lara-Rallo (2009) who has used the notion of 'cabinet of curiosities' in her analysis of *Possession*.

of the Renaissance and the mnemotechnics of the ancient Greeks and Romans. In this essay, she connects the set of the York Mystery Plays in the ruins of St Mary's Abbey in York, which she remembers from childhood, with their symbolic transposition in *The Virgin in the Garden*, and the iconography of Elizabeth I with a series of analogies relating to Frederica, the novel's protagonist. She also claims having been haunted by memories that seemed to solicit 'a place, a hearing' (ibid.: 61), proving that in her fiction, she was seeking *lieux de mémoire*, or memory sites, of a literary kind, aiming to preserve a wealth of authorial voices which have become threaded in her mind. As she pointed out in an interview: 'I learn things by heart very easily, and my mind is possessed by very long quotations, which sing about when I'm sitting in taxis' (Wachtel 1994: 81).

The term *lieux de mémoire* was introduced into the social sciences by the historian Pierre Nora in a highly influential work on French collective memory, which he edited between 1984 and 1992. His project originated as a response to what came to be perceived as a 'crisis of French national identity' (Whitehead 2009: 141) and as a strategic tool for the innovation of historical research. This field of enquiry suggests a different set of narratives from those available to the literary imagination and, in particular, from those spun by A.S. Byatt in her fiction. However, Nora's argument is that we are obsessed with memory because we have destroyed it with historical consciousness. In his 1984 introduction to the first volume of *Les lieux de mémoire*, which also appeared later as a separate article in English, he claimed that modern times had led to both an acceleration of history and the growth of historiography, and to the vanishing of actual *milieux de mémoire*, of 'real environments of memory' (Nora 1989: 7). Therefore, he thought it necessary to create an inventory of French *lieux de mémoire* or memory sites, placing them symbolically 'between memory and history', as the title of his preface suggests. This fundamental opposition between memory and history was outlined as follows:

> Memory is life, borne by living societies founded in its name. It remains in permanent evolution, open to the dialectic of remembering and forgetting, unconscious of its suggestive deformations, vulnerable to manipulation and appropriation, susceptible to being long dormant and periodically revived. History, on the other hand, is the reconstruction, always problematic and incomplete, of what is no longer. Memory is a perpetually actual phenomenon, a bond tying us to the eternal present; history is a representation of the past. (ibid.: 8)

Nora goes on to suggest that such *realms of memory*, where 'memory crystallizes and secrets itself' (ibid.: 7), have emerged at specific historical moments marked by a turning point or break with the past. Such critical turning points are, for example, the time of industrialization and consequent disappearance of the paesantry, of nation building, decolonization and the tearing away of traditions and identities caused by the wars of the twentieth century. Placed in the interstices between memory and history, memory sites are therefore meant to provide a set of mental tools anchoring the French national past into consciousness: emblems, commemorations, rituals, calendars, textbooks or even mottos, such as 'Liberté, Egalité, Fraternité', are among the examples fulfilling this function. To all of them, Nora attributes a 'material, symbolic, and functional' dimension, which is a pre-requisite for their existence (ibid.: 19).

Meanwhile, Nora's approach to historical research has become widespread. Despite the identity politics that could be associated with it, this strand in memory studies has been so successful that publishers have commissioned similar projects in countries such as Germany, Italy, Spain and the Netherlands, as historian Pim den Boer notes in his contribution to *Cultural Memory Studies* (Erll/Nünning 2008: 22). This circumstance may ultimately serve a comparative approach which is urgently needed in order to create a kind of transnational identity politics: 'in order to instruct their young citizens, European countries need teachers with at least a degree of knowledge, affection, and sympathy for Europe' (ibid.: 24).

Although Pierre Nora's important project lies outside the immediate context of our reading of A.S. Byatt's work, the conceptual use of the term *loci memoriae* or realms of memory originates, for both novelist and historian, in the same ancient sources, which Nora also acknowledges in a final note to his theoretical introduction (see Nora 1989: 25). Indeed, the term harks back to an ancient tradition which Frances Yates has famously related to the tradition of the Elizabethan memory theatre in *The Art of Memory* (1966).

In the Renaissance, the *memory theatre* was an architectural building mapping the secret structure of the universe and conceptualizing all knowledge through striking allegorical sculptures and paintings. The most famous of the Renaissance memory theatres was planned by Giulio Camillo, an eclectic Humanist 'hailed as "the divine Camillo"' by his contemporaries (Yates 1966: 130). A man of letters and philosophy, 'Friulian and cosmopolitan' and 'a master rhetorician' (Bolzoni 2001: xiv), he had been much admired at the French court of Francis I as well as in Italy. Giulio Camillo had planned his memory theatre as a wooden construction, a complex structure which only survived as a conceptual framework in *L'idea del theatro* (1550), a short treatise he had written just before his death. A system of images, painted by great artists like Titian, were meant to symbolize all scientific knowledge available to mankind. As for the actual structure, this resembled a Vitruvian amphitheatre with a tiered, semicircular auditorium rising 'in seven grades or steps, which are divided by seven gangways representing the seven planets' (Yates ibid.: 136). The planets were those currently known at the time, symbolizing the divine macrocosm of alchemical astrology.

Because Camillo was fully acquainted with the Hermetic-Cabalist tradition and Neoplatonist philosophy, his theatre can be considered as 'the incarnation of the myths of the century: it unites repertories of words and images; it utilizes both the mechanism of the logical and rhetorical diagram and the magical fascination of the icon' (Bolzoni ibid.: xvi). In fact, each of the seven gangways described by Yates, who relied on Camillo's treatise for a reconstruction of the original plan (Yates ibid.: folder between 144–145), had seven gates or doors decorated with countless images, associated with both classical mythology as well as all forms of creation in an expanding universe (Yates ibid.: 141). While 'his imaginary gates are his memory places, stocked with images', it even appears that 'under the images there were drawers, or boxes, or coffers of some kind containing masses of papers, and on these papers were speeches, based on the works of Cicero, relating to the subjects recalled by the images' (ibid.: 144).

As Paolo Rossi notes in his *Logic and the Art of Memory* (Rossi 2000) Camillo's work was closely related to the mnemotechnical tradition, but it paved the way for further developments in the art of memory. Both Camillo and, later, Giordano Bruno replaced the traditional *loci* of mnemotechnics, to be pictured in the mind, with 'external loci', so as to express 'the eternal knowledge of all things' (Rossi 2000: 75). Thus, the artificial *ars reminiscendi* became gradually associated with hermetic knowledge and all wisdom. Giordano Bruno's complex mnemonic systems consisted of intricate revolving wheels symbolizing everything in existence, solar systems, natural elements and minerals, geometrical designs, music and all possible inventions, even including 'pincers and combs' (Draaisma 2000: 41).

Although memory studies encapsulate a complex nexus in the interplay between temporality and spatiality and the concomitant disciplines pivoting around these central terms, it is chiefly the idea of spatiality which governs Byatt's approach to memory. The concept is indeed grounded in the ancient past and in Plato's idea of memory as a wax tablet bearing the inscription of sense perception as an object of thought. In Plato's dialogue *Theaetetus* (360 BC), Socrates describes memory in this way, i.e. as a seal imprint, adding that the wax tablet was a gift of Mnemosyne, the mother of the Muses.[4] This classical idea has continued to interest poets and philosophers to this day. Aristotle, Augustine,

4 Plato's metaphor is well-known and is frequently mentioned in memory studies. Cf. Draaisma (2000: 24–25); Yates (1966: 36); Whitehead (2009: 15–18); Assmann (1999: 151–153).

Wordsworth, Freud, Bergson and Proust all had something to say in the discursive field of memory, but it is chiefly memory as the basis of the learning process that sets Byatt's art of recollection in motion.

Byatt has explicitly acknowledged the influence of Francis Yates's exploration of the *Art of Memory* (1966) in her own essay on the interplay between memory and literary invention, which I have mentioned above. The art of memory as an inner pictorial technique that may aid the process of memorization provided the ancient Greeks and Romans with a first rhetorical strategy to recite long speeches in public. I shall return to this early system of mnemonics in the context of Byatt's novel *The Virgin in the Garden* in Chapter 1, but here I wish to stress the visual and spatial aspect underlying it. Its invention is attributed to the Greek poet Simonides of Keos and is narrated by Cicero in *De oratore*, who tells of a poet who was dining in the house of a rich man where a banquet was held.[5] Having left his seat temporarily to meet two visitors outside, Simonides miraculously escaped the catastrophe when the roof of the house collapsed, killing everybody else. Left with the task of identifying the disfigured victims before their burial, Simonides was able to do so by remembering their sitting order. Therefore, he concluded that the orderly arrangement of place and images – of *locus* and *imagines* – localities and facts pictured as images function 'as a wax writing tablet and the letters written on it' (qtd. in Yates: 2).

In relating her childhood memories of the York mystery plays, Byatt demonstrably created a personal system of mnemonics on the basis of her reading of Yates. Weaving together place and the various inscriptions constructed in her narrative, the *imagines* or *phantasma* described by the ancients, the novelist acts as a mnemonist engaged in mapping the orderly arrangement of memory traces along the path of an archaeological site or architectural building.

In the transition from classical antiquity to medieval culture, and from Renaissance to later epochs, the art of memory became gradually more introspective. As the historian Raphael Samuel argues in his preface to *Theatres of Memory*, Romanticism continued to build on time's ruins but focused on involuntary acts of recall as against 'memory training and conscious acts of will' (Samuel 1994: ix). Memory became subjective and 'a plaything of the emotions' and 'history began where memory faded' (ibid.).

The centrality of place to cultural memory was taken up again by Maurice Halbwachs in the first half of the twentieth-century. Halbwachs, who was a

5 Two more sources relate the myth of the poet Simonides, namely Quintilian's *Institutio Oratoria* and the anonymous tract *Ad Herennium* (See Yates 1966: ch. 1).

student of Henri Bergson and had studied the psychology of memory, was also influenced by the sociology of Emile Durkheim. He became convinced that individual memory becomes displaced and absorbed into collective memory in the changing interaction between individuals and society since 'it is individuals as group members who remember' (qtd. in Whitehead 2009: 129). It follows that in establishing the link between social groups and collective memory, he highlighted the mutable shape of memory, which is carried by social groups in their interrelation with time and place.[6]

While Halbwachs's theory of collective memory became highly influential in the social sciences, Aby Warburg's concept of cultural memory and, in particular, of a memory of art connecting different ages and cultures, was of paramount importance for the overall discursive field. Warburg was an art historian and cultural anthropologist who had tried to understand the cultural process informing the transmission of symbols and rituals in ancient cultures and primitive art. As expounded in his famous conference delivered in Kreuzlingen in 1923 and first published in 1939 in the *Journal* of the Warburg Institute in London (Warburg 1998), he was especially preoccupied with the survival of archaic rituals in Native American cultures, as well as with the relation between antiquity and Renaissance art.[7] Having understood that ancient terrors may re-emerge as sources of energy in artistic form, he coined the term *Pathosformeln* to describe the affective energy that became engraved in human memory and found expression in art (cf. Ginzburg 1986: 31–35; Erll 2005: 19–22; Erll and Nünning 2006: 15; Assmann 1999: 373). His project for an exhibit, an atlas entitled *Mnemosyne*, was conceived 'to illustrate the world's memory of images, which crosses the chronological and spatial borders of epochs and countries' (Erll and Nünning 2006: 15). As Astrid Erll and Ansgar Nünning observe in their contribution to *Literature and Memory* (ibid.), Warburg's theory can be applied to literature as well, since 'the

6 In outlining Halbwachs's theory of *mémoire collective* and *cadres sociaux*, Astrid Erll speaks of a 'sozial geprägte individuelle Gedächtnis' (Erll 2005: 15) and Luisa Passerini aptly observes in her afterword to the Italian edition of Halbwachs's *La mémoire collective* that 'the process of selecting and giving shape to remembrance has often to do with power' (Passerini 1996: 190 my trans.).

7 Well-known is, for example, his contribution to the study of astrological images portrayed in a cycle of fifteenth-century fresco paintings in Palazzo Schifanoia, Ferrara, frequently mentioned in scholarly activities, as the exhibition guide *Il cosmo incantato di Schifanoia. Aby Warburg e la storia delle immagini astrologiche*, edited by Cinzia Fratucello and Christina Knorr in 1998, shows. On Warburg's engagement with art and the survival of classical tradition see Gombrich (1970) and Ginzburg (1986: 29–106).

memory of literature is based on a resemiotisation of signs, on a process which re-charges elements of old texts with meaning' (ibid.: 15). This idea has significant implications for the theory of intertextuality in our reading of Byatt's work, which will be discussed in Section iv.

As I have already suggested, it is virtually impossible to offer an exhaustive overview of the history of cultural memory, of an idea which interconnects diverse fields of studies in a crucial nexus of 'metaphorically coded clues to a semantic deep structure' (Harth 2008: 85). It would be tempting, for example, to refer to Ernst Cassirer's important theory of symbols and their interrelation with language and culture in conjunction with the work of Aby Warburg, but this would lead us into a far too broad area well beyond the scope of the present study. What is evident, however, is that the notion of cultural memory intersects numerous contributions across many disciplines in different countries. In Germany, the field has been systematized earlier or more intensely than elsewhere perhaps, as Astrid Erll illustrates in her *Kollektives Gedächtnis und Erinnerungskulturen* (2005: 2–5). Erll's volume is a competent study which in itself demonstrates the results of restless academic endeavours aimed at systematizing a complex interdisciplinary area. Erll belongs to a generation of younger scholars, but it was the influential work of Jan Assmann which started off the process.

Jan Assmann built on the work of Maurice Halbwachs by formulating a clear distinction between cultural and communicative memory. He considered that each culture develops a kind of connective structure (*konnektive Struktur*) interacting with a set of relations and norms tied to a social and temporal dimension.[8] While communicative memory has a limited temporal horizon of approximately eighty to a hundred years depending on the living memory of three to four generations of people, cultural memory is chiefly concerned with events beyond living memory.[9] Not only does culture bind human beings to their immediate future by creating a horizon of experiences, actions and expectations; it also binds their past to their present by adapting and re-enacting the founding memories of their community, including images and narratives from earlier times, within their present horizon.[10] Assmann repeatedly insists on the notion that

8 ‚Sie wirkt verknüpfend und verbindend, und zwar in zwei Dimensionen: der Sozialdimension und der Zeitdimension' (Assmann 1997: 16).

9 The notion of a gap between a community's recent and remote past is known to scholars as *floating gap* and derives from Jan Vansina's ethnological studies which Assmann explicitly refers to (1997: 48–49).

10 Cf. Assmann ibid.: 'Sie bindet den Menschen an den Mitmenschen dadurch, daß sie als "symbolische Sinnwelt" (Berger/Luckmann) einen gemeinsamen Erfahrungs-,

rituals, ceremonies and commemorative practices all ensure the transmission of cultural memory, shaping myth and historical narratives.[11]

Because of his field of expertise, Jan Assmann drew on ancient history to illustrate the workings of cultural memory, in order to establish the interconnection between collective memory, written culture and ethnogenesis ('den Zusammenhang von "kollektiver" Erinnerung, Schriftkultur und Ethnogenese' – Assmann 1997: 19). Here, the notion of a tightly-knit set of references evoking improbable myths of origin or potentially rigid ideas of a unified culture becomes problematic. After all, stressing the notion of group memories may justify the claim that memory studies simply reflect a kind of narrow ethnicity (cf. Whitehead 2009: 2–3). The point is worth bearing in mind since, as I shall argue, A.S. Byatt may be seen to conjure up similar kinds of mnemonic processes when giving shape to her personal reinvention of England in *The Virgin in the Garden*. Significantly, a parallel issue has been raised by Alexa Alfer and Amy J. Edwards de Campos in their general discussion of Byatt's characterization of fictional types, when they observe that the author's

> powerful images of humans as types, composites or mere representatives of a species [...] point to a more complex issue that remains unresolved in Byatt's *œuvre* to date, namely the question of the extent to which human fate is written by biological *and* discursive forces, and the extent to which understanding these forces may yet be capable of bringing freedom.
>
> (Alfer and Edwards de Campos 2010: 8)

I shall return to this relevant point later in my study, but what can be added here is that while A.S. Byatt operates within the field of literary invention and a wholly imaginative fictional process, Jan Assmann's theory of cultural memory aims at an interpretation of intellectual culture as a whole and has therefore far-reaching implications for the human sciences.[12]

Erwartungs- und Handlungsraum bildet, der durch seine bindende und verbindliche Kraft Vertrauen und Orientierung stiftet'.

11 'Der Modus der fundierenden Erinnerung arbeitet stets - auch in schriftlosen Gesellschaften - mit festen Objektivationen sprachlicher und nichtsprachlicher Art; in Gestalt von Ritualen, Tänzen, Mythen, Mustern, Kleidung, Schmuck, Tätowierung, Wegen, Malen, Landschaften usw., Zeichensystemen aller Art, die man aufgrund ihrer mnemotechnischen (Erinnerung und Identität stützenden) Funktion dem Gesamtbegriff 'Memoria' zuordnen darf. [...] Durch Erinnerung wird Geschichte zum Mythos' (ibid.: 52).

12 Dietrich Harth observes, for example, that the 'relationship of the theory of *Kulturelles Gedächtnis* to controversial questions of identity-creating politics of memory does, though, draw attention to a difficult aspect of the concept' (Harth 2008: 93).

In outlining his theory, Jan Assmann was joined by his wife Aleida Assmann, a literary scholar whose main research has focused on cultural memory and trauma studies. In *Erinnerungsräume* (1999), Aleida Assmann has broadened the heterogeneity of the concept outlined by Jan Assmann by including a new dichotomy of terms, i.e. memory as *ars* and *vis*, which partially re-proposes the opposition between cultural and communicative memory. Memory as *ars* relates to the archival function of memory, whereas memory as *vis* relates to memory as a living force capable of activating memory in time (27–30). Both terms are complementary and are further elucidated through the additional notion of *Funktions-* and *Speichergedächtnis* 'functional and archival or storage memory' (133). Functional memory is embodied, living memory and represents only a selection of the sheer mass of knowledge contained in archival memory. By contrast, storage memory is disembodied, undifferentiated and bears no direct link with the immediate present.

Through her extensive publication output and academic activities, Aleida Assmann has continued to draw attention to the social function of memory in its interaction with performative media, commemorative practices, historical knowledge and generational dialogue. Tellingly, she has qualified her activity as a kind of therapeutic intervention into social and political processes (qtd. in Erll 2005: 4). However, the question remains as to whether theoreticians of the trauma paradigm in the humanities in general are 'interested in the empirical phenomenon of trauma and the traumatic experiences of actual people' (Kansteiner and Weilnböck 2008: 232).

Without wishing to venture into the specific area of memory and trauma, which reaches into the insoluble problem of how to represent trauma in culture, I wish to refer here to those aspects in Aleida Assmann's theory which are useful for an interpretation of Byatt's texts. Relevant aspects focus on her detailed analysis of the kind of imagery that writers, artists and thinkers of different epochs have associated with human memory. In a chapter entitled 'Zur Metaphorik der Erinnerung' ('On the Imagery of Remembrance'; ibid.: 149), she distinguishes metaphors in terms of the medium used to convey their basis of analogy, beginning by listing metaphors referring to writing or writing instruments, such as Plato's wax tablet, De Quincey's palimpsest or Freud's 'mystic writing pad', also called *Wunderblock*. Secondly, she lists metaphors associated with the idea of a building or a storage space gathering images present in the mind, which resembles the *locus* or mental space devised by mnemotechnics and which can also be thought of as a library, much like the library in the castle tower in Spenser's *The Faerie Queene* (Book II). Assmann sees such metaphors as dependent on the idea of a spatial order which structures the free flow of impressions and memories lodged in the mind. She makes the useful observation that when the metaphor refers to space which is structured, it is suggestive of media, symbols or patterns connected with the very idea of the archive or repository of memory, which she generally refers to as *Modelle des Speicherns* 'storage patterns' (ibid.: 162). In contrast, when this space appears disorderly, invisible or inaccessible, the metaphor is to be associated with unbidden recollection.

In 'Memory and the Making of Fiction', Byatt describes in great detail her own kind of iconic memory and the metaphors generated in it. She especially refers to two types of mental pictures which she associates with the writing process as it unfolds. The first is one of 'feathers – being preened, until the various threads, with their tiny hooks and eyes, have been aligned and the surface is united and glossy and gleaming' (Byatt 1998: 65). The second image is that of 'a fishing net, with links of various sizes, in which icons are caught in the mesh and drawn up into consciousness – they come up through the dark, gleaming like ghosts or fish or sparks, and are held together by the links' (ibid.). These powerful analogies convey something essential about the nature of cognitive processes regulating mnemonic activity and cultural construction through a network of associations. Evoking the concept of synaptic connections storing memories in the neural system, they give it a poetic expression, shifting it from the sphere of neuroscience and psychology to the realm of the literary imagination.

These metaphors point towards both a deliberate act of recollection and a systematic network of narrative 'links' which reorganize and store experience. Byatt's mental imagery is therefore suggestive of both cognitive and cultural processes of memory interrelating mind and place. Her remarks on the York Mystery Plays of her childhood, which I mentioned earlier, highlight this kind of mnemonic imagery further. As the author observes, those ruins 'spoke to some primeval schema for human narrative with which I was already working' (ibid.: 61).

In Aleida Assmann's survey of mnemonic imagery, one encounters also metaphors in which the temporal dimension is predominant, emphasizing a sense of oblivion, discontinuity and decay, as well as the unpredictable nature of memory. Of all the metaphors associated with memory, the one coined by Virginia Woolf in *Orlando* stands out for its vividness. Here, memory is first personified in the figure of a capricious seamstress whose work is unpredictable, and then compared to a line of underwear fluttering outdoors in the wind:

> Memory runs her needle in and out, up and down, hither and thither. We know not what comes next, or what follows after. Thus, the most ordinary movement in the world, such as sitting down at a table and pulling the inkstand towards one, may agitate a thousand

> odd, disconnected fragments, now bright, now dim, hanging and bobbing and dipping and flaunting, like the underlinen of a family of fourteen on a line in a gale of wind.
> (Woolf 1990: 49)

Assmann suggests that this metaphor evokes the free flow of associations normally attributed to episodic memories, characterized by the erratic quality underlying their basic structure, which fascinated Virginia Woolf (Assmann 1999: 160–161). At the same time, the image of a line of underwear fluttering in the wind in a colourful arrangement captures something of the pattern normally associated with spatial memories without appearing, however, fixed in a rigid form. This particular metaphor strikes me as a complete opposite to the kind of tightly-knit patterns described by A.S. Byatt in her essay on 'Memory and the Making of Fiction'. Yet in their opposition they also seem to complement and qualify each other.

To sum up: while A.S. Byatt's image of a feather and fishing net suggests a deliberate act of recollection and a systematic network of narrative 'links' which reorganize and store experience, Virginia Woolf's sewing and laundry line metaphors convey the quality of involuntary memories surfacing freely into consciousness, highlighting a sense of discontinuity and disjunction between the self and the orderly arrangement associated with consciousness. If Woolf's rhythmic diction ('hanging and bobbing and dipping and flaunting') captures the irregular flow of perception and the potential disruptions of time which cannot be accommodated within the structure of a plot, Byatt's gleaming icons 'are caught in the mesh' and, by contrast, given a fixed shape.

In closing this preliminary overview of theories of cultural memory relating to Byatt's work, I wish to return briefly to an earlier point raised in my discussion of critical responses to the author's fiction. There are obvious connections between narrative, ethnography, cognitive science and intertextuality in Byatt's handling of mnemonic processes interrelating with a tightly-knit framework of cultural references giving shape to a personal reinvention of England in her long series of novels. When approaching these texts through the lens of a general theory of cultural memory, however, the danger is to superimpose a rigid structure onto writings which remain primarily works of fiction and should be read as such, i.e. as the expression of the literary imagination transcending any normative function.

In addressing the theme of memory, which undeniably runs through much of Byatt's work, I hope to show how this is embedded in the very structure and shape of the novels discussed. Rather than superimposing a large theoretical framework on the novels, I wish to engage more closely with Byatt's texts and show how her narratives since her early work have been ingrained with the theme of memory, partly anticipating perhaps a theoretical discussion that became prominent at the turn of the millennium. I suggest that the intellectual concerns underpinning the fiction of A.S. Byatt are all housed in the freedom, the non-normative, non-taxonomic, non-systematizing play of fictional creation.

iii. Visual Culture

Byatt's interest in art is well-known. Much of her work contains references to portraits of historical characters as well as visual representations of still life, landscape paintings or interior milieus. Aiming at a detailed rendering of life and culture at distinct periods of time, she explores the many facets of the past with consummate energy across a broad canvas. What seems remarkable is that in seeking to represent a comprehensive image of an epoch, the novelist sets the special tension existing between words and things in motion, interrelating an ancient art of memory grounded in the use of vivid imagery not only with pictorial representation and contemporary visual culture, but also with shifting modes of perception and processes of cognition.

Byatt's range of themes has given rise to a substantial strand of research exploring the interconnection between visual and verbal art in her novels. Much has been said, for example, about the function of ekphrastic descriptions in *Still Life* (1985) and *The Matisse Stories* (1993). Elizabeth Hicks (2010) has dealt extensively in her monograph with this aspect of Byatt's fiction, while several shorter scholarly contributions have also examined Byatt's ekphrastic descriptions of artwork (see Meyer 2012; Stewart 2009; Stewart 2008; Spinozzi 2006; Sorensen 2004; Worton 2001; Rippl 2000; Bigliazzi 1999).

Ekphrasis is a specific rhetorical term derived from late antiquity, when rhetoricians developed a theory to describe or 'tell (*phrazo*) in full (*ek*)' about any object or event (Webb 1999: 13). This was conceived of as a mode of speaking that would capture the attention of an audience through vividness (*enargeia*) and *hypotyposis* (*hypotypoein*: to sketch), so as to conjure up an absent subject matter in the listeners' minds (*evidentia*) (cf. Webb: 11; Tripp 2013: 57). Tellingly, the ancient sources refer to 'a speech which leads one around (*periegematikos*), bringing the subject matter vividly (*enargos*) before the eyes' (Webb ibid.: 11). While highlighting the quality of vividness in the evocation of images, this definition also refers to the inner activity of the mind, suggestively moving as in slow motion. This detail is significant if we consider that *ekphrasis* became mostly associated with the description of static objects. Nonetheless, for the ancient rhetoricians, its subject matter could also contain 'a description of a person, a place, even a battle, as well as of a painting or sculpture' (Webb: 8).

In her detailed exploration of the genre,[13] Webb uncovers 'the meaning of 'ekphrasis' in its original context' (ibid.: 11), showing that the rhetorical tradition of the first century AD proposed a range of subjects suitable to ekphrasis, which included 'persons (*prosopa*), places (*topoi*), times (*chronoi*) and events (*pragmata*)' (ibid.: 11) but did not focus on how the visual arts could be translated 'into a verbal medium' (ibid.: 8).

As Webb further explains, the term underwent subtle changes of meaning until, in the mid-twentieth century, it became associated exclusively with the description of a work of art. While Leo Spitzer is credited to have coined the new definition of the term, i.e. '*ekphrasis*, the poetic description of a pictorial or sculptural work of art' (qtd. in Webb: 10), Roland Barthes seems to have conflated modern and ancient definitions in his discussion of ekphrasis in 'The Reality Effect'. Omitting any reference to actions or events, he overlooked the absence of any specific reference to works of art in discussions of *ekphrasis* by the ancients, thus 'limiting its subject-matter to the static, the objectified and, of course, associating it with the work of art' (ibid.: 12). Webb's fascinating account of the history of the term refers, therefore, to an almost imperceptible change of meaning, highlighting a constantly evolving and diverse 'invented tradition of a genre' (ibid.: 18).

In her own essay 'Still Life/Nature Morte' (1991) and in *Portraits in Fiction* (2002) Byatt comments at length on the special tension existing between words and things, as well as between portraits and characters, emphasizing 'the constructive visualising work' which readers must do (Byatt 2002b: 2).

Surveying the history of mnemonics from ancient culture to the Renaissance construction of imaginary memory buildings, Byatt moves along a path which establishes correspondences between the microcosm of the mind's images and the macrocosm of an ideal universe. *The Virgin in the Garden* illustrates this gradual passage from a textual to a visual culture by focusing on the life experiences of a young woman approaching adulthood and grappling with various forms of cultural expression, including her tentative appreciation of Renaissance paintings and her active participation in the staging of a verse play in the role of Elizabeth I. When television finally enters the novel, the process

13 Although *ekphrasis* is usually thought of as a technique or verbal strategy, Webb refers to it as a 'genre' or 'trope' (7). Similarly, Mitchell defines it as 'the name of a minor and rather obscure literary genre (poems which describe works of visual art) and of a more general topic (the verbal representation of visual representation)' (Mitchell 1995: 152).

of transition towards an increasingly pervasive visual culture is foregrounded and becomes more prominent, until *A Whistling Woman*, which I shall discuss in Chapter 4, captures the mesmerising and manipulative workings of television on people's consciousness, associating them with the mimetic games of *Alice in Wonderland*. As will become apparent, the author deals with the impact of television on national and popular culture in both of these novels, addressing a multiplicity of issues which have engaged theoreticians of visual studies ever since Marshall McLuhan declared that 'the medium is the message'.

Although the interrelation between verbal and pictorial representation in Byatt's novels has been sufficiently debated in criticism, very little has been said about her fictional rendering of the performing arts and of televised culture in particular. With the exception of Renate Brosch, who has dealt with the performative aspects of visualisation, staging and narrativisation in Byatt's novels at a more structural level (Brosch 1999), this significant theme has received comparatively little attention. By contrast, it seems important to highlight Byatt's imaginative rendering of a gradual transition from a textual to a visual culture and to show how this is achieved in the shape of her novels.

As regards Byatt's aesthetic views, these have been influenced by artists from the nineteenth and twentieth centuries, in particular the Pre-Raphaelites, Van Gogh and Matisse, though her novels contain allusions to works by many more painters, including Caravaggio, Tintoretto, Velasquez, Mondrian and Patrick Heron, to name just a few. Frequently, the author probes the limitations and potentialities of art in evoking the authenticity of lived experience, thus conflating texts and images in an intermedial framework. Her novelistic practice relates therefore to the much debated question of realism and pictorial representation which, ever since Plato challenged the mimetic role of the visual arts in *The Republic*, has gained a special hold on Western imagination.

A.S. Byatt actively engages with these issues, lending her contemplative gaze at both static and moving images in the unfolding of her novels. Tellingly, her appreciation of visual art is indebted to E.H. Gombrich, who famously discussed the notion of the 'innocence of the eye' in *Art and Illusion* (Gombrich 1972: 250–251). Having examined John Ruskin and Roger Fry's ideas about sense perception and painting, Gombrich observed in this text that an unbiased or innocent eye, capable of perceiving form and colour unmediated by previous knowledge, 'is a myth' (ibid.: 251). Taking her cue from these observations, Byatt tests the theoretical notion of a childish response to light and colour by describing a baby's first impact with sense perception at childbirth in *Still Life*, which I shall discuss in Chapter 2. Translating complex theoretical issues into literary form, she surveys therefore the history of aesthetics and visual culture, evoking the pleasure of thinking in pictures. As has been noted, visual art appeals to her because it functions as a separate semiotic system, but also because it nourishes both verbal art and her greed for knowledge in a way which Gombrich may best explain:

> The Greeks said that to marvel is the beginning of knowledge and where we cease to marvel we may be in danger of ceasing to know. The main aim I have set myself [...] is to restore our sense of wonder at man's capacity to conjure up forms, lines, shades, or colors, those mysterious phantoms of visual reality we call 'pictures'. (Gombrich 1972: 7)

Given A.S. Byatt's declared admiration for the ideas expressed by the influential art historian (cf. Tredell: 68), we may detect her nod of consent to the statement above. It is in the wake of these remarks that Chapter 2 of the present study will attempt to highlight the intellectual concerns embedded in the narrative of *Still Life* and demonstrate how Byatt's approach to memory conflates questions of sense perception in relation to visual phenomena as well as reflections derived from art theory.

iv. Intertextuality

As well as exploring significant aspects of visual culture, A.S. Byatt pays tribute to a variety of language forms in her novels. The interplay between memory and intertextuality is, as anticipated in Section ii, at the heart of her work. Countless intertextual allusions derived from both literary and not-literary texts are assembled within the structure of her novels, which can be seen to assume a hermeneutic function in relocating the great bulk of her personal and cultural memories. As I shall illustrate in the chapters devoted to both *The Virgin in the Garden* and *Babel Tower*, extracts from newspaper cuttings, televised speeches, scientific reports and legal jargon, all fall into shape in various ways in her novels. In *Possession*, which will be the focus of Chapter 5, the reflections of both literary scholars and fictional characters inhabit the imaginary world of the novel, itself transformed into a papery museum or favourite textual location for Victorian culture.

As for the actual term, *intertextuality* has played a vital role ever since Julia Kristeva first employed it. Long before it became a critical tool underpinning the rationale of many postmodern novels, including works by Jorge Luis Borges, Umberto Eco, John Fowles, A.S. Byatt, David Lodge and Italo Calvino, Julia Kristeva coined the term to illustrate the interdependence of literary texts and the implicit dynamism generated in the process. Drawing on Mikhail Bakhtin's concepts of *dialogism*, which in turn highlights the *polyphony* or co-existence of a plurality of diverse voices in the novel,[14] Kristeva stresses the complexity of this form of exchange involving more than a mere interaction between a writing subject and an addressee. In an essay contained in *Desire in Language* (1980), she expounds on Bakhtin's attempts to define these different dialogic modes, interrelated with a structural and linguistic approach, in the following terms:

> The word's status is thus defined *horizontally* (the word in the text belongs to both writing subject and addressee) as well as *vertically* (the word in the text is oriented towards an anterior or synchronic literary corpus. (66)

Her insight results in the well-known conception of the literary text 'as a mosaic of quotations' (ibid.), implying that 'any text is the absorption and transformation of another' (ibid.). Thus, the emphasis is on the literary text as the expression of different discourses or sign systems which interrelate and influence one another. For Kristeva, 'the notion of *intertextuality* replaces intersubjectivity, and poetic language is read as at least *double*' (ibid.).

As Graham Allen points out in his successful contribution to *The New Critical Idiom* series, Kristeva writes on Bakhtin at a time of transition during the mid-sixties, characterized by a shift towards the disruption of stable meanings and objectivity, i.e. from structuralism to post-structuralism (Allen 2000: 3–4). Tellingly, she introduces 'a psychoanalytic component to Bakhtin's dynamic linguistics – or seen conversely, she brings his dynamic linguistics, an incipient theory of the speaking subject, to her psychoanalysis' (Becker-Leckrone: 93).

Following on both Bakhtin and Kristeva's ideas, Roland Barthes develops a theory of intertextuality which further undermines the stability of meaning in textual culture. Since every cultural phenomenon is the expression of a system of signs and every act of writing is the result of a proliferation of preceding texts, a fact which places the writer in dialogue with his/her forerunners, all literary texts may be said to be composed impersonally. The text is now 'a multidimensional space in which a variety of writings, none of them original, blend and clash. The text is a tissue of quotations drawn from the innumerable centres of culture' (Barthes 1977: 146). The implications of these theories result in what Barthes calls 'the death of the author', according to which only the reader is thought to be in a position to receive the full plurality of all the echoes created in the cultures surrounding us. Yet, not only does Barthes claim that 'a text's unity lies not in its origin but in its destination', but also that the reader is now 'without history,

14 The specific term Bakhtin introduces to denote the diversity of languages intersecting each other is *heteroglossia* (cf. Bakhtin 1981: 291).

biography, psychology' (ibid.: 148) since he is merely positioned at the intersection of numerous writings, fragments, rumours, myths.

Parodic echoes of these influential theories notoriously nourish A.S. Byatt's bestselling novel *Possession*, in which one of the protagonists, the namesake Roland, is characterized as embodying aspects of the culture that dominates individuals and their subjectivity in the last decades of the twentieth century. As we shall see in Chapter 5, Roland sees himself 'theoretically, as a crossing-place for a number of systems, all loosely connected' and lacks any coherent idea of self (Byatt 1991: 424).

Intertextuality underpins also A.S. Byatt's long series of novels, weaving together a tangle of language forms which appear to be in search of a textual *locus*. Indeed, all her fiction builds intertextual links as complex structures conflating text-specific information with background knowledge. Not only does the author seem to rely on a fundamental concept emerging from literary theory to construct her narrative, but she also combines it with a cognitive approach, as I wish to demonstrate in this study.[15] A significant example of this elaborate intertextuality is, as will be shown in the following chapter, the insertion of an extract from Churchill's speech celebrating the coronation of Elizabeth II in chapter 27 of *The Virgin in the Garden*, followed by the media coverage of the event occurring in 1953. As if wishing to rescue those language forms from the threat of oblivion, the author relocates them within the memory theatre of her narrative, placed at the intersection between memory and intertextuality.

Renate Lachmann has much to say on the theoretical convergence of these two concepts. Although her field of expertise is Russian modernism, we can draw on the general premises of her work to highlight the interplay between cultural memory and intertextuality, which is at the heart of Byatt's work. Lachmann's observations are contained in a volume entitled *Gedächtnis und Literatur: Intertextualität in der russischen Moderne* (1990) which, in its English translation, bears an introduction by Wolfgang Iser (1997).

Lachmann's exploration of culture as a system generating an expanding network of interlinking processes and her conception of intertextuality as 'an act of memory' (Lachmann 1997: 15) offer opening keys to Byatt's intellectual meditation in her novel series. Taking her cue from Frances Yates and some of Leonardo da Vinci's aphorisms in the *Profezie*, Lachmann retraces the legacy of mnemotechnics and its reception in Western culture, having its starting point in the legend of the Greek poet Simonides, the inventor of the science of recollection.

15 For a cognitive approach to intertextual theory see Panagiotidou (2012).

As I pointed out in Section ii, Simonides miraculously escaped a catastrophe where a banquet was held and was left with the task of identifying the disfigured victims before their burial, which he was able to do by remembering their sitting order. Therefore, Lachmann suggests that the beginning of this tradition is 'marked by a myth of origin with death as its central argument' (4) and further illustrates the content of the legend related by the classical sources. The idea that death interrelates with a need to preserve lost memories reasserts itself in some of Byatt's works, which I have discussed elsewhere.[16] Here, I merely wish to draw on Wolfgang Iser's remarks in his introduction to Lachmann's study *Memory and Literature.*

Following the theories of the Russian semiotician Jurij M. Lotman, Iser reminds us that 'cultural memory is collective memory which cannot be genetically transmitted' (xii), and then goes on to suggest:

> Meaning [...] can no longer be located in the text proper but arises out of the points of intersection at which different contexts clash, collide, overlap, interpenetrate, or are telescoped into one another. Thus meaning appears as something intangible; at best it can only be pinpointed as an operation that feeds a recall of other texts into a semantic project that is in the making.
>
> (Iser 1997: xvi–xvii).

Iser also compares the workings of cultural memory to neural networks active in the brain, a trope in itself reminiscent of a number of images Byatt employs in her writing. According to Iser:

> If memory is considered as a plurality of locations in which the different activities of preserving, recalling, remembering, and forgetting are lodged, intertextuality provides an exact image of what neurophysiologists maintain to be the nature of memory. Even the shifts through which these activities are hooked up with one another correspond to what occurs in the brain, thus allowing us to experience the operation of a locally ramified memory. (ibid.: xvii)

In turn, the metaphors of a feather and a fishing net, which Byatt describes in her essay on 'Memory and the Making of Fiction' (ibid.), are suggestive of the multi-layered structure of narrative and the endless ramifications of memories shaped by language. They stand out for their vivid, iconic quality and seem to convey something essential about the nature of memory, cognitive processes and

---

16 In *The Biographer's Tale*, for example, the author smuggles the photographs of the corpses of Francis Galton and Henrik Ibsen teasingly into the novel, while in her autobiographical short story in the homonymous collection *Sugar*, A.S. Byatt muses on the nature of fiction, memory and death. Cf. Cambiaghi (2005a).

cultural construction through a network of associations. More generally, they may also be seen to symbolize the writing process as it unfolds, in its interrelation with memory, cognition and creativity. These metaphors form a cluster of interrelated patterns which re-emerge in various ways in Byatt's long narrative, drawing on countless intertextual forms binding memory to both its cognitive and cultural context.

Hence, Iser's idea of a 'locally ramified memory' interlocks with A.S. Byatt's imagery of a feather and fishing net underlying her fiction and symbolizing the multi-layered structure of her narrative, as well as the endless ramifications of memories shaped by language. Significantly, this literary construct will also be nurtured by metaphors associated with the neurosciences and the physiology of the mind in *A Whistling Woman*, the final volume in the tetralogy charting the old philosophical debate of the mind-body problem. As I shall illustrate in Chapter 4, the climax of this novel occurs when a multi-disciplinary conference on the relation between body and mind takes place at a fictional university in Northern England. Translating scientific concerns into the plot of her narrative, Byatt captures therefore a whole intellectual climate and the reflections of an age dominated by new developments in technology and the neurosciences. Thus, intertextuality provides the ideal pattern for Byatt's organization of narrative, interconnecting people, culture and society in the fictional world of her long series of novels. Not only does it prove a useful strategy in the construction of narrative, but it also encapsulates the mnemonic function of literature in 'the representation and transmission of knowledge' (Lachmann 2008: 306).

Finally, intertextual theory also involves identifying various forms of intertextuality within texts. Gerard Genette provided a systematic approach to working out a taxonomy of intertextual categories in his influential study *Palimpsestes: La littérature au second degré* (1982), contributing to dismantling the assumption that literary texts are enclosed, separate objects. He identified five types of intertextual links between texts: intertextuality, paratextuality, metatextuality, hypertextuality, and architextuality. As Lara-Rallo succinctly elucidates, '[t]hey operate on different levels of abstraction, ranging from the effective presence of one text in another (as in quotation, allusion, and plagiarism), to the abstract connection of any text with the generic category to which it belongs' (2009b: 100).

In Germany, Ulrich Broich and Manfred Pfister edited a volume entitled *Intertextualität* (1985), mapping the field of intertextual phenomena and distinguishing between marked or unmarked quotations, explicit or implicit intertexts. A useful term was coined by Wolfgang G. Müller (1991) to designate the interrelation existing between characters of different texts, i.e. *interfigurality*. This concept implies that authors may borrow characters from other texts in order to suggest common character traits through analogies or names. They may also *re-configure* a group of characters from different works in a new fictional situation. Although the present study does not entail a detailed classification of the various intertextual forms operating in Byatt's narrative, interfigurality is an interesting device that can be observed in her fiction.

v. Blending Theory

Byatt's characteristic way of incorporating cultural knowledge into her novels by creating characters that may represent distinct disciplines or even the *Zeitgeist* in which the novels are set, has led me to investigate the pattern underlying her narrative mode. From what I have already observed, it is apparent that Byatt favours complex narrative structures, allowing her to store and reorganize experience, knowledge and imaginative subject matter. As I have tried to elucidate, the endless ramifications of memory and the complex operations of the mind inform some of the ruling metaphors structuring the plot of her novels, as well as the way in which the writing process unfolds through a network of associations. Accordingly, the images of a feather and fishing net to describe the nature of cognitive processes provide the link for her characteristic narrative process, which allows us to tease out some of the questions embedded in Byatt's novels for further reflection.

The all-inclusive, erudite quality of her writing, encompassing different forms of knowledge as well as imaginative subject matter, seems to chart a space in which thinking and knowing may ideally co-exist. We may ask, therefore, how precisely the author accommodates the broader concerns of her intellectual work into an imaginative framework, and whether any specific structures of learning can be detected beneath the surface of her narrative.

With Wolfgang Iser, we may say that 'culture as the latest target area in the study of humankind trains our gaze on both the need and the capacity of human beings to build their own world' (Iser 2007: 318). Writers are by definition 'worldmaking' individuals generating alternative stances from which to reflect on the complexity of the universe. Being immersed in a world of ever-growing complexity and contingency, the novelist may use all the tools at her disposal to master control of her world picture. In the case of A.S. Byatt, the novel even seems to stand at an angle between the need to create fictional worlds and yet 'say something of cognitive consequence about reality' (Gibson 2007: 2). But how precisely does knowledge interlock with the imaginative quality of her storytelling?

One way to answer this question is to consider the ancient practices of memorization and Renaissance forms of systematizing thought derived from antiquity in the light of recent cognitive theories developed by Mark Turner. Turner is a cognitive scientist who, in cooperation with Gilles Fauconnier, has tried to investigate how humankind has come to develop skills that allow for the construction of meaning and memorization. Wishing to investigate the very sources of knowledge and creativity, Turner and Fauconnier have developed a theory, known as *conceptual blending* or *conceptual integration*, which seeks to illuminate the human capacity for thought and language. Claiming that 'complex blending is always at work in any human thought or action but is often hard to see' (Fauconnier and Turner 2002: 25), they observe that this capacity has developed over thousands of years, characterizing both art, science and everyday human activity. For Fauconnier and Turner, human beings develop thought and language by drawing on different domains of knowledge and experience and by interrelating these domains with one another. This means that human beings construct meaning by creating new mental spaces, namely temporary frameworks drawing on previous conceptual domains. Fauconnier and Turner describe the essence of this process as matching or conflating two input spaces in order to project part of those inputs into a new mental space. This is the *blended space*, a compression of input spaces which then becomes the *emergent structure* (ibid.: 41–42), which can be generated in three ways: 'through *composition* of projections from the inputs, through *completion* based on independently recruited frames and scenarios, and through *elaboration* ('running the blend')' (ibid.: 48).

In *The Artful Mind* (2006), Turner further observes that the strongest form of conceptual integration characterizing human beings is 'double scope blending', described as 'the crucial incremental cognitive capacity that makes it possible for human beings to create and share art' (Turner 2006: 94). And just as individuals, cultures 'work hard to develop integration resources that can be handed on with relative ease' (Fauconnier and Turner 2002: 72). They do so by creating methods 'for setting up a blend' (ibid.: 72) and one such an example of a suitable method for ensuring the transmission of knowledge is the ancient art of memory earlier described. Following the observations of the cognitive anthropologist Edwin Hutchins, Fauconnier and Turner point out that the art of memory 'invites us to create a blended space in which items to be remembered are objects along a familiar path and, as such, take on the inevitable sequence that would be perceived by a traveler along it' (ibid.: 72).

Blending theory built on earlier studies of metaphor, famously discussed by Lakoff and Johnson in 1980, who claimed that 'most of our normal conceptual system is metaphorically structured' (Lakoff and Johnson 2003: 56). They understood metaphor as a 'cross-domain mapping in the conceptual system' (Popova

2014: 247) and considered that conceptual structure 'is not merely a matter of the intellect' but affects 'all the natural dimensions of our experience, including aspects of our sense experiences: color, shape, texture, sound, etc.' (Lakoff and Johnson ibid.: 235). Tellingly, they saw that art can also structure our experience 'in terms of these natural dimensions' and that '[w]orks of art provide new experiential gestalts and, therefore, new coherences' (ibid.: 235).

These broad theoretical observations may illuminate the characteristic narrative pattern informing much of Byatt's fiction, grafted by a process of accumulation of characters, symbolic and semantic structures, never-ending and spiralling, like the double helix of the DNA or Pieter Brueghel's painting *The Tower of Babel*. *Babel Tower*, the third novel in Byatt's tetralogy, would ideally provide the appropriate terrain to highlight the author's characteristic narrative pattern in relation to blending theory, which could also be applied successfully to the whole of the tetralogy. Indeed, if story and projection are essential to human thought and concepts can be defined as 'packets of meaning' (Turner 1996: 57), A.S. Byatt may be said to make a paradigmatic use of all the functions underlying the creative process: by continually blending together different forms of knowledge and imaginative storytelling, she produces an increasingly rich narrative that makes up the space of her novels.

vi. Chapter Outline

My specific focus is on Byatt's major novels interlocking with some of the above theoretical categories. My choice of texts depends on the range of issues involved in dealing with Byatt's work and the need to keep my argument sufficiently cohesive. I have chosen to focus my argument on the way her works relate to the overarching theme of the art of memory and have followed the order of their publication. In Chapter 1, I trace the shift from the arts of memory of the classics (*ars memoriae*) to their Renaissance reenactment, which I discuss in relation to *The Virgin in the Garden*. Here, I explore the author's densely layered narrative underpinned by an elaborate system of mnemonics, which I read as a memory theatre of a literary kind. My aim is to show how the novelist turns an ancient and long forgotten art into a conceptual framework accommodating different forms of memory within her fictional recreation of the 1950s. The interplay between verbal and visual culture providing one of the themes of the narrative, is also foregrounded in this opening chapter. Byatt's evocation of Renaissance art and other cultural forms available to post-war English society illustrate in fact a gradual transition towards a visual culture, anticipating later developments in the tetralogy when television becomes more pervasive.

Leaving aside the elaborate Renaissance allegory underlying the narrative in *The Virgin in the Garden*, Chapter 2 focuses on *Still Life*, a novel preoccupied with the question of pure representation and the functions of language as a vehicle for direct description. I illustrate the intellectual concerns underlying the novel and show how these become translated into fictional form through the author's handling of ekphrasis and visuality. In turn, these issues are shown to interrelate with Byatt's approach to memory as regards its iconic and spatial aspects. Most importantly, the novel introduces a concern with the cognitive aspects of memory, with questions of sense perception in relation to visual phenomena, thus conflating learned reflections derived from art theory with a fictional plot. The excerpt portraying a baby's physiological reaction to light at childbirth provides the focus of my analysis, showing the point of convergence in the novel for the cultural and cognitive functions of memory. In parallel, I draw attention to how *Still Life* historicizes visuality through the paradigmatic institutional context in which it is enacted – the museum. Memory is here conceptualized as an overarching category interrelating different modes of thought and ways of apprehending the world. At the same time, a wealth of intertextual allusions provide an equivalent mnemonic space within the novel, which I show to be embedded within a specific literary tradition relating not only to the evocation of childhood, but also to questions of sense perception and mental processes. What I wish to highlight in my reading of *Still Life* is the subtle craft intertwining the disparate strands of the narrative, which previous critical studies have mostly examined in relation to its aesthetic concerns or questions of mimetic representation probing the limits of language.

Chapter 3 explores the intricate symbolic network woven by A.S. Byatt in *Babel Tower*, where language is the dominant concern of the novel. It aims at showing how a complex narrative structure interrelates with a broad social and intellectual background, mingling fiction, critical discourse and other modes of non-verbal representation. Highlighting the individual images governing the structure of her work brings into focus the extraordinary mosaic of intertextual allusions assembled in the novel. The chapter also aims at demonstrating how this pattern of textual interconnectedness maps a fragile order onto an increasingly fragmenting social and cultural scene, reflected in the life of its protagonist. Formally, this is Byatt's most experimental novel, flamboyantly expressing the author's fundamental concern with the origin and creative potential of language, as well as its inherent limitations. Readers may be baffled by the complex mishmash of parodic forms embedded in the narrative. Yet, these are a clear reflection of a postmodern project famously theorized by social and cultural theorists.

Chapter 4 deals with the interplay of gender and the cognitive function of memory in *A Whistling Woman*, the fourth novel concluding Byatt's quartet. Close attention is paid to both the symbolic function of language, reflecting the gender-related concern of the novel, and the broader social and intellectual themes underpinning the narrative. The novel foregrounds imminent changes brought about by the sexual revolution and the counterculture of the sixties. It also highlights the unresolved question of body and mind deploying science as its main thematic and metaphoric elements. As television becomes the most prominent medium for addressing these central concerns, the novel enacts a gradual transition towards visual culture, when women's issues become the subject of talk shows. Therefore, I wish to highlight how the novel imaginatively recreates the virtual reality of television, interrelating complex issues relating to technology, the physiology of mind and cognitive processes.

The final chapter revisits Byatt's most famous novel, *Possession.* Although it is placed at the end of the present study, this work precedes chronologically the publication of *Babel Tower* and *A Whistling Woman*, marking a significant watershed in the development of the writer. Critical responses to this award-winning novel soon proliferated, addressing Byatt's treatment of Victorian culture in its dialogue with a twentieth-century sensibility, postmodernism, myth and Romance. My analysis of the novel is arranged according to the three temporal planes underpinning its framework. I aim to bring out the polyphony of the many voices woven into the novel, highlighting the range of textual and contextual references that define its cultural scope and justify the claim of its mnemonic function.

I have been engaged in research on A.S. Byatt's work for a long time. Over the years, I have marvelled at the author's capacity to intertwine various forms of knowledge and map a fertile dialogue across disciplines in artistic form. Her fiction can both entertain and educate, opening up the space of the novel for new possibilities of encountering both science and art, high and low culture. We may become lost or engrossed in her expansive novels, featuring a myriad ideas and complex imagery, but ultimately these seem to encompass a large display of blended spaces mapping a huge palace of memory. Indeed, the connection between creative and scholarly modes operating in her work can be seen to serve a kind of museological practice, which the culture of modernity and postmodernity has only enhanced. A recent collection of essays entitled *The Exhibit in the Text*, edited by Caroline Patey and Laura Scuriatti (2009), fruitfully addresses this cultural practice with regard to various authors during the nineteenth and twentieth centuries. This aspect of Byatt's work continues to solicit my attention and informs the present study.

1. A Memory Theatre of Words: *The Virgin in the Garden*

The Virgin in the Garden (1978) harks back to a double time level, Elizabethan England and Coronation year 1953. It is Byatt's third novel, following *The Shadow of the Sun* (1964) and *The Game* (1967), and initiates a long narrative in four volumes that began to appear in 1978. While the overall publication of this ambitious project spans some twenty-five years, with the last novel appearing in 2002, the whole sequence covers the period from Elizabeth II's coronation to 1970. Each novel is then preceded by a prologue, which adds to the structural complexity of the project. For example, the prologue to the second novel in the series affords a fleeting glimpse into a later period coinciding with a real-life event, the Post-Impressionist exhibition held at the Royal Academy of Arts in 1980, described in the opening pages. The setting of each novel within a specific time frame with multiple flashbacks and proleptic anticipations contained in the prologues, shows that the narrative is firmly rooted in a chronology of events shifting constantly back and forward, inviting the reader to compare and assess the development of characters and situations spanning more generations and creating the impression of a symbolic distillation of cultural and historical processes. Chronicling a segment of English provincial life through the case history of a lower-middle-class family, the tetralogy can be read both as a *roman fleuve* and as a female *Bildungsroman*. Each novel is interrelated through a large group of characters appearing intermittently throughout the sequence; yet, they can all be read as separate works. Finally, the series also qualifies as a long novel of education charting the lived experience of two sisters achieving maturity. Their experiences are to be read as representative of women's achievements in society during the two decades in which the novels are set.

This chapter focuses on *The Virgin in the Garden* and seeks to illuminate the tightly-knit framework of cultural references that make up the space of the novel. This densely layered narrative is underpinned by an elaborate system of mnemonics which I read as a memory theatre of a literary kind. Conflating myth and Renaissance culture with the historical present in its imaginative reinvention, Byatt's novel turns the ancient art of memory into a conceptual framework that may accommodate different forms of memory as well as her sense of the past. In what follows, I shall refer to some of the initial concepts discussed in the introduction in order to illustrate how Byatt's tetralogy grew out of the procedures of an ancient and long forgotten art, which has not been a common practice in the tradition of the novel.

Visual and verbal expressions of learned and popular culture are frequently woven together in the opening novel to convey a broad vision of shared memories, shaping the landscape of mental and social lives in the provincial microcosm of a Northern English community. Accordingly, an early reviewer writing for *The New York Times Book Review* described the novel as 'grave, solid, ample as a Yorkshire tea' (Dinnage 1979: 20), translating the many themes and tropes underlying the narrative into a colourful metaphor.

Looking back on this early novel from the vantage point of our present time, we may be struck by the conceptual framework underpinning the whole sequence, which this first novel only begins to convey. Despite the intricacy of its narrative and the density of ideas characterizing it, Byatt's project is informed by a greater degree of coherence than one might at first assume, and it is only by thinking of her work to-date as a complex creation that may be striving to achieve a kind of unified broad vision, that we can begin to explore her writing in its full scale.

The conceptual framework of Byatt's *roman fleuve* may gain in coherence if one focuses on the overall concerns overarching the entire project, since the author interrelates the workings of memory, both individual and collective, cognitive and cultural, with the fabric of her novels. Here, the past emerges as an elaborate reconstruction of social history in which fiction and cultural memory are mingled. However, because her fiction integrates both the cognitive and cultural aspects that cluster around the representation of the past, Byatt's exploration entails more than a mere historical revisiting of a quintessentially English social landscape.

Byatt's reinvention of England occurs on several levels and under a variety of aspects. Stylistically, *The Virgin in the Garden* merges a realist framework with Renaissance allegory; it moreover employs a comic fictional mode which undermines the mythical allusions embedded in the narrative contrasting the two 'Elizabethan' periods. Language here is highly self-conscious and metaphorical, dwelling deliberately on countless intertextual allusions enhancing the expressive potential of the text. The language and works of Shakespeare, Spenser, Keats and the Metaphysical Poets, to name but a few, haunt the narrative at every turn, reminding us of times past and of the cultural forms that have shaped them.

This evocation of the Renaissance and literary works from other periods of English literature is further enhanced through the interplay of word and image, visual and verbal culture, illustrating the shifting dialogue between these forms of art and providing one of the themes of the narrative. Indeed, though *The Virgin in the Garden* encompasses a more traditional picture of society reflected in the theatricality of popular drama and the cultural forms available to post-war English society, the media also play a key role throughout the long series of novels and become subject to extensive scrutiny. Television here makes its first appearance, offering us a glimpse of the 1953 coronation of Elizabeth II, which the inhabitants of a small provincial town in Northern England are able to watch on the tiny screen in their homes. By the end of the tetralogy, the role of television will become much more pervasive, reflecting a gradual and relentless transition towards visual culture permeating all facets of reality and replacing obsolete forms of communication. Therefore, in my reading of these novels, the interplay of word and image provides a link between the theatricality of Elizabethan culture evoked in *The Virgin in the Garden* on the one hand, and the social effects of televised culture further explored in *A Whistling Woman* on the other. It also anticipates the new tension between high and low culture characterizing the transition to a postmodern world as portrayed by the author in her later works.

Further thematic aspects of the novel focus on the changing predicament of women and the family in post-war English society through the intertwined fate of two sisters who, as they come of age, are confronted with their first major choices. As Ruth P. Feingold (2013) has shown in her interpretation of the novel, these changes are portrayed as private rites of passage, mirroring the large-scale social rituals occurring at the national level. Thus, birth, childhood, education, adolescence and marriage find an echo in the public rituals characterizing Coronation year 1953, when the Queen takes on her predestined role and Great Britain seeks to define itself as a modern nation in the post-war and post-imperial world. Brief extracts of media commentaries inserted into the novel offer a sample of the national grandeur accompanying the event. Yet, their effect is immediately undermined by comic motifs surrounding the life of the characters in the plot, who are involved in fragile liaisons of erotic power. Cast in an atmosphere reminiscent of *A Midsummer Night's Dream*, their small-scale tales of love and loss detract from the main action in the novel, revolving around the staging of a fictional verse play to mark the celebrations of the royal event.

Aside from these allegorical and metaphorical patterns, the plot focuses on the microcosm of the Potters, a lower middle-class family residing in the small Yorkshire town of Blesford. They are a bookish, lively and agnostic family headed by a willful and eccentric father who resembles F.R. Leavis in his manner of teaching and in his moral convictions. The family includes the already mentioned two highly literate sisters, Stephanie and Frederica, and an inarticulate younger brother, Marcus, who is gifted, however, with exceptional visual powers and the ability to work out complex mathematics. Their mother Winifred is the patient and passive endurer of much of the tension generated within the family.

The novel orchestrates a large number of characters and a prologue, set in 1968, which retrospectively looks back on the main action of the narrative, thus employing anachrony, specifically temporal prolepsis, in Genette's terms (Genette

1976: 83–134). In the course of the novel, Stephanie marries a well-meaning curate, Daniel Orton, which causes a stir in the family and meets with the disapproval of her father and sister. In contrast, Frederica pursues activities of an intellectual nature. At the same time, she experiences the first pangs of romance and tries to rid herself of her virginity. The playwright Alexander Wedderburn, whose verse play *Astraea* is performed in the course of the novel to mark the celebrations for the crowning of Elizabeth II, becomes a secret object of desire and the focal point for many attempts of seduction in the novel, while the younger Marcus Potter falls victim to the undesired attention of a science teacher showing signs of mental instability.

Inevitably, the question of the past and its literary representation links up with a whole discursive field which has long engaged with notions of Englishness and identity. Admittedly, Byatt's novel captures a specific historical moment as the point of intersection for many strands in the narrative, in which two young women coming of age seek to define their adult selves through a network of relations and in opposition to their immediate world (cf. Samuel 1989: preface x–xvii). On the surface, Coronation lends this narrative a seemingly monolythic view of the past but, as has been noted, this is mainly a trope for the narrative of domesticity characterizing the life of women in the early Fifties (Feingold 2013: 73–74). At a metafictional level, however, *The Virgin in the Garden* does provide its own reflections on questions of identity and belonging, as the opening prologue makes clear. How the author encompasses these thematic concerns in her handling of mnemonic processes will be the object of Section 1.4 below.

If the main action in the novel is easily summarized, its structural complexity represents a challenge of a different kind and the real focus of my enquiry. Byatt accommodates a vast amount of knowledge in her work, weaving together local politics, media coverage of the Coronation event, retrospective comments on the rhetoric employed for the occasion, views on education, gender, family values and government policies, all intertwined with a thick layer of intertextual allusions from Shakespeare, Milton, Marvell, Keats, T.S. Eliot and the Metaphysical Poets. They all feed into the imaginary palimpsest for the English literary canon which the novel revisits and celebrates. The overall effect may be baffling but the ambitious quality of the enterprise is noteworthy, bearing comparison perhaps with the activity of a curator engaged in furnishing the halls of a museum. Indeed, the concept of the museum may provide us with a suitable critical tool to open up her work for further inspection, since it is in a museum that we can accommodate a vast amount of knowledge such as we find displayed in Byatt's work. However, it is more accurate to think of her novel as a memory theatre of a literary kind, because it is the Renaissance notion of the memory theatre which underpins the whole narrative structure of *The Virgin in the Garden*, producing a set of motifs which will resurface openly in the final volume *A Whistling Woman*, albeit in a somehow different shape.

Before analysing the implementation of this concept in *The Virgin in the Garden*, I shall return once more to the notion of the *ars memoriae* and the layer of associations it evokes (1.1). I will then discuss how the notion of the memory theatre intersects the tradition of Elizabethan culture and the English Renaissance in the novel (1.2), considering the play of images and garden motifs in the narrative (1.3) and situating the cultural rituals enacted in the novel within the discourse of Englishness and the new Elizabethan epoch (1.4).

1.1 *Ars memoriae*, Renaissance Memory Systems and Frances Yates

Section ii of my introduction pointed to Byatt's essay 'Memory and the Making of Fiction' (1998), in which the author comments on the interrelation between memory and literary invention, highlighting her personal system of mnemonics and the way in which they have become intertwined with the history of ideas, culture and community. In this essay, she connects the York Mystery Plays of her childhood, which she remembers vividly as an event generating great popular excitement, with their symbolic transposition in the structure of *The Virgin in the Garden*. She also describes how, having read Frances Yates's study of Elizabethan symbolism *Astraea* (1975), the iconography of Elizabeth I became intertwined with a series of analogies relating to Frederica, the novel's protagonist cast as the young Elizabeth I in the fictional play within the novel. The Queen celebrated by court poets as Virgo-Astraea, the Virgin Goddess of Justice already known to Latin poets (see Yates 1977: 29–31), produced many mythological echoes in Renaissance culture. Thus, the pagan goddesses Artemis, Astarte and 'the turret-crowned Cybele, the goddess of the groves, queen and huntress, chaste and fair' (Byatt 1998: 62) became associated with the Virgin Queen, who famously replaced the image of the Virgin Mary when puritan iconoclasm did away with all tangible signs of Catholicism. Further allusions to Gloriana and Belphoebe from Spenser's *Faerie Queene* add to the layer of associations.

Byatt repeatedly alludes to this set of analogies in her critical writings, including *Portraits in Fiction* (2002: 4) and the introduction to her first novel *The Shadow of the Sun* (1991), first published in 1964 as *Shadow of a Sun*. She stresses how she became preoccupied with 'the problem of female vision, female art and thought, using these images' (Byatt 1991: xiv) and how the representational problem of invoking an alternative myth for female creativity led her 'to substitute a female mythology for a male one' (qtd. in Dusinberre 1983: 193). In a characteristic move that allows her to conflate complex imagery with a multiplicity of meanings, the author creates 'a kind of *grammar* of constructing narratives' (Byatt 1998: 66) and inscribes her own sense of the past onto a specific location, coinciding with the ruins of St. Mary's Abbey in York where the Mystery Plays were enacted. Having been haunted by memories that appeared to solicit 'a place, a hearing' (ibid.: 61), the author looks for memory sites of a literary kind which will help her preserve a wealth of authorial voices that have become threaded in her mind. As I have already indicated, this densely layered web of allusions interrelates with the notion of the memory theatre, the ideal destination for Byatt's dialogic engagement with the literary past. It also provides a first example of a blended space in which different forms of knowledge, connected with distinct input spaces (the embedded symbolic images), are compressed and projected onto a new domain, which is the new blended space or emergent structure of the novel with its alternative symbolism.

I have elsewhere commented on the significance and function of the memory theatre in Byatt's work (Cambiaghi 2004; Cambiaghi 2005a). Its conceptual framework and characteristic structure has also been described in the introduction to the present volume (1.2). This concept interlinks with an ancient tradition harking back to Greek and Roman times, when the art of memory was developed as a kind of inner pictorial technique to aid the process of memorizing long speeches to be recited in public. Three classical sources relate its conception, i.e. Cicero's *De Oratore*, Quintilian's *Institutio Oratoria* and the anonymous tract *Ad Herennium* (see Yates 1966: ch. 1). According to this technique, a series of places or *loci* was imprinted in the memory of the speaker and associated with images (*imagines*) which would facilitate the resurfacing to consciousness of the thoughts and words to be spoken in public. These *loci* were to be arranged in the mind's eye as an architectural building, 'not omitting statues and other ornaments with which the rooms are decorated' (ibid.: 3). The speaker would then have to imagine going through the rooms and re-visit the various sites 'drawing from the memorised places the images he has placed on them' (ibid.). Thus, the orderly arrangement in the sequence of places on the trajectory through the building would ensure the process of recollection, and the visual faculty of the mnemonist would essentially enable the act of recall.

This long forgotten art, which belonged to the art of rhetoric used by the ancient orators, was resurrected in the 1950s by Paolo Rossi and Frances Yates. Both scholars explored its interrelation with a new figurative language produced by medieval art, and with the Renaissance philosophy of the Neoplatonists (Rossi

1960; Yates ibid.). The conception of memory theatres and other intricate mnemonic systems produced by Italian Renaissance humanists and philosophers, such as Giulio Camillo (1480–1544) and Giordano Bruno (1548–1600), emerged from this very culture, which was grounded in the mystical traditions of the Hebrews (Cabala) and the philosophies of the Egyptians (*Corpus Hermeticum*) and also influenced Elizabethan England (Yates ibid.: 135–136; 260–265, 320 ff.). More specifically, Yates associated the *ars memorativa* of the ancient Greeks and Romans with the Elizabethan memory theatre of Robert Fludd (1574–1637), whose ideas were founded on the philosophy of the Neoplatonists and the Hermetic and Cabalistic tradition.

Fludd believed in 'the principle of *coincidentia oppositorum*, whereby contraries are contained within each other' (Schmidt 2001: 76), and in the claim that the microcosm mirrors the image of the universe (Yates ibid.: 321 ff.). He also believed that a kind of mystical alchemy could lead to the understanding of the universe. Therefore, he conceived of a space which could represent the microcosm of the human mind, mirroring the harmony of celestial bodies. His memory system is closely related to that of Giulio Camillo, who had planned his own memory theatre as a wooden construction, as outlined in 1.2.

This architectural building, which only survived as a conceptual framework described in Camillo's *Idea del Theatro* (1550), was presented to the average viewer 'as a large machine capable of producing texts and knowledge […] the ultimate computer' (Bolzoni 1991: 23). It was also meant as a guide into more hidden levels of reality and into the divine, since the seven pillars on which the building rested symbolized both the seven planets and the Sephiroth, marking the path to 'the seven peaks of mystical rapture' (ibid.). Camillo's theatre had been much admired at the French court of Francis I and Yates considers that Fludd may have heard of it when he visited France (ibid.: 336). Viglius Zuichemus, a correspondent of Erasmus, is even quoted to have written:

> They say that this man [Camillo] has constructed a certain Amphitheatre, a work of wonderful skill, into which whoever is admitted as spectator will be able to discourse on any subject no less fluently than Cicero. I thought at first that this was a fable until I learned of the thing more fully from Baptista Egnatio. It is said that this Architect has drawn up in certain places whatever about anything is found in Cicero… Certain orders or grades of figures are disposed… with stupendous and divine skill. (Yates ibid.: 130–131)

His letter conveys a sense of wonder for the Renaissance man who would earn 'the accolade of greatness at the time: "divine"' (Mack 2003: 16).

While Camillo's construction was an architectural building mapping the secret structure of the universe and conceptualizing all knowledge through striking allegorical sculptures and paintings, Fludd's memory system was really a *stage* deprived of an auditorium and placed in heaven (ibid.: 329). Yates further elaborates on the significance of this distinction, suggesting that Fludd's memory system may be related to the original design for Shakespeare's Globe Theatre, mixing zodiac signs and the spheres of the planets to produce a place of popular public entertainment (ibid.: 342 ff.). She details the way in which Camillo and Fludd's memory theatres differ as follows:

> There is in both cases a distortion of a 'real' theatre for the purposes of a Hermetic memory system. Camillo distorts the Vitruvian theatre by transferring the practice of decorating with imagery the five entrances to its stage to the seven times seven imaginary gates which he erects in the auditorium. Fludd stands with his back to the auditorium and looking towards the stage, loading with imaginary imagery its five doors, used as memory *loci*, and distorting the stage for his mnemonic purposes by crushing it into a memory room. (Yates ibid.: 367)

Thus, in both cases the theatre represents a creative transformation of the art of memory which has become externalised into a Renaissance building symbolizing the universe – 'a kind of epistemological planetarium displayed so as to be recollected' (Mack 2003: 16) – but while Camillo places his viewer onto the stage and has him look towards the auditorium, deprived of an audience and decorated with images, Fludd ignores the auditorium and conceives of his memory system as a stage, with its five doors to be used as memory places.

The interconnection of these elaborate memory systems, which also involved the work of other 'Renaissance occult memory artists' (Yates ibid.: 230), such as Ramon Lull, Pierre de la Ramée (generally known as Peter Ramus) as well as Giordano Bruno, is a broad and complex subject which has been studied extensively in the years when Frances Yates was writing (cf. ibid.: 232) and cannot be expounded fully here. What interests me for the purpose of the present study is to illustrate how an idea which has travelled across the centuries and produced enthrallingly complex schemes in the mind of Renaissance thinkers could influence the conception of a twentieth-century novel. The English Renaissance was clearly receptive to this transfer and it was a desire to encompass all knowledge into a universal framework that motivated the 'memory artists' of the period in their attempt to comprehend the ideal and essential structure of reality. As Paolo Rossi writes in his preface to the 1960 edition of *Clavis Universalis* (tr. *Logic and the Art of Memory* 2000), which Yates acknowledges in her preface to *The Art of Memory*,

> [t]hey formulated systematic rules for improving the memory, compiled grandiose encyclopaedias and complicated 'theatres of the world', sought to reduce the complexities of human thought to a primordial 'alphabet' of simple notions, and harboured

> pansophic aspirations and hopes for a universal reformation and pacification of humankind. (Rossi 2000: iv)

From a twentieth-century perspective, their attempt to construct total encyclopaedias and classify the world in an orderly scheme can be compared to the operations of a computer storing and processing memory through data compression, an observation which has frequently been made (see Matussek 2001) and also finds its way into Byatt's later works, as will be shown in connection with *A Whistling Woman*. Musing on the interrelation between memory and fiction, 'on the interlocking systems of mnemonics that constitute a novel in progress' (Byatt ibid.: 64), the author describes her writing as 'large static structures of mnemonics to put things into, to remember their relations' (ibid.: 66). Thus, beneath the surface of her novel, we can begin to detect the design of her personal memory theatre – a visual arena for her fictional recreation.

1.2 A Memory Theatre, a Literary Pageant and Elizabethan England

Byatt's reinvention of England in her novel series can ultimately be read as a memory theatre in fictional form, namely as a symbolic architectural project that systematizes both her imaginative and learned subject matter. The conceptual influence of this visual technique of recollection is particularly evident in *The Virgin in the Garden*, where the author intertwines the iconography of Elizabeth I with a series of analogies relating to Frederica. As already noted, Byatt derives her conception of visual mnemonics from Frances Yates's study of both *The Art of Memory* and of Elizabethan symbolism and the imperial theme in the sixteenth century in *Astraea*. Let us now consider how this symbolic structure is mapped onto the novel which, as the author tells us, grew out of an unfinished doctoral dissertation on religious allegory in the seventeenth century (Byatt 1993: 3). I suggest that the conceptual framework connected with the art of memory may have served the need to structure a densely layered narrative resulting from this earlier scholarly project.

The Virgin in the Garden unfolds as a series of narratives corresponding to individual chapters whose titles refer to spatial locations ('In the Tower', 'Masters' Garden'), mythological, literary or role figures ('Paterfamilias', 'Anadyomene'), or else historical, religious and personal events marking rites of passage in people's lives ('Easter', 'Annunciation', 'Coronation', 'Saturnalia'). They may also bear titles containing intertextual allusions, such as 'Women in Love', 'Prospero', 'Comus' or 'Ode on a Grecian Urn'. Each title allows the narrator 'to play games on a metafictional level' (Fludernik 2009: 24) and comment symbolically on the plot conveyed by realistic means. Thus, for example, the title of Lawrence's novel *Women in Love* appears in chapter 4 of *The Virgin in the Garden* as a reminder of a potential parallel between the young Potter sisters and Lawrence's characters.

Although this is a mere detail in a short chapter, Lawrence haunts the imagination of Frederica throughout the tetralogy and is the focus of many ideological and moral conflicts. Central among them is the generational conflict between Frederica, her siblings and their father, Bill Potter. This puritan teacher of Leavisite convictions, 'who has broken out of a stifling Nonconformist background' (Preston 2012: 191), is the 'Paterfamilias' of the title in ch. 20. Agnostic and ambitious for his children to invest in their talents, he has an outburst of rage when he learns that his eldest daughter Stephanie wants to marry 'a fat curate' (Byatt 1994: 259). Committed to the idea of reforming culture and community, he admires Lawrence's liberating values, while Frederica remains critical of Lawrence's treatment of women in his fiction.[17] As will be subsequently shown, this battle of ideas reaches its climax in *Babel Tower*, the third novel in the series.

Since 'the art of memory is like an inner writing' (Yates ibid.: 6) where the images (*imagines*) function as letters arranged in a script, Lawrence is present in Byatt's text as a mnemonic image encapsulating his fictional world. Hence, the reference to *Women in Love* in chapter 4 of *The Virgin in the Garden* evokes chiefly a topos in the characterization of two sisters conversing about their lives. The opening lines of both Lawrence's and Byatt's chapters are worth quoting, as they are suggestive of the author's intertextually mnemonic practice:

> Ursula and Gudrun Brangwen sat one morning in the window-bay of their father's house in Beldover, working and talking. Ursula was stitching a piece of brightly-coloured embroidery, and Gudrun was drawing upon a board which she held on her knee. [...] both had the remote virgin look of modern girls, sisters of Artemis rather than of Hebe. Gudrun was very beautiful, passive, soft-skinned, soft-limbed. She wore a dress of dark-blue silky stuff, with ruches of blue and green linen lace in the neck and sleeves; and she had emerald-green stockings. (D.H. Lawrence 1979: 7–8)

> The sisters sat by Stephanie's electric fire in nightclothes. Stephanie was dripping, injecting milk into the increasingly bedraggled but still living kittens. She wore striped Marks and Spenser's boys' pyjamas, rather large, inside which her rounded body seemed formless and elusively bulky. Frederica affected a long white nightdress with full sleeves, and a yoke of broderie anglaise threaded with black ribbon. (Byatt 1994: 58)

17 For an indepth discussion of Byatt's response to D.H. Lawrence in her fiction see Preston (2012).

The two passages differ in their description of specific details concerning the characters' appearance, but they are essentially similar in their evocation of an atmosphere foregrounding the relationship between sisters. Furthermore, the second excerpt hints symbolically at Stephanie's future as a young mother by casting her as a gentle animal lover and carer of kittens. Lawrence's pre-text contains significant allusions to Greek mythology, with Hebe personifying youth, and the image of Artemis as virgin-huntress underlies the narrative of both novels. The subtle interrelations existing between the two texts refer us back to the notion of interfigurality, described in the introductory chapter (iv). The attentive reader will be alert to the fact that a hefty dose of metafictional commentary is frequently let in through carefully placed intertextual clues, though s/he needs not be conscious of it. Hence, references to previous texts make it possible to weave together a densely layered pattern of connections that both activate and reinscribe the literary voices of the past kept in the cultural archives of tradition, so as to re-stage the author's own sense of the literary past and map its development through conceptual images. A similar strategy affording parallels with the art of memory as mentioned above underlies each chapter title. I shall return to some of these thematic links in the relevant sections.

The chapters of *The Virgin in the Garden* are arranged in three parts, which have allegorical titles. Part I, 'A fugitive virtue', draws on Milton's polemical tract *Areopagitica* (1644), which is on the subject of licensing, freedom of speech and the power of the intellect to embody moral life.[18] 'A flowery tale' (part 2) hints at Renaissance patterns of birth and rebirth, affecting language and characters as through an ideal transmutation between words and things. This is a clear evocation of T.S. Eliot's account of the 'dissociation of sensibility' occurring in the seventeenth century, when thought became separated from feeling and the language of the Metaphysical poets ceased to flourish. Eliot expressed these views in a famous essay on 'The Metaphysical Poets' (1921) and Byatt has openly acknowledged that 'the play in my novel, and the novel itself, are nostalgia for a *paradis perdu* in which thought and language and things were naturally and indissolubly linked or, to use an Eliot metaphor, fused' (Byatt 1993: 9–10). This also explains why the characters in the novel

18 'I cannot praise a fugitive and cloistered virtue, unexercised and unbreathed, that never sallies out and sees her adversary, but slinks out of the race, where that immortal garland is to be run for, not without dust and heat' (Milton 2005: 349–350).

are 'haunted by dreams of wholeness and completion, of 'breaking through' into a state in which mind and body, word and thing, would be one' (Hanson 2000: 23). Finally, 'Redit et Virgo' in part 3 is a clear reference to Virgil's Fourth Eclogue predicting a new golden age coinciding with the return of Virgo-Astraea, for which Byatt draws on Yates's study *Astraea*.[19] All this shows that Byatt has recast the localities and facts pictured as 'images' – namely the *imagines* and *loci* of ancient mnemotechnics – so as to evoke a whole period, the first Elizabethan age, and to make it overlap with the crowning of Elizabeth II in 1953, parading like a procession or a pageant under the reader's eyes. Consequently, the allegorical denomination of parts and chapter titles allows the narrator to comment symbolically on the plot and mark a visual and conceptual trajectory along the space of the novel.

This kind of tightly organized mental space becomes externalized in the shape of the novel; it is suggestive of a storage pattern connected with the very idea of the archive or repository of memory. It also affords an example of the development of a literary work out of the procedures of the art of memory, which has not been a common practice in the tradition of the novel. Memory has emerged at the turn of the Millennium as a key word underlying the way in which cultures and societies construct their identity and orient their future by selecting, organizing, and passing on the knowledge of the past via archives and memory sites, including rituals and oral traditions. Yet, the *ars memorativa* of the ancients does not seem to have affected the genre of the novel in a recognizable way, so much so that Frances Yates could state in her classic study that 'the influence of the art of memory on literature is a practically untouched subject' (312). She does, however, trace a distant precedent for this kind of relation between the art of memory and literature in the work of the Renaissance philosopher Giordano Bruno *La Cena de le Ceneri*, published in England in 1584 (tr. *The Ash Wednesday Supper* 1995). While the work of Giordano Bruno does not bear any direct relation to Byatt's novel, it is relevant in the overall development of a genre having a distant precedent in Renaissance culture (see Yates 1964; Yates 1966: 199–230, 243–319).

---

19 'Iam redit et virgo, redeunt Saturnia regna', i.e. 'now comes back the virgin, now returns the reign of Saturn' (Yates 1977: 33). As Yates suggests, the golden age epitomizes the Augustan rule and the revival of empire which greatly influenced the Elizabethan age, since 'the unmarried state of the Queen is exalted into a symbol of the imperial virgin Astraea which fills the universe' (ibid.: 59).

Bruno was in England from 1584 to 1586 and became acquainted with such men as Sir Walter Raleigh, Sir Philip Sydney and Sir Fulke Greville.[20] He was introduced to the court of Queen Elizabeth and spoke of her as the 'unique Diana' and as 'Diva Elizabetta' (qtd. in Yates 1977: 84). It was also in London that he wrote one of his most controversial works, *De l'infinito, universo e mondi* (*On the Infinite Universe and Worlds*), which may have precipitated his conviction by the Inquisition (Yates 1964; Aquilecchia 2001: 48–50; 71–91). Transcending the ideas of Copernicus, whose theory on heliocentricity he had followed, Bruno had come to conceive of the universe as infinite, devoid of centre and circumference. His *Ash Wednesday Supper*, however, does not openly describe a mnemonic system but a set of dialogues or conversations in prose interspersed with sonnets, which a group of lively characters exchange while strolling the streets of Elizabethan London. On his way to supper in the house of Sir Fulke Greville, the learned philosopher Theofilo converses with a number of characters about astronomy and, among other things, the theory of Copernicus.

Tellingly, *La cena de le ceneri* contains an invocation to the Muses and Mnemosyne, the goddess of Memory:

> a voi Muse d'Inghilterra dico, inspiratemi, suffiatemi, scaldatemi, accendetemi, ambiccatemi, et risolvetemi in liquore, datemi in succhio, et fatemi comparir non con un picciolo [,] delicato, stretto, corto, et succinto epigramma: ma con una copiosa et larga vena di prosa lunga, corrente, grande, et soda: onde non come da un arto calamo, ma come da un largo canale mande i rivi miei. Et tu Mnemosine mia ascosa sotto trenta sigilli, et rinchiusa nel tetro carcere dell'ombre de le Idee, intonami un poco ne l'orecchio.
>
> (Bruno 1955: 17)

> To you, Muses of England, I say: inspire me, breathe on me, warm me, ignite me, distill and resolve me into liquor, make me into juice and make me utter not a small, feeble, narrow, short and succinct epigram, but an abundant, broad vein of lengthy, fluent, grand and steady prose, whence my rivers will not be fed as from a narrow stream but as from a capacious channel. And thou, my Mnemosyne, who art hidden under thirty seals and shut up in the bleak prison of the shadows of Ideas, harmonize a little in my ear.
>
> (Bruno 1995: 84–85)

This excerpt hints at the 'thirty seals' of Bruno's arcane and complex theory of concentric seals and shadows symbolizing everything in existence, which I mentioned in the introduction. On the subject, Bruno had written a treatise, *Triginta*

20 A different authoritative source marks April 1583 as the date of Bruno's arrival in London, where he found hospitality in the home of the French Ambassador (see Aquilecchia 2001: 34).

sigillorum explicatio (*On the Thirty Seals*) and a book, *De umbris idearum* (*On the Shadows of Ideas*).

Yates claims that in *La cena de le ceneri*, Bruno uses a topographical setting, 'the Strand, Charing Cross, the Thames, the French embassy, a house in Whitehall, on which to remember the themes of a debate about the Sun at supper' (ibid.: 311). The debate interrelates with Bruno's views about Christianity and the rebirth of 'magical religion heralded by the Copernican Sun' (ibid.). It is also characterized by the use of allegory within a mnemonic, topographical structure, since the characters of the *Cena* have to face many obstacles on their way to Supper. This text is significant because it shows how 'the streets of memory places' can become populated with characters and also become 'the backcloth for a drama', as Frances Yates has suggested (ibid.: 312).

Similarly, Byatt intertwines her visual pattern of narrative and mnemonics with a wealth of learned material throughout her series of novels, while her geographical setting alternates between Northern Yorkshire and London in the overall narrative of her tetralogy. In this overarching comparison of narrative related to the art of memory, we may observe similar features. Both Bruno's text and Byatt's novel resort to a topographical setting to arrange their subject matter and facilitate the process of memory; both employ allegory in order to comment symbolically on the plot and also insert complex ideas into their prose and dialogues spoken by the characters in the texts. As will be shown in a later chapter, Byatt's final volume *A Whistling Woman* even incorporates a whole theoretical debate among scientists about the workings of cognitive processes and the function of memory. This debate will take place in the same Renaissance building, now converted into the fictional university of North Yorkshire, where the characters involved in the staging of the verse play *Astraea* discuss the iconography of the cult of Elizabeth I in *The Virgin in the Garden*. Significantly, it is the garden of this Elizabethan mansion which provides the ideal setting for the staging of Alexander Wedderburn's verse play.

1.3 The Play of Images and Gardens: The Visual Process

Before I turn my attention to the staging of the play and the concomitant cultural rituals enacted in the novel, let me stress again that the link between spatiality and visuality is an essential component of the narrative. The author is acutely aware of issues concerning the nature of form and representation of the visible world and in the above mentioned essay on 'Memory and the Making of Fiction' (ibid.), she claims having a strong eidetic mnemonic faculty. Her own system of mnemonics may resemble abstract paintings or the rising of geometrical structures associated with a text in the making.[21] Therefore, it is significant that in *The Virgin in the Garden*, Byatt endows Marcus Potter, the youngest character in the family at the centre of the novel, with an exceptional capacity for visualising and performing complex mathematical operations by thinking in geometrical forms.

In the novel, these geometrical forms multiply and pattern the narrative structure of different episodes. Thus, the Elizabethan garden functions as a conceptual frame for different 'inset structures' (Fludernik 2009: 156) intertwining the plot and various secondary episodes, enacting a protracted *mise-en-abyme*. This is a concentrated redoubling of other narratives and intertextual references which proliferate producing a kaleidoscope of images and iconic signs. As Lucien Dällenbach's well-known study *The Mirror in the Text* well illustrates, its 'essential property' is to bring out 'the meaning and form of the work' (1989: 8). Accordingly, we have the garden of the title as well as real and symbolic gardens, such as the gardens around the Blesford Ride School, where both Bill Potter and Alexander Wedderburn teach, and the walled Master's garden outside the church, where Stephanie and Daniel's wedding reception takes place. During the wedding ceremony, 'the congregation swayed like a windy garden, tilting helmeted and floral heads to see the bride' (*Virgin*: 342) and when Daniel and Stephanie make love, Stephanie perceives 'the inner spaces of her body [… as a] clear landscape […] coming out into fields of flowers, light green stalks, airy leaves, bright flowers moving and dancing in wavering tossing lines to the blown grass of a cliff' (*Virgin*: 372–373). As has been noted, this passage evokes ideas of fertility and growth but also connects the female body with an affirmative sense of 'renewal and rebirth rather than Christian repudiation of the body' (Hanson 2000: 136). Conversely, the field and Bilge Pond where Marcus Potter experiences visionary moments of hallucinations is an open and threatening space, increasing the boy's loss of touch with the real world.

The episodes concerning the life of this younger character belong to the intricate sub-plot of the novel and can only be summarized here. Marcus is prone to psychic outbursts of light, a phenomenon frequently referred to as photism, which renders him an isolated figure within his articulate and intellectual family. Unfortunately, he is subject to the influence of a dotty science teacher 'who thinks him a visionary in the tradition of Blake' (Schumann 1983: 115) and

21 'My own structures are rather like abstract paintings - a rising series of increasingly acute triangles in complementary colours may represent one text in construction, a series of concentric spirals, or even a double helix, another' (Byatt ibid.: 66).

wishes to experiment with the paranormal on him. On the subject of Marcus's reputed autism and exceptional visual and mathematical faculties, Judith Plotz has written perceptively that the characterization of Marcus Potter is inscribed within the Romantic tradition of the visionary child (Plotz 2001). Similarly, Olga Kenyon had observed in an earlier essay that Marcus 'has elements of the child-seer, but bereft of religious blessing' (Kenyon 1988: 69), connecting his experiences with those of the child in Wordsworth's *Prelude*. However, as both Alexa Alfer and Michael J. Noble have claimed in their introduction to a co-edited volume, 'his remains a profoundly "dissociated sensibility" at sea in a fictional world that has so much invested in Eliot's myth of modernity's fall from "undissociatedness"' (Alfer and Noble 2001: 7).

Throughout the novel, we are invited to reflect on the peculiarities of the visual faculty and the nature of mental processes engrained in personal experience. Each character is shown to respond differently to experiences that are mediated either through words or images. Stephanie, for example, a much more literary and articulate character than Marcus, is equally gifted when it comes to memorizing abstract knowledge as well as images and objects that meet her eye. A teacher of English who sacrifices her vocation to family life and motherhood, Stephanie reflects on the changes in education that her short-lived professional experience has made apparent to her. In chapter 11, titled 'Play Room', an external voice overlapping with her own observes that memory training is no longer fashionable, noting that:

> There are fashions in habits of mind as in habits of gear, and memory banks went out, a little after the time of this story, a little after the Coronation of Elizabeth II, as memory theatres had gone out with the Renaissance, and with memory banks went works of art that were themselves memory-banks, went tradition and the individual talent, the Bible, the pantheon, the different organisations of other languages. (Byatt 1994: 142)

This kind of authorial comment shows the extent to which A.S. Byatt feels the weight of an Eliot-like tradition she has inherited and of which she feels part. It also invites the reader to reflect on the peculiarities of a visual faculty which had once required a far greater capacity of concentration, skill and attentiveness than our contemporary visual culture demands of us. In order to capture the precise correlation between space, orderly arrangement and image, the mind's eye must scan images slowly, in an orderly and analytical manner,[22] a process

---

22 See Bolzoni 1991: 9–34 (here 13): 'Perché lo spettacolo della memoria si metta in moto e funzioni, bisogna che l'occhio della mente percorra le immagini in modo lento,

towards which Byatt seems naturally inclined: 'I know that I know certain things and I know them in visual shapes' (Tredell 1994: 67), is one of her paradigmatic statements on the relation between visual and verbal processes that engages her attention in fiction as well as in critical commentary. Even more telling in this context, is her description of one of her earliest experiences in childhood demonstrating the importance of vision underlying her novels: 'And then I remember, when I was a small child, being frightened of shapes moving on the ceiling at night – there was a tree outside my bedroom – and thinking, do I think this is a bear, no I don't think this is a bear, but it means that there are things you can see and not see' (ibid.).

Apart from telling us something about mental processes engrained in personal experience, these remarks are interesting in that they interrelate with fundamental observations on the nature of form and representation of the visible world, such as have been raised in scholarship by E.H. Gombrich. In his *Art and Illusion* (1972), the art theorist highlights how primitive art and child art have been assessed since the nineteenth century. Both use a language of symbols rather than natural signs and the child 'does not look at trees; he is satisfied with the conceptual schema of a tree' (76). These reflections shed light on Byatt's comments. Indeed, the novelist has frequently referred to Gombrich when trying to illustrate her own ideas about the nature of thinking with visual images, as I pointed out in the introduction. In an interview with Nicolas Tredell, she comments on Gombrich's insights about how artists adjust acquired schemata in order to draw the things they see (Tredell ibid.: 68).

Byatt's correlation of the two cognitive levels regarding visual and linguistic processes is all the more significant because it also reveals her own experience in overcoming a divide between pictorial art and abstract knowledge which is deeply embedded in the puritan tradition of her home culture. Having attended a Quaker school, she notes that 'the Quakers, because they have so few rules, put enormous moral pressure on you and this becomes a kind of imprisoning… On the other hand… Quaker emphasis on silence creates an awareness of the value of words, of what they can do, and *it also reminds one*

---

ordinato, analitico. L'arte della memoria richiede una visualità molto lontana dalla nostra, una visualità capace di far sprigionare dall'immagine tutti i messaggi di cui è stata investita, una visualità, quindi, attenta a cogliere tutti gli aspetti del rapporto fra l'ordine, lo spazio, l'immagine stessa, oltre a ripercorrere il gioco di relazioni fra parti e tutto, fra pluralità e unità'.

of what words can't do, of where their limits are, which a novelist needs to know' (Dusinberre 1983: 188).[23]

The implications embedded in these remarks are particularly relevant for *The Virgin in the Garden*, where the young Frederica is described as being singularly unequipped to comprehend the iconography of Renaissance paintings, although she is well versed in literature. This is especially evident in chapter 13 entitled 'In the Humanist's House', where Frederica and other characters are invited for a guided tour by its rich owner Matthew Crowe. Significantly, the tour starts in the luxuriant garden surrounding Long Royston, which had been planted according to the prescriptions of Francis Bacon's essay 'Of Gardens', and ends in a library full of pictures and Ovidian echoes, which dazzle the young protagonist. Inevitably, we are reminded of Dorothea Brooke, George Eliot's protestant heroine cast in a similar predicament in *Middlemarch*, when she visits the Vatican Museums on her wedding journey to Rome and feels overwhelmed by the sight of classical art and the beauty of naked sculptures, those 'strange ancestral images and trophies gathered from afar' (Eliot 1985: 224). In Byatt's novel, both the garden and the picture gallery are parodic instances of a bygone world resonating distant echoes. Because they are set in a Northern landscape, they are associated with 'a very strong Puritan element' (Dusinberre ibid.: 190) which the author traces back to the original project at the heart of her novel, i.e. her abandoned dissertation on religious metaphor in the English Renaissance.

This incompatibility between Protestantism and the visual process connected with the art of memory had already been remarked upon by Frances Yates. In one of the chapters devoted to Giordano Bruno in *The Art of Memory*, she had observed that in the Elizabethan world 'the Protestant educational authorities, and probably public opinion generally, were against the art of memory' (ibid.: 261). One can therefore all the more appreciate the cross-cultural significance and historical resonance of this episode in the novel relating to Frederica's encounter with the visual arts and their erotic power.

1.4 New Elizabethans

Let me now illustrate how Byatt's distinct lingering gaze becomes enacted in *The Virgin in the Garden* which, like the other volumes in the series, is a long and complex work. I would like to highlight some central chapters which are cornerstones in its conception, such as the prologue set in 1968, that is a time

23 *Emphasis added.*

following the main events chronicled in the novel, and the chapters entitled 'In the Humanist's House', 'Coronation', 'Saturnalia' and 'Queen and Huntress'. All of them, in fact, intertwine the theme of memory, identity, culture and community in a variety of forms, casting the many characters in the novel as New Elizabethans. This notion has recently re-emerged in the aftermath of the London Olympics and Jubilee celebrations to describe a patchwork of variously defined ideals and values in the years surrounding the Coronation of Elizabeth II and assess their legacy in contemporary culture. Curiously, Byatt's novel seems to anticipate the need for a retrospective glance at those years and thus offer a perspective from which to explore the spirit of the age. In order to keep my argument cohesive, I shall deal with the prologue after discussing the chapters I have indicated.

In the chapter 'In the Humanist's House', Frederica is invited by a wealthy cultural impresario and art connoisseur, Matthew Crowe, to visit his stately home. Earlier in the novel Crowe is characterized as a kind of Prospero with a genius for organization, capable of enlivening a whole community and masterminding a festival which is 'to be his *magnum opus*' (ibid.: 83). The garden of his Elizabethan mansion provides the ideal setting for the celebration of Coronation year 1953 and Frederica will act the role of the young Elizabeth I in the verse play *Astraea* performed as a tribute to the newly crowned Elizabeth II. Having gathered in his home all the actors involved in the production of *Astraea*, including professional and non-professional actors, he leads them into the library 'where various sketches and mock-ups' are 'displayed' (175). Among them are Alexander Wedderburn's drawings for the play, demonstrating the playwright's interest in 'portraits, miniatures, the garments themselves' (176) which he has studied meticulously in the Victoria and Albert Museum. Repeatedly, the novel self-consciously incorporates unobtrusive reflections on the nature of parody and historical representation through Alexander's viewpoint. Tellingly, he remains throughout the narrative a detached observer of all kinds of performances, seeing various forms of parody around him, including the clothes that many women wear when he first enters the novel and appears in the prologue.

While the iconography of the cult of Elizabeth I is discussed in detail by Matthew Crowe and Frederica in this chapter, the myth of the historical Elizabeth as both Virgin Queen and hermaphrodite gives rise to complex meditations on the subject of female creativity and power. Wishing to instruct Frederica about the significance of various mythological allusions to female figures of power, Crowe initiates a long discussion on the paintings hanging on the walls of his library, illustrating Ovid's *Metamorphoses*. One of the images Frederica sees is:

> a plaster frieze running round the Great Hall, under the gallery. She had taken in no more than a vague impression of forest trees, naked running figures and animals, in chalky relief. Now, staring obediently at this, she saw that the figures were both vigorous and slightly wooden, an uneasy marriage of the English and the classical. She located a man becoming a stag, a creature whose tortured energy of metamorphosis was something like that of the foliate men in Southwell Minster: stretched sinews, hardening distorted feet, spreading ribcage, branching horns, creamy-furred dewlap and opening muzzle-mouth under a human brow. (178–179)

The ekphrastic description details Ovid's figures in the process of being painfully transformed. Frederica recognizes Actaeon turned into a stag and torn to pieces, promptly associating the classical myth of Diana and Actaeon with something she remembers from Southwell cathedral in Nottinghamshire. Similar depictions of Ovid's tales appear as Frederica ventures further into the house, until the cruel story of Marsyas flayed by Apollo is revealed to her in all its erotic sadism (Cox 2013: 265–266). Needless to say, the learned impresario, 'small, cherubic, red and shining' (Byatt 1994: 85), plans to initiate the young protagonist into both aesthetic and sexual education. Though Frederica is repelled by the sadism of the myth, her exposure to Ovid's depictions does foreshadow her subsequent sexual experience in this very place. Indeed, looking at 'Venus hunting the errant Cupid' (179), Frederica judges 'the whole thing' as 'a continual allegory' (ibid.).

This seductive vision is followed by scenes foregrounding Elizabeth I as a focal icon in Crowe's stately home. Frederica stops in front of a portrait of the queen as 'Polyolbion-Virgo-Astraea' (181), which seems modelled on the frontispice of Michael Drayton's topographical poem: 'under its literally landscaped draperies it was heavy and exuberant, castle-crowned. The left hand held a naked sword; [...] the cornucopia rose powerful and huge, a stiff curving horn, a river of plenty' (ibid.). Symbolizing harvest as well as the head of the Body Politic, Elizabeth as Astraea multiplies the countless intertextual allusions underlying the narrative. What follows is a tour of the State Bedrooms: 'These were cosmologically named, Sun, Moon and Planets, opening into each other, each containing a huge curtained bed under an elaborately painted ceiling' (ibid.). Thus, the world view characterizing Renaissance England, intertwined with the neoplatonic conception of the universe as the Great Chain of Being of the Elizabethans, pervades the microcosm of Long Royston.[24] Crowe's select guests will soon be involved in the staging of a play which will subvert the many roles assigned to them off-stage. Illicit love affairs and secret meetings take place in

24 On the subject of Byatt's evocation of the Great Chain of Being in the novel see Celia M. Wallhead's in-depth commentary (Wallhead 1999: 204–211).

Crowe's stately bedchambers, governed by celestial powers mirroring the order of creation. Ironically, Frederica will gain an overview of her recent initiation into matters of life and aesthetics when she finally escapes the grip of Crowe's seductive power. In an amusing scene portraying her as small scale 'Queen and Huntress' in ch. 35, Frederica hastens to leave the premises of this wealthy Tudor home, passing through:

> the long galleries, in moonlight and dark, stopping for a moment under the iconographical representation of Elizabeth with the cornucopia. She shifted the knot in the towel over her own shoulder, which pulled like Scotland over Polyolbion's, and made a sketchy obeisance to the squat figure. She herself had no river, no cornucopia, no golden fruit. (437)

Thus, the frequent juxtaposition of life, 'fleeting, accidental, entailing constant changes, with works of art, permanent and static' (Kuzniar 2012: 196) marks Frederica's rite of passage into adulthood. The young Frederica who, in this novel, is little more than an adolescent, undergoes a number of developments which are reflected in the wider cultural context in which she moves. This is the macrocosm of the ideal universe portrayed in classical mythology and Elizabethan culture, though the reality of the novel transforms those very images into comic motifs for entertainment.

In the course of the novel Frederica is cast as the young Elizabeth in Wedderburn's play *Astraea*. Thus, she performs a theatrical role in a public performance coinciding with an official event while, on a private level, she experiences her first sexual encounter. In a sort of small-scale parodic game, her bodily changes mirror metaphorically the fate of the Virgin Queen, Elizabeth Tudor. There is implied irony in this choice of subject matter of course, because all the characters in the novel are somehow mirrored in those of the Elizabethan setting, starting from Frederica in the role of the Queen, who 'needed no consort' and was 'her own heir', as she authoritatively claimed in her speeches to Parliament (Jordan 1990: 160). The governing principle of a central metaphor – the Virgin Queen – is therefore refracted into multiple references and different levels of signification, enacting a protracted *mise-en-abyme*. As I have already indicated, this is a concentrated redoubling of other narratives and intertextual references which proliferate, giving shape to a kaleidoscope of images and iconic signs, which the title of Byatt's novel had already announced.

The scenes describing the preparations for the staging of the play are interspersed in fragments throughout the narrative and occupy various chapters, including first auditions, rehearsals, opening and last performances. Furthermore, the playwright's reflections on the language adopted for his allegorical verse drama underlie the various phases of production. Wedderburn strives to achieve a 'renaissance of language, florid and rich and muscular' (417). He had meant to recapture that fusion between words and things which T.S. Eliot had theorized in his essay on *The Metaphysical Poets*, earlier referred to. Writing in the wake of T.S. Eliot and Christopher Fry, he considers that:

> What he had made was so dense: thick, like all good fifties verse drama, with witty imagery, which meant jostling suns and moons and swans and gossamer and flowers and stones, and again thick with the specificity of the visual imagination of a playwright who designed his own costumes, chestnut and twilight velvets, packed radiant pleats and gilded stitchery of which actuality could only be a shadowy representation. (417–418)

In retrospect, he will understand that his obsession with the need to renovate the genre through a cluster of connections harking back to Renaissance verse is illusory and 'a false beginning' (15).

Yet, the novel does something different than simply re-stage with nostalgic grandeur the idea of a past historical moment. When the inhabitants of this small provincial community in Northern Yorkshire gather in the private home of one of its members to watch the coronation of Elizabeth II on television, the Queen has become a mere icon on a tiny screen, bearing no comparison with the Darnley portrait of Elizabeth I reproduced on the posters hanging outside the National Portrait Gallery in London and described in the prologue preceding the main narrative. At the threshold of a new visual culture heralded by the new mass medium, the Queen has become:

> a matt and twinkling tiny doll, half an inch, an inch, two inches, a face maybe eight inches across, grave or graciously beaming, a black and white smiling image of pleated linen and cloth of gold and shimmering embroideries in mother-of-pearl shades [...] (315)

She has turned into a mere glittering sign whose function remains on the surface that of an *imago agentes* – i.e. of a conceptual memory image governed by the same principles laid down by the art of memory of the ancients as described by Frances Yates. Television by contrast is the new *locus* of the mind mirroring its movements. Byatt is therefore asking profound questions about the nature of ritual, tradition and the individual talent, and the thick layer of intertextual references including excerpts of newspaper cuttings and official discourses, incorporated into this chapter (ch. 27), demonstrates the extent of her enquiry.

A significant example of this elaborate intertextuality is the insertion of an excerpt from Churchill's speech celebrating the coronation of Elisabeth II in tones of archaic grandeur:

> 'Let it not be thought that the age of chivalry belongs to the past. Here, at the summit of our worldwide community, is the lady whom we respect, because she is our Queen, and whom we love because she is herself. Gracious and noble are words familiar to us all in courtly phrasing. Tonight they have a new ring in them because we know that they are true about the gleaming figure whom Providence has brought to us in times when the present is hard and the future is veiled'. (316)

At the same time, we should also bear in mind that the novel bears the imprint of T.S. Eliot's *Four Quartets*, which obsessively re-echoes in Frederica's mind: 'In a Proustian way too, as she acquired age, she came to associate her obsession with the *Four Quartets* with the Coronation, with the Coronation's gestures towards England, history and continuity' (319). Inevitably, the allusion links the historical moment in the novel's fictional plot to Eliot's idea of history and tradition in 'Tradition and the Individual Talent', evoking the notion 'not only of the pastness of the past, but of its presence' and of the necessary co-existence in the writer of the plurality of voices which have preceded him:

> the historical sense compels a man to write not merely with his own generation in his bones, but with a feeling that the whole of the literature of Europe from Homer and within it the whole of the literature of his own country has a simultaneous existence and composes a simultaneous order. (Eliot 1973: 2014)

With hindsight, Frederica will also fully acknowledge the pastness of the past, and the elusive nature of an event whose reality can only belong to the past. The following retrospective comment highlights just this disjunction between the illusory power of narrative and the perception of an event confined to a specific time and social context:

> It had tried and failed to be now and England. There had been other worse failures. In the sense in which all attempts are by definition not failures, since now *is* now, and the Queen was, whatever the People made of it, crowned, it *was* now, and England. Then. (319)

As well as including the comments of ordinary people watching the event on the tiny screen, this chapter also reproduces the media coverage of the Coronation, followed by a retrospective commentary on the rhetorics informing the speeches of journalists and politicians, and what the novel therefore does is to disclose the so-called politics of consensus. Significantly, words such as 'national' and 'identity' are voiced with implicit self-awareness by an anonymous character in the prologue to the novel, who has declined an invitation to attend the opening of a theatrical performance in which Flora Robson plays Elizabeth I at the National Portrait Gallery. Indeed, he rejects those terms. Alexander Wedderburn, the playwright who makes his début in the course of the novel, picks up on this casual remark and comments further:

> He considered those words, once powerful, at present defunct, national and portrait. They were both to do with identity: the identity of a culture (place, language and history), the identity of an individual human being as an object for mimetic representation. (Byatt 1978: 7)

It is the year 1968, a time following the incidents narrated in the main plot which take place in 1953. Yet, these carefully placed observations anticipate the erosion of a sense of national identity which would become a target of much social and scholarly criticism in the age of postcolonial literary theories.

The prologue contains many details which may be easily overlooked at a first glance. For example, when Alexander Wedderburn notes the reproductions of the Darnley portrait of Elizabeth I on the railings outside the National Portrait Gallery which he is about to enter, we may not be immediately aware of the embedded significance of these iconic reproductions. They announce the theme of the exhibition 'People, Past and Present', calling for a retrospective glance that also suggests an invitation to review and assess the national past by comparing it with the present. The androgynous power exercised by the Tudor Queen in the patriarchal sixteenth century has long been an object of scholarly discussion (cf. Jordan 1990; Doran 2003), but what the novel does is to contrast it implicitly with the role assigned to women in post-war English society. It is interesting to note in this regard that when the novel was being written, new iconographic interpretations of the portraits of Elizabeth I had just been published by Frances Yates and Roy Strong, the former director of the National Portrait Gallery (see Brosch 1999). Therefore, it is all the more significant that these real-life characters appear in the prologue among the select guests attending the theatrical performance, which is part of the exhibition held at the National Portrait Gallery. Tellingly, 'the large, contemplatively vague figure of Dr. Frances Yates' (*Virgin* 11) is clearly visible in the crowd and we learn that her 'writings on the images of Elizabeth Tudor as Virgo-Astraea' (ibid.) have had a profound influence on Alexander's life. Ironically, the fictional playwright 'amuses himself by counting powerful women' (ibid.) among the many guests taking their seats in the gallery, but most of all his attention is captured by the portrait of the Virgin Queen hanging there, which the novel ekphrastically describes:

> There she stood, a clear powerful image, in her airy dress of creamy stiff silk, embroidered with golden fronds, laced with coral tassels, lightly looped with pearls. She stood and stared with the stillness and energy of a young girl. The frozen lassitude of the long white hands exhibited their fineness: they dangled, or gripped, it was hard to tell which, a circular feathery fan whose harsh whirl of darker colours suggested a passion, a fury of movement suppressed in the figure. There were other ambiguities in the portrait, the longer one stared, doubleness that went beyond the obvious one of woman and ruler.

> The bright-blanched face was young and arrogant. Or it was chalky, bleak, bony, any age at all, the black eyes under heavy lids knowing and distant. Her portraits had been treated as icons and as witches' dolls: men had died for meddling with them in various ways, such as stabbing, burning, piercing with hog's bristles, embedding in poison.
>
> She herself had been afraid, but had not lost her head. (12)

The passage conveys the elaborate splendor of the queen's appearance as portrayed in the Darnley Portrait; yet, it also describes her as set apart, as an individualized subject capable of capturing the imagination of a modern viewer. Thus, the portrait of the Virgin Queen is used not only to evoke a sense of the past, but also to highlight the complex relation between painted figures and characters in fiction. Indeed, the symbolic power of this visual image hovers over the whole narrative, since some of the characters see themselves reflected in it as in a mirror. This becomes evident when Frederica is cast as the young Elizabeth in the course of the novel, aided by her complexion and physical features, which are said to resemble those of the Virgin Queen. In the prologue, this physical resemblance is reinforced through a parodic reference to fashion and clothes, so much so that Frederica appears to Alexander, who is observing the scene, as a novel Britomart from Spencer's *Fairie Queene*:

> Frederica, in a kind of brief knitted corselet of dark grey wool with a glitter in it, and boots with a metallic sheen, was Britomart, her hair itself cut into a kind of bronze helmet, more space-age, maybe, than Renaissance. (ibid.: 12)

This playful allusion announces a kaleidoscope of images which proliferate in the novel, conflating the dual time level of the narrative and enacting a protracted *mise-en-abyme*, as I have already indicated. Accordingly, if Britomart is the female knight of chastity in search of her lover in the *Faerie Queene*, the young Frederica is involved in a similar quest. Ironically, she falls in love with Alexander, the androgynous and self-sufficient playwright who remains mostly aloof and is also reluctantly involved in an extra-marital affair with Jennifer Parry, the wife of a German master at Blesford Ride School. Placed against the backdrop of classical mythology and Elizabethan drama, these incidents become comic motifs for entertainment.

Meanwhile, on the square outside teeming with 'military jackets from Vietnam and the Crimea' (*Virgin* 8) a hippie crowd of tourists offers a panoramic view of the 'cultural carnival of London in the Swinging Sixties' (Alfer and Edwards de Campos 2010: 41), anticipating a future time level and creating a tension between the static quality of pictorial images and the manifest theatricality of lived experience. Thus, the structure of the novel emerges as a formidable space housing a vast array of individual images and historical moments that can be perceived as transitory or fragmented and yet are capable of generating a memorable narrative of what it was like to come of age in the early Fifties for a New Elizabethan.

As I have tried to show in this chapter, Byatt's reinvention of England connects Renaissance art and other cultural forms available to post-war English society with a tightly organized symbolic space derived from the ancient art of memory. I have read this elaborate system of mnemonics as a memory theatre of a literary kind that systematizes learned and popular culture as well as the author's memory of the Fifties as an imaginative and personal reinvention. Drawing on classical and Elizabethan conceptions of the art of memory and prompted by her reading of Frances Yates, I detail how the novelist turns an ancient and long forgotten art into a conceptual framework underpinned by a topographical setting, meaningful inscriptions and conceptual images, to portray a segment of English social and cultural history. In the process, the novel anticipates later developments in British culture when visual art and media become gradually more prominent. In the following chapter I wish to illustrate how this gradual transition becomes enacted in *Still Life*, the sequel to *The Virgin in the Garden*.

2. Painted in Memory: *Still Life*

Still Life (1985) was conceived in contrast to *The Virgin in the Garden*, a novel steeped in metaphors and Renaissance allegory which became transmuted into a flowery and densely layered narrative, as I have tried to show. Commenting on the gestation of the second novel in the series, the author noted that this was informed by her reflections on the Imagist poets and their capacity for accurate and vivid description. William Carlos Williams's dictum 'No ideas but in things', a frequently quoted line from Book I of his poem *Paterson* (1946), seemed to offer a solution to the problem Byatt was grappling with when she set to work on *Still Life*. Having probed 'the infinitely extensible cross-referencing of *The Virgin*' (Byatt 1993: 11), she wished to return to the question of representation pure and simple, exploring the basic functions of language as a vehicle for direct description. In an authorial aside towards the end of the novel, the narrator makes these concerns unambiguously explicit:

> I had the idea, when I began this novel, that it would be a novel of naming and accuracy. I wanted to write a novel as Williams said a poem should be: no ideas but in things. I even thought of trying to write without figures of speech, but had to give up that plan, quite early. (Byatt 1986: 301)

Thus, *Still Life* can be seen to retrace the strands of an old theoretical dilemma having its origin in Plato's notion of mimesis and the adequacy of pictorial representation as discussed in Book X of the *Republic* and further developed in Aristotle's *Poetics*. The relationship between art and life, between an image and the real is one of the leitmotifs woven into the aesthetic and conceptual fabric of the novel. Moving between these two opposing worlds, the novel even explores the possibilities of language devoid of any metaphors to describe reality, broadening the scope of its theoretical investigation through narrative.

In this chapter I wish to illustrate the intellectual concerns underpinning *Still Life* and the way in which these become translated into an artistic and fictional form. After some broad considerations regarding the conceptual frame of the novel, I shall illustrate the functioning of the prologue for the novel, highlighting the subtle play of correspondences that operate in connection with the main narrative. Subsequently, I shall analyse the author's handling of ekphrasis and visuality in *Still Life*. This interlocks with the author's manipulation of spatiality and links up with Byatt's approach to memory, as I indicated in the introduction (1.2).

While the overall narrative remains couched within a realist frame, *Still Life* begins to create a tension between realism and postmodern reflexivity by juxtaposing a close dialogue with the visual arts on the one hand and metafictional commentary on the other, heightening the self-consciousness of the narrative voice. It could even be argued that Byatt adopts the theme of visuality in order to pose the question of knowledge, a point which had already been made in an early review of the novel (Westlake 1989). This allows her to deal more extensively with the iconic aspects involved in systematizing her subject matter. As I noted in the preceding chapter (1.3), these iconic aspects consist in 'large static structures of mnemonics to put things into', which the author compares to abstract paintings that may resemble 'a rising series of increasingly acute triangles in complementary colours' in her essay 'Memory and the Making of Fictions' (ibid.: 66). For Byatt, memory and visualization are strictly interdependent and characterize her cognitive process.

The novel creates a kind of *trompe l'œil* effect when unobtrusively translating images derived from artworks in order to describe a certain landscape or an interior setting. At the same time, it also incorporates fragments of the letters of Vincent Van Gogh to his brother Theo in order to sound the aesthetic ideas informing the novel and bridge the gap between visual and verbal modes of perception. What is presented in the novel is a gradual unfolding of a *mise en scène* relying both on memories of artwork and knowledge. Consequently, the notion of a museological practice which criticism has recently adopted in order to define Byatt's characteristic approach to memories of things past, seems appropriate (Rippl 2001: 242; Lara-Rallo 2009: 221; Steveker 2009: 112).

In an age fraught with new digital media increasing our exposure to hypermediated spaces (Bolter and Grusin 2000), the interaction between image and text has become something of a *cliché*. Therefore, Byatt's engagement with this theme may seem of scarce consequence for the contemporary sensibility, though we need to bear in mind that *Still Life* was published in 1985 and critical attention regarding the iconological aspects of the novel was set in motion well after the publication of the acclaimed *Possession* in 1990.

Still Life can then be seen to anticipate what has become a pervasive theme in the age of digital graphics and multimedia. Some of the theoretical and aesthetic ideas underlying the novel find their place in the history of representational practice, since the author explores the limitations of the realist text in its dialogue with the visual. In the process, both text and image become increasingly fragmented, mirroring the rise of metafictional narrative and the cross-breeding of new narrative forms in the age following the time in which the novel is set – the late 1950s.

These changes are signalled by the prologue, proleptically set in 1980 at the time of the Post-Impressionist exhibition held at the Royal Academy of Arts in London. Arresting the linear narrative of the preceding novel, *The Virgin in the Garden*, which ended in the domestic space of a private home and left many characters with unresolved futures, the prologue to *Still Life* shifts our attention to the opening of a real-life event. The interactive gaze of the visitors viewing the row of Van Goghs and Monets hanging on the walls of the museum marks the pivotal focus of the scene, foregrounding Alexander Wedderburn, now aged sixty-two, as he signs the Friends' book and approaches the many paintings on exhibit, including Van Gogh's *Poets' Garden*.

Both Michael Westlake and Renate Brosch have aptly identified the 'play of looks' (Westlake 1989: 33) or 'visuelle Interaktion von Betrachtern' ('visual interaction of beholders'; Brosch 1999: 55) in the prologue as a crucial moment of signification for the underlying theme of visuality in *Still Life*. Although large portions of the novel engage with a multiplicity of themes ranging from science, sociology, religion, linguistics and philosophy for which various characters act as mouthpieces, the prologue foregrounds the overarching theme and metaphorical focus of the novel, which needs to be further illustrated before moving on to the novel itself. Let us consider therefore how the fictional characters enter the exhibition.

2.1 Strolling the Gallery of Memory

Frederica and Daniel arrive separately. As the narrative outlines, they respond differently to the paintings on display; this reveals distinct aspects of their individual character (Rippl 2000: 526). While the museum functions as a conceptual frame for different inset structures corresponding to the characters' individual stories,[25] the paintings observed bring out their emotional responses or else

25 Elizabeth Wanning Harries dwells on the question of narrative framing in Byatt's fiction, aptly suggesting that '[t]hese opening frames, whether they take place in the future or in the distant, symbolic past, situate the reader at a remove from the events of the primary narratives. Like a picture frame, they oscillate between the inside and the outside, belonging neither to the space within the frame or to the world outside it' (Harries 2008: 87). See also Harries 2001 for further discussion on 'New Frames for Old Tales' (Harries 2001: 104–134).

connect with some aspects or episodes in their life. As in *The Virgin in the Garden*, the narrative enacts a protracted *mise-en-abyme*, i.e. a concentrated redoubling of other narratives which proliferate producing a kaleidoscope of images.

Daniel, a practical man whose life is marked by personal tragedy due to the early death of his wife Stephanie, needs to keep active and continues to carry out community work in his role as a curate. Drawn to the exhibition in the hope of discussing practical matters with Frederica, he lacks the concentrated artistic appreciation which his young, intellectual wife was able to bestow on literature. The canvasses on the museum walls only remind him of reproductions of the same paintings he has seen in hospital corridors or other public buildings, though, glancing at Van Gogh's *Harvest*, he notes that 'Van Gogh himself had died mad and despairing in such surroundings' (ibid.: 4). In the figure of Daniel Orton the author has cast a type who is capable of empathetic feelings towards other people's distress, but cannot easily transcend contingency and lacks an immediate aesthetic and sensuous response to images.

Frederica, on the other hand, now a successful journalist and art critic, enters the exhibition and attracts the immediate attention of John House, the curator of the Post-Impressionist exhibition mounted at the Royal Academy. Indeed, the author takes this character from real life, since John House famously co-directed the 1980 exhibition at the Royal Academy and co-edited the catalogue for this event. In the prologue, he is 'accompanied by a smallish woman in a pine-green tent-like coat' (ibid.: 3) who appears to look at Frederica with an 'absent-minded scanning attention' (ibid.). Critics have recognized the identity of the author behind this anonymous character (Westlake 1989: 33; Brosch 1999: 55; Campbell 2004: 67; Boccardi 2013: 30), a detail which Byatt has confirmed in conversation (Byatt 1997b). It will be recalled that the same playful allusion to both fictional and real-life characters also characterized the prologue to *The Virgin in the Garden*, with its unobtrusive reference to Frances Yates and other glittering personalities attending the 1968 theatrical performance at the National Portrait Gallery.

Thus, the mutual gaze of various guests directs the reader's attention through the museum galleries, where Frederica also meets Alexander, now a successful playwright and 'a connoisseur of garments' (ibid.: 4). He is struck by the new style in clothes Frederica is wearing and compares them to those worn by the surrounding crowds, which appear to him as a form of parody: 'Fifties *and* post-impressionist, thought Alexander, connecting. She came up and kissed him. He remarked on the parody-young. She took the point eagerly' (*Still Life*: 5).

A first mark of discontinuity in the chronology of the narrative is evident in the prologue, introducing 'a postmodern project containing gaps, broken lines, fragmented experience and open endings' (Campbell: 68). Yet, as Boccardi argues, any temporal rupture is offset 'by an overwhelming sense of historical continuity which transcends the exact dating of the action and reaches backwards to a national past that is still present and available either in its cultural artefacts or in attempts at their modern recreation' (Boccardi ibid.: 45). While the post-impressionistic paintings on exhibit cannot possibly be thought of in terms of a British national heritage, the setting in which they appear is that of a major British institution, and Boccardi is clearly referring to those aspects of popular culture that Alexander is viewing as parody. The novel arises out of this incongruity. It creates endless forms of reproduction, 'mirrored exercises in revisiting the past' (Lara-Rallo 2009: 224), while seeking to accommodate shifting modes of apprehending the world in the time in which the characters are placed.

Accordingly, we follow Frederica and Alexander as they cast a critical glance at 'Man with the Axe' and 'Still-Life, Fête Gloanec' by Gauguin, commenting on the androgynous features of the figure portrayed in the first painting and only symbolized in the second (Figs. 1 and 2). Aloof and self-sufficient, Alexander is frequently associated with the theme of androgyny and we learn elsewhere that he feels drawn to figures like Rodin's *Danaïde* and Picasso's *Boy with a Pipe* (*The Virgin in the Garden*: 135–136).[26] Similarly, the question of gender identity informs Alexander's reflections on the subject of female creativity and power in the cult of Elizabeth I in the earlier novel. These mnemonic details underlie the conversation between Frederica and Alexander on Gauguin's 'Man with the Axe' and 'Still-Life, Fête'. For Frederica, who, at the time in which the prologue is set, has already escaped marriage to a violent husband who has tried to hit her with an axe, Gauguin's painting contains an indirect allusion to her married life, which had been confined to a wealthy country house with Gothic overtones.

The second painting, bearing Madeleine Bernard's signature but produced by Gauguin, has been interpreted as a tribute to the woman admired by Gauguin (Brosch 1999: 55). Within it

26 The theme of androgyny and the consequent ambiguity is here connected with creativity and art. Byatt inherits from Coleridge and Virginia Woolf the idea of the androgynous mind, in which masculine and feminine elements are evenly balanced (Dusinberre 1983: 192).

Fig. 1: Paul Gauguin. *Man With an Axe*. Private Collection. The Yorck Project (2003) *25.000 Meisterwerke*. CD-ROM. Berlin: The Yorck Project. Gesellschaft für Bildarchivierung. No.10187.

> various inanimate objects, two ripe pears, a dense bunch of flowers, swam across a bright red table-top rimmed with a black ellipse. The picture was signed 'Madeleine Bernard', and Alexander told Frederica that Gauguin had flirted seriously with that young woman, had characterised her, as was fashionable at the time, as having the desirable, unattainable androgynous perfection, complete sensuality combined with unattainable self- sufficiency. Frederica informed him from the catalogue that the vegetation was supposed to be a jocular portrait by Gauguin of Madeleine, the pears her breasts, the dense flowers her hair.
> (*Still Life*: 6)

However, Alexander's playful comment that the pears could be read as 'partly male' (ibid.) highlights the question of how females have been portrayed in art (Hicks 2010: 113). Thus, Frederica and Alexander's views on the painting bring into focus the question of gender, defining its embedded symbolism as androgynous. In the painting itself, the soft colours of red, orange and brown fade into

Fig. 2: Paul Gauguin . *Still Life Fête Gloanec*. Musée des Beaux-Arts d'Orleans. Wildenstein, Daniel (2001) *Gauguin. Premier itinéraire d'un sauvage*. Catalogue de l'œuvre peint. Vol. 2. Milan: Skira. 435.

one another, while the outline of the objects portrayed is not clearly drawn, except for the two pears and fruit in the foreground, which are painted in green.

In her study of ekphrasis and intermediality, Gabriele Rippl aptly observes that Byatt's novel includes quotations from exhibition catalogues and that the narrative voice in *Still Life* frequently speaks as a professional guide or as a curator of the exhibition on show, thus contributing to popularizing the artworks described, reinscribing them into cultural memory (Rippl 2005: 290).[27]

Frederica and Alexander then move on to the 'Olive Pickers' by Van Gogh, painted when the artist was confined to the asylum at St. Rémy. The painting gives rise to reflections on the symbolic significance of the trees in connection with Van Gogh's mental distress. In turn, these are interpolated with quotations from Van Gogh's letters to his brother Theo, lending the narrative depth and a measure of authenticity.

---

27 'Byatts Roman nimmt aber nicht nur Zitate aus Ausstellungskatalogen, d.h. nichtfiktionalen Texten, in sich auf, sondern besitzt selbst über viele Passagen den Charakter eines Ausstellungskataloges oder Museumsführers, wenn die "Kuratorin" Byatt Gemälde vor den Augen der Leserinnen ausbreitet, sorgfältig archiviert und damit im kulturellen Gedächtnis aktiviert' (Rippl 2005: 290).

Daniel, whose attention to the paintings is only intermittent, cannot associate the image of the olive trees with the Garden of Gethsemane, as Frederica and Alexander do. For him, the experience of suffering and death cannot easily be transcended or translated into a symbol, though he is quick in acknowledging the paradox that reproductions of Van Gogh's paintings of orchards and olive trees appear 'all over the walls of other asylums now, to cheer people up' (ibid.: 8).

Although Daniel remains a secondary character within the overall quartet, we frequently encounter him in association with experiences of loss and death. Dressed in black because of his social role, he is often left pondering the agony of death or, as later in *Babel Tower*, even the effects of capital punishment in the stillness of a church while looking at the reproductions of Rubens's *Deposition* and Holbein's *Dead Christ*.

The underlying theme of mental suffering, death and the visionary artist is a well-known topos in cultural and medical history, which appears intermittently throughout Byatt's long series of novels. In *Still Life*, it is countered most emphatically by the theme of growth, birth and creation in relation to different forms of vision, which are discussed both in a realistic and metaphorical fashion. Byatt has frequently described *Still Life* as her 'biological novel' (Murdoch 1985: 29), stating that in this novel, she wished to lay bare the mere facts of existence stripped of any symbolic allusion, i.e. birth, life and death. A concomitant aspect of this significant range of themes is also the separation between body and mind which the novel explores with regard to questions of gender and science, paving the way for further developments in *A Whistling Woman*, as shall be shown in a subsequent chapter.

In questioning the denotative power of language, the author delves into a vast theoretical array which she projects onto Alexander Wedderburn. His views and aesthetic concerns guide us into the world of Vincent Van Gogh. At the start of the prologue, we learn of Alexander's attempt to portray the painter's private world and art in his second major play, *The Yellow Chair*, first performed in 1957. Just as the symbolic power of the Virgin Queen portrayed in the Darnley Portrait hovered over the whole narrative of *The Virgin in the Garden*, Van Gogh becomes a kind of memory image and a central icon in *Still Life*. The interpolated fragments of his letters to Theo reveal his patterns of thought and language, expressing his art through words.

The first painting Alexander sees in the exhibition is 'The Poets' Garden' (Fig. 3), one of a series of works painted in Arles in 1888. It was meant as a decoration for the bedroom Gauguin would occupy in the *Yellow House* which the two artists shared. The Prologue includes an ekphrastic description of the

Fig. 3: Vincent Van Gogh. *The Poet's Garden* III. Private Collection. Hulsker, Jan (1996) *The New Complete Van Gogh: Paintings, Drawings, Sketches*. Revised and enlarged edition of the catalogue raisonné. Amsterdam: Meulenhoff. 433.

painting as Alexander sees it –'a whirl of yellow brushstrokes, a viridian impasto, a dense mass of furiously feathered lines of blue-green' (ibid.: 2). It also quotes a portion of Van Gogh's letter relating the circumstances in which the painting was produced.[28] We learn from Van Gogh's letter that he linked the garden he saw from the *Yellow House* with Petrarch and Boccaccio, who had resided in nearby Avignon:

> I am seeing the same cypresses and oleanders … But isn't it true, this garden has a fantastic character which makes you quite able to imagine the poets of the Renaissance strolling among these bushes and over the flowery grass? (ibid.: 2)

We also learn of Alexander's difficulties in 'finding an appropriate language for the painter's obsession with the illuminated material world' (ibid.) when

28 See <http://www.artic.edu/aic/resources/resource/272> for an analysis of the artist's painting. Cf. also Rippl (ibid.: 525 and 6n).

at work on his play *The Yellow Chair.* From the vantage point of his achieved maturity, he muses on his desire 'to write a plain, exact verse with no figurative language, in which a yellow chair was the thing itself, a yellow chair, as a round gold apple was an apple or a sunflower a sunflower' (ibid.: 2).

Tellingly, this fascination with the power of words and paint to represent objects is foregrounded on the opening page. Two of the epigraphs preceding the novel contain quotations from Marcel Proust. Byatt discusses his influence on her writing in an essay entitled '*Still Life/Nature morte*', highlighting a fundamental distinction between metaphoric names and *les mots*. Proust argues as follows:

> Les mots nous présentent des choses une petite image claire et usuelle comme celles qu'on suspend aux murs des écoles pour donner aux enfants l'example de ce qu'est un établi, un oiseau, une fourmilière, choses conçues comme pareilles à toutes celles de même sorte.
>
> (qtd. in *Still Life*, n. pag.)[29]

This is a quotation from *Du côté de chez Swann*, which Byatt selects as one of the epigraphs for *Still Life* to convey the relevance of Proust's observations on precise language and direct description for her writing, at a time when she is trying to avoid the use of figurative language. As we know, the novel demonstrates the failure of this attempt, but Proust's emphasis on simple denomination, associated with the language used in primary education to depict and classify objects, prompts Byatt's experiment.

In her essay, Byatt refers to Michel Butor's analysis of *A la recherche du temps perdu*, showing how works of art in Proust's novel become 'metaphors for Proust's undertaking, the colour patterning of imaginary paintings, stages, music, spills over into and patterns the shape and texture of the *Recherche* itself' (Byatt 1993: 10). As Elizabeth Hicks notes in her comparative analysis of Byatt's and Proust's handling of verbal still life in their work, Butor demonstrates how 'Proust sets up metaphorical chains linking the fictional artworks to the text in which they are embedded' (Hicks 2010: 39–40).[30] For Byatt, this 'is a classic description of coherent *thinking with* metaphors' (ibid.: 10).

Despite her fascination for Proust's aesthetic views on the denotative power of language, Byatt maintains in the above essay that language is always also

29 The quotation also appears in 'Still Life/*Nature morte*' (Byatt 1993: 18).

30 Drawing on Butor's essay 'The Imaginary Works of Art in Proust', Hicks provides further examples of how metaphorical names link up with pictorial works in Proust (ibid.: 40 ff.). Butor remarks that 'Elstir [Proust's fictional artist] will disclose fields of reciprocal metaphors, two different vocabularies which in the given picture will reveal one another, particularly the earth and the sea' (Butor 1970: 161, qtd. in Hicks ibid.: 40).

inherently metaphorical and that 'the thing itself' ultimately defeats precise description. Instead, as Kelly suggests, things are loaded 'with meaning that is endlessly circulated and refashioned' (Kelly 1996: 76).

These intellectual concerns, which the author shares with both her fictional playwright and the narrator in *Still Life*, are put to the test within the novel itself. Below, I seek to articulate the various phases of this programmatic set of intentions as they unfurl and shape out in the novel.

2.2. The 'Bright' Fifties: Birthing, Vision, Art and Ekphrasis

As I hope to show, visuality fulfils multiple functions in the novel: on the one hand, Byatt explores it in connection with theories of representation in order to test the power of visual and verbal language to describe reality; on the other hand, visuality is also historicized because of the paradigmatic institutional context in which it is enacted –the museum. Both functions converge and materialize in the prologue, but they are also further explored in the novel itself, incorporating many examples of re-description of artwork. The reader need not be aware of their presence within the text, since the many instances of re-description are often smuggled into the main narrative unobtrusively. Yet, their presence should be noted if we wish to gain an insight into Byatt's characteristic mode as a novelist.

A brief outline of the plot is at this stage necessary. The novel revolves around the new household of Stephanie and Daniel Orton in the Northern province, where Stephanie gives birth to her two children and also takes care of both her uncongenial mother-in-law and her brother Marcus, who is recovering from a mental breakdown. Meanwhile, Frederica, who is Stephanie's sister and Daniel's sister-in-law, travels to Southern France as an *au pair* before returning to England to study English at Cambridge. Marcus discovers a new interest in the natural sciences and Alexander Wedderburn writes a new play on Van Gogh, focusing on his art and his relationship to his brother Theo. The artist's interpolated letters to him provide one of the leitmotifs of the novel. Indeed, Van Gogh pervades the entire narrative in different ways, both as a central icon affecting the imagination of the fictional playwright and through the many redescriptions of Van Gogh's mimetic images –the sunflowers and irises, the yellow chair, the sea landscape on the Southern French coast and other scenes of domesticity, which I shall refer to later in this chapter.[31]

31 The influence of Van Gogh on Byatt is further illustrated in an essay entitled 'Van Gogh, Death and Summer' contained in *Passions of the Mind* (Byatt 1993: 292–332). For a detailed discussion of Byatt's handling of this theme in *Still Life* see Sorensen (2004).

A number of new characters, who will reappear in the subsequent novels, make their first appearance in *Still Life*. Among them Gerard Wijnnobel, a Dutch linguist and polymath destined to become the Vice-Chancellor of the new, fictional University of North Yorkshire at Long Royston; Jacqueline Winwar, a promising student of science; Vincent Hodgkiss, a philosopher who is knowledgeable about Wittgenstein's reflections on the logic of colour, and Gideon Farrar, a new parish vicar of dubious morality whom Richard Todd has succinctly described as: 'coarse-grainedly committed to a 1950s version of muscular Christian socialism, to be transformed, in *Babel Tower* in the 1960s, into a charismatic evangelism' (Todd 1997: 52). This comment is far-reaching, since it reveals an aspect of how the sixties will be portrayed in *Babel Tower*, the sequel to *Still Life* in the tetralogy.

Numerous incidents interrelate in the novel, building a dense net of cross-references and multi-perspectival enquiry into human nature, social history, artistic and natural phenomena. A satisfactory, concise survey of the many strands woven together in this complex tapestry of fictional invention almost defies description. However, by adopting the notion of visuality as a signpost for the intersection of the many strands in the novel, it is possible to uncover the main threads or sub-text underlying the narrative. Thus, we observe how the ekphrastic description of Van Gogh's paintings is followed by intertextual echoes of Wordsworth's verse, illuminating Byatt's portrayal of birth and childhood experience. But how do these visual and poetic references interlink exactly in the narrative?

For instance, the realistic first chapter describing Stephanie's visit to the antenatal clinic, in which she seeks to read William Wordsworth's 'Lucy' poems while standing in line for her medical examination, anticipates chapter 7, entitled 'A birth', describing in vivid detail her labour while trying to remember, in its early stage, lines from Wordsworth's *Ode: Intimations of Immortality*. The rhythm of the lines – 'The Rainbow comes and goes. And lovely is the Rose' (*Still Life*: 91) – is meant to assist the young mother as she tries to walk up and down the hospital room and work with the rhythms of labour. Unfortunately, her instinctive response to the onset of labour is contrary to the hospital procedures current at the time and Stephanie is prevented from continuing to walk by unsympathetic nurses, cast as 'representatives of a repressive institution' (Cosslet 1989: 272).[32]

---

32 Byatt's fictional representation of childbirth and the concomitant handling of the gendered body-mind dichotomy is an absorbing aspect of *Still Life*, which has already been dealt with in criticism (Cosslet ibid.; Steveker 2009: 65–73). Significantly, the

These Romantic overtones are clearly not fortuitous, since Wordsworth's exploration of childhood offers a vision of human consciousness in the various stages of its development. It is through memory that the poet famously portrays the growth of his artistic self in *The Prelude*, a poem that profoundly affects Stephanie before her wedding, when she dreams of losing contact with her inner self and the life of the mind in *The Virgin in the Garden* (Campbell ibid.: 76). Memory is then an overarching category conceptualizing a mode of thought and also incorporating exemplary Romantic poetry into the narrative, serving as a 'mnemonic space' or 'intertextual depository' (Steveker ibid.: 115). Furthermore, Byatt relies on this tradition in order to describe one of the most enigmatic characters in the tetralogy, Stephanie's younger brother Marcus. As I have already mentioned in the previous chapter, Judith Plotz has written perceptively on this troubled 'child seer' (ibid.: 33) with regard to *The Virgin in the Garden*, highlighting his exceptional visual and mathematical faculties, as well as his reputed autism.

In *Still Life*, Byatt partly collapses this Romantic vision by portraying Stephanie's gradual perception of herself as being 'sunk in biology' (13) from the moment she enters the ante-natal clinic. Dozing 'open-eyed, looking up at slits of light' (ibid.), she tries to concentrate on 'A slumber did my spirit seal', reading slowly: 'No motion has she now, no force' (ibid.). Weaving together carefully placed intertextual lines from Wordsworth's 'Lucy' poems within the narrative, the author creates a well-known, paradigmatic Barthesian effect –a 'rustle of language' (*bruissement de la langue*), i.e. a tissue of subtle allusions and countless echoes shedding light on Stephanie's present state, but also prefiguring her future death. In fact, Lucy has no clear identity in Wordsworth's series of poems. She remains a character connected to nature, existing between the spiritual and the human.

At the same time, the realistic provincial setting in the novel provides an ironic context for the handling of this Romantic ideal. Nonetheless, the author builds on this cultural legacy in order to portray the baby's first response to light experience at birth, and it is at this point that the Wordsworthian pre-text intersects

---

author's questioning of patriarchal structures characterizing society in the fifties does not appear sufficiently equipped to undermine the body-mind dichotomy, though it certainly exposes 'this opposition as a socio-cultural construct' (Steveker ibid.: 73). What interests me here though is to highlight the subtle craft intertwining disparate strands of the narrative in order to create an artistic *vision* of a given time, informed by a vast range of ideas and patterns of thought.

pictorial and visual culture, as well as matters of sense perception and cognition. Let us take a closer look at the relevant passage in the novel, offering us a description of this brand new vision, following the actual rendering of the birth experience. The scene is portrayed first through conventional realistic means from the mother's point of view:

> The green nurse was pressing the suddenly diminished hump: *push*, she said: and as the rhythm died the body pushed for the last time and Stephanie heard the liquid slither of the afterbirth. The boy wailed again, and the woman saw, beyond her feet and the stained sheets, the purple nurse carrying the small bloodred body compact on one hand. She closed her eyes and lay back, solitary, surprised to be solitary, to hear the beat of her own life only, after so long. (*Still Life*: 93)

Following a longer description of Stephanie's harrowing labour, this passage, describes the emergence of a new life from the mother's body in plain language, conveying the essential details of a natural process in a simplified form, where the primary colours associated with the stained sheet, the bloodred body, and the purple nurse provide a bright plane of colour for the scene portrayed. Its visual quality is matched by the sound of the baby's wailing and the beat of the mother's heart, which can now be heard separately. Thus, the bare facts of biological life appear here almost as a mimetic description on a 'still life' canvas and we are reminded of Stephanie's initial foreboding in the opening chapter of the novel, when she reflects that she is 'sunk in biology' (*Still Life*: 13).[33]

Subsequently, we are offered an insight into the mother's perception of ecstatic feelings at the sight of her newborn, as well as a description of her bodily response and mental process of acknowledging the presence of the boy, whom she finally addresses as you: 'There was her body, quiet, used, resting: there was her mind, free, clear, shining: there was the boy and his eyes, seeing what? And ecstasy' (ibid.: 94). In the bright new daylight, the emphasis is on the baby's eyesight and a question is asked as to what he may be able to see, which is only taken up again towards the end of the chapter, after numerous other incidents involving life in the ward and family visits. Subsequently, the perspective shifts to that of the newborn:

> The child opened his eyes and turned his head from side to side and saw light. He saw light as through water, or it could be said that he saw the air as a thick, translucent

33 Waiting in line in the ante-natal clinic, Stephanie adds that this 'was not a complaint [since] [b]iology was very interesting. She had never imagined it could be so wholly voracious of time and attention' (*Still Life*: 13).

> medium, so that the wide swathe of light that scarfed and followed his slow-moving gaze was streaked and stroked with delicate repeated dashed and flashes of pale violet (from the irises) and chrome yellow (from the daffodils). Light was like the close roof of a sphere within which he lay. (ibid.: 107)

This excerpt is part of a much longer passage in which the baby's physiological reaction to his present state is rendered in terms of light and colour. The narrator pauses on details of sense perception, depicting the air 'as a thick, translucent medium' (ibid.). Vision and bodily experience are foregrounded. It is at this point that the novel conflates observations regarding the physiology of mind and brain with questions of visual perception, enacting its own 'cognitive turn'. In the background, Byatt places her memories of the cultural context in which women gave birth in a particular time and place.[34]

As these sensory perceptions expand, the narrator becomes gradually more obtrusive, adding a layer of knowledgeable expertise to the phenomena described:

> The light, modulated by his tears and the hazy matter of his eye, was a warm light, with the soft light of the flowers spread and diffused in it, though it is not possible for me to say whether he in any way associated synaesthetically the ideas of warmth and light, one necessary to him, one new to him. The particles he saw in the flowing waves of light were streaked with the colours of the flowers, mauve, lilac, cobalt, citron, white-gold, sulphur, chrome, though of course he could not name or distinguish these divisions of light as he could not see the lip of the iris, the frilled trumpet of the daffodil.
>
> If he had been capable of simile, which he was not, he could have said that the glistening particles he saw were like overlapping transparent fish scales. Or he could have said they were like delicate quills, arching back to feathery trails of waving light in plumes. Or like small, curving, repeated candle flames. [...] He had watched lightless amniotic fluid and now he saw the light. Who can possibly say if those parts of the brain which become the rods and cones of vision had any precognition, any preparatory dream of light, in that darkness, before it flooded in? (ibid.: 107–108)

Time and again, the author delves into 'a universal language of colour, a primary language, a divine alphabet of colours and forms' (ibid.: 79), the same palette which, as Matthew Crowe tells us when discussing the nature of colour with Vincent Hodgkiss and Edmund Wilkie in chapter 6, the symbolists of Van Gogh's time had known and shared. Colour and shape are equally essential in

34 See Tess Cosslett's perceptive account of how childbirth is portrayed in Byatt's novel (Cosslett 1989).

bringing an image before the mind and the inner activity of the baby's mind is here portrayed as moving in slow motion.[35]

In the above passage, the range of colours described fulfil a double function, both mimetic and self-referential. The narrator muses on the sensuous and concrete feel of colour adjectives in connection with a vase of flowers the newborn baby perceives through 'the hazy matter of his eyes' (ibid.). At the same time, naming them on the written page also involves an enquiry into the cognitive status of colour, which the novel self-reflexively incorporates. The baby's bodily sensations reach 'those parts of the brain which become the rods and cones of vision' (ibid.), while the author/narrator strives to capture all the variables of colour through words that are also marvellously metaphorical. As Worton notes in his analysis of Byatt's visual language, 'terms such as "cobalt blue" evoke minerals and mines as much as a deep bright blue' (2001: 23).

The flux of light and colour in which Stephanie's baby is immersed suggests more than a powerful description of bodily sensations and cognitive processes. It also evokes a whole series of associations and literary allusions which coalesce into a kind of unified vision steeped in Romantic notions about the visual faculty and imagination. It is no coincidence that Byatt devoted one of her early critical works to Wordsworth and Coleridge (1970), in which she commented on their ideas about nature, light and the picturesque as foreshadowing 'the use of light by Turner and the Impressionists' on landscape (Byatt 1970: 279).

The poets' interest 'in the power of the eye to perceive light' permeates the pages of *Still Life*, connecting the art of Van Gogh with phenomena relating to visual perception and the visual faculty. Hence, Wordsworth's line 'The sunshine is a glorious birth' from his *Dejection Ode* (1802) reverberates through Byatt's description of childbirth in the above passage, much as Coleridge's ideas about 'lights, chemical lights, firelight' (Byatt ibid.: 276) set down in his Notebooks and re-assembled in the subliminal world of *The Rime of the Ancient Mariner* seem to inform the novelist's visual language. Indeed, if we are to follow these clues closely, it appears that Byatt's chosen metaphors for her characteristic mnemonic processes may derive from this very source. An early study of Coleridge's poems by J.L. Lowes (*The Road to Xanadu*

35 One is reminded of the early definition of ekphrasis by the ancient rhetoricians, suggesting that the evocation of vivid images in the mind entailed its own inner movement (see Introduction iii).

1927) helps us uncover the hidden references behind Byatt's intertextual and iconic memory.[36]

In this influential study, Lowes highlights Coleridge's use of intertextual sources in his poems, derived from his copious reading. Lowes traces a significant range of words, such as 'phosphorescent sea' (ibid.: 38), 'fishes' leaving behind a 'luminous' track (ibid.), 'the hooks and eyes of the memory' (44), 'luminous creatures … "*shining*" white, and blue, and "glossy" green' (46), fish 'scales … powdered with red' (47), to the texts Coleridge was reading when composing *The Rime of the Ancient Mariner* (1798). Not surprisingly, these words reappear in a slightly metamorphosed fashion in the above passage from *Still Life* as 'overlapping transparent fish scales' (ibid.) and 'delicate quills, arching back to feathery trails of waving light in plumes' (ibid.), which strikingly resemble the mental pictures Byatt associates with her writing process as it unfolds.

Again, those images of 'feathers being preened […] with their tiny hooks and eyes […] glossy and gleaming' described in her essay 'Memory and the Making of Fiction' (ibid.), which I mentioned in the introduction, resurface in the context of *Still Life*. In the above passage, they exemplify the nature of cognitive processes characterizing the visual faculty in a new born baby, but they also interrelate with the notion of the innocent eye discussed by Gombrich in *Art and Illusion* (1972).[37]

As already noted, Gombrich proved that an unbiased or innocent eye, capable of perceiving form and colour unmediated by previous knowledge, 'is a myth' (Gombrich 1972: 251). In her novel, Byatt puts these observations to the test by giving them literary expression, while also expounding the underlying intellectual argument. Towards the end of the chapter, the narrator reminds us that 'even the innocent eye does not simply receive light: it acts and orders' (*Still Life*: 108–109).[38]

The actual birth so vividly described in the above passage from chapter 7 is conceived literally as a journey of the human body through light, which seems a

36 I wish to thank Joyce Crick for kindly pointing this study out to me.

37 As I pointed out in Section iii of the introductory chapter, Byatt's appreciation of visual art is indebted to E.H. Gombrich. Interviewed by Nicolas Tredell, she stated: 'One of my great heroes is Gombrich, and one of the great moments in Gombrich is when he says Giotto never drew a sheep, he saw other sheep that people had drawn and corrected them against reality' (Tredell 1994: 68).

38 In *Art and Illusion*, Gombrich states that 'whenever we receive a visual impression, we react by docketing it, filing it, grouping it in one way or another' (Gombrich 1972: 251). Byatt's description of Stephanie's baby's first response to light is a clear echo of this observation. See also the preceding introduction (iii).

distant evocation of Dante's description of the Empyrean in *The Divine Comedy* (Paradise, Canto XXX) when, approaching the highest heaven, the poet becomes gradually enveloped and blinded by a dazzling light of intellect and love. Although no direct reference indicates that Byatt has Dante's lines in mind, her description of birth is a potent evocation of a well-known topos and of Dante's spiritual journey towards pure light. Dante's lines read as follows:

Noi siamo usciti fore
del maggior corpo al ciel ch'è pura luce:
luce intellettüal, piena d'amore;
amor di vero ben, pien di letizia;
letizia che trascende ogne dolzore.

(Par. XXX 38–42)

We have issued
from the largest body to the Heaven of pure light,
light intellectual, full of love,
love of true good, full of joy,
joy that surpasses every sweetness.[39]

This journey is conceived as a passage from the ninth sphere or *primum mobile* circling the earth, into Heaven. Significantly, Dante refers to the ninth sphere as 'maggior corpo' ('the largest body') and names the pure light towards which the poet is ascending 'luce intellettüal'; hence, this passage from body to light is a crucial stage in the journey towards pure understanding and pure light.

Even though Byatt may not have drawn on Dante's text, we know that her unfinished dissertation 'on the nature of religious metaphor –the relations between the world of sense and the world of spirit' underlies the genesis of *The Virgin in the Garden* (Byatt 1993: 17). Indeed, the idea that birth resembles a journey of the human body through light is connected with Plato's conception of the soul. For Plato, 'the soul is like the eye […] radiant with intelligence' (Plato, *Republic* VI, 508). Hence, a well-known topos underlies both Dante's spiritual journey towards pure light in *Paradiso* and Byatt's description of Will's birth. The parallel is striking, notwithstanding the obvious replacement of a medieval conception of the universe with a secular one, informed by the art of Van Gogh and the cognitive sciences rather than a theological order and Christian dogma.

39 This is the English translation of Dante's Paradiso by Robert Hollander and Jean Hollander (2007) with facing Italian text.

It is no coincidence that, in an essay written for the centenary of Van Gogh, the novelist dwells on the painter's idea of 'light in the midst of darkness' (qtd. in Byatt 1993: 297) and his rejection of religion connected with 'images of churches shrunk in the light of the starry night, or battered in the darkness' (ibid.). Tellingly, she is attracted by Van Gogh's notion of 'the symbolic sun' deriving 'as much from the nineteenth-century religious emblem books and prints as it does from the substitution of natural energy for divine' (ibid.).

Still Life is imbued with the secular debate between words and paintings, between the image and the language used to describe it and much of this debate revolves around Van Gogh. Even when seeking to represent different colour shades, the author is guided by Van Gogh's own thoughts on 'the importance of representation without a system, without reasoning' (ibid.: 301).

Similar reflections are scattered throughout the novel, not only in connection with the figure of Alexander Wedderburn who is engaged in the writing of a new play focusing on the life of Van Gogh. Also the young Frederica is subject to the same theoretical battle between words and colours when, on the Southern French coast, she tries to capture in writing the landscape of Provence, for which, however, she lacks an appropriate way of seeing, as the narrator makes clear:

> Pigment is pigment and light is light in any culture. But words, acquired slowly over a lifetime, are part of a different set of perceptions of the world, they have grown with us, they restrict what we see and how we see it. (*Still Life*: 59)

By contrast, we are confronted with Van Gogh's 'precise aesthetic expectations' (ibid.: 60) and the results of his artistic endeavour:

> Provence is as he painted it, we use his images as icons by which to recognize certain things, the cypresses above all, the olives, some configurations of rock and vegetation, the line of the Alpilles, the plain of the Crau, the light itself. (ibid.: 60)

Thus, the novel articulates the representational problem of dealing with patterns of thought preceding our perception of the world. In so doing, it exemplifies a wealth of theoretical problems which have long been associated with post-structuralist thought –the relationship among signs and shifting forms of signification.

As I mentioned earlier, the connections between these theoretical ideas and *Still Life* are clearly expounded in 'Still Life/*Nature morte*' contained in *Passions of the Mind* (1993), in which Byatt outlines the interlocked issues recurring in her novel. Among them, she dwells on Ricoeur's philosophical discussion of metaphor in *La Métaphore vive* (1975) as well as Michel Foucault's discussion of the relations between 'words and things, thoughts and sensations' (Byatt

1993: 16) in *Les Mots et les choses* (1966). She sees Van Gogh as offering 'an objective correlative' (Byatt ibid.: 14) for her attempt to capture 'both things and metaphors' (ibid.) and elects his sunflowers as supremely mimetic icons or Gestalts, conflating both the principle of identity and difference within a single semantic area. Following Paul Ricoeur, these are the principles defining the structure of likeness in a metaphorical scheme (Ricoeur 1977: 193–199). Byatt is fascinated by the act of understanding involved in a metaphorical scheme, when the mind forms a picture or Gestalt between two terms 'in which the similarity coheres' (ibid.: 15). The pictorial dimension at stake in the metaphorical process is what allows Byatt to intertwine different patterns of thought and cultural metaphors.

Van Gogh is a pivotal figure in the novel, 'a talisman, a symbol of plain seeing in a book that purports to do without symbols' (Sorensen 2004: 68). Even the fictional characters are placed against the background of his painted landscape, rendered through ekphrastic descriptions. In the introduction to the present study, I noted the meaning of the term *ekphrasis*, derived from late antiquity and associated with the description of objects, places, people and even battles. As already explained, this rhetorical term underwent in time subtle changes of meaning, becoming mostly associated with descriptions of static objects until, in the mid-twentieth century, it became exclusively connected with descriptions of works of art. Byatt's approach to ekphrasis, exemplified by her many descriptions of artwork, is in line with the latter meaning of the term.

Chapter 6, entitled 'Seascape', illustrates her approach further. The scene depicts a group of English tourists attending a beach party, which Frederica joins, recognizing some of her friends among them. In the background, we view a familiar scene with boats which are:

> unchanged since Vincent Van Gogh had spent one week there in June 1888 and had painted them, red, and blue, green and yellow, with coloured delicate masts erect, and the slanted, tapering yard-arms crossing each other on the pale mackerel sky. Their lines were curved and beautiful [...]. (ibid.: 72–73)

The simplicity of the lines and the radiant colours in Van Gogh's painting (Fig. 4) are matched by the author's plain description, aiming at conveying the same outline of shape with accuracy and dense brush strokes. The fishing boats stand out in their referential status as mere objects, as things foregrounding their intrinsic qualities. Hence, William Carlos Williams's dictum 'No idea but in things' illuminates the scene, while pointing to the realist conventions from which the novel originates.

Fig. 4: Vincent Van Gogh. *Fishing Boats on the Beach at Saintes-Maries*. Van Gogh Museum, Amsterdam. Walther Ingo F. and Rainer Metzger (1989) *Vincent van Gogh, Sämtliche Gemälde*. Vol. 2. Köln: Benedikt Taschen Verlag. 355.

Let us recall that the author seeks to follow the principle of 'words as mimesis of things' attributed in criticism to Flaubert but also recognizable in the novels of Ford Madox Ford. In her essay 'Still Life/Nature Morte', Byatt quotes Ezra Pound's comments on Ford, reminding us that he was an impressionist for whom 'this word did not carry [...] primarily connotations of randomness' (ibid.: 12). Instead:

> He was dealing mainly with visual and oral perceptions, whereinto come only colours, concrete forms, tones of voices, modes of gesture. Out of these you build sane ideogram.
> (qtd. in Byatt ibid.: 12)

This remark highlights the link between the principles of realist fiction and the Imagist movement, showing the range of ideas informing *Still Life*. Tellingly, these indicate both a connection with the empirical tradition in which the novel is embedded ('no ideas but in things' ibid.) as well as the shift towards pictorial language.[40]

For Alexander the playwright, 'a man haunted by voices' (ibid.: 70), Van Gogh is a source of inspiration and the means through whom to reflect on problems of perception and notation, precision and expressiveness. Ch. 14, entitled 'Figures of Speech', casts him as a successful advisory producer working in Broadcasting House and sharing a mansion flat in central London. He is a paying guest of the Pooles, a family of five who, like him, have moved down to the capital from the Northern province. Sitting at a breakfast table, Alexander notices that communication in the family is largely centred on the materiality of objects. He then muses on the nature of verbal and pictorial representation and finds that language is insufficiently equipped to convey the immediacy of experience and the fullness of what the eye perceives. Striving to describe the colour of a plum, Alexander observes that:

> A writer aiming for unadorned immediacy might say: a plum, a pear, an apple, and by naming these things evoke in every reader's mind a different plum, a dull tomato-and-green specked Victoria, a yellow-buff globular plum, a tight, black-purple damson. If he wishes to share a vision of a specific plum he must exclude and evoke: a matt, oval, purple-black plum, with a pronounced cleft. (*Still Life*: 164)

Time and again, long passages of metafictional commentary alternate with minute descriptions of domestic space, still lives or visual phenomena. Because 'writing involves a phenomenology of perception' (Stewart 2008: 59), the narrator goes at great length to register different ways of seeing and representing material objects, aspiring to emulate the painter while also exploring the gap between writing and painting.

Domesticity in the Pooles' home may hide the fragility of human relations or the constraints imposed by marriage on their lives. By contrast, Van Gogh's painting *Still Life with Blue Enamel Coffee Pot, Earthenware and Fruit* (Fig. 5) which Alexander thinks of frequently while writing his play, seems to counter the tensions underlying domestic life and suggest a different sort of harmony. We learn that Alexander 'had trouble with the disposition of colour-adjectives in his play' and we also gain a sense that his inner frame of mind may be partly reflected in that of the painter who, like him, 'had feared and fled the domestic and had also idealised and desired its order, its ceremony' (*Still Life*: 166).

40 For a discussion of how the empiricist tradition has structured English discourse see Easthope (1999: ch. 4). This point has also been raised by Rippl (2000: 527).

Byatt inserts into her novel a letter by Van Gogh to his brother Theo, containing a precise description of the above painting. After having succinctly described the painting in her own words as 'a clean, bright paradox, still and very much alive, held together by the contrast and coherence of blue and yellow' (ibid.), she quotes Van Gogh's letter as follows:

> A coffee pot in blue enamel, a cup (on the left) royal blue and gold, a milk jug checkered light blue and white, a cup (on the right) white with blue and orange patterns on a plate of earthenware yellow-grey, a pot of barbotine or majolica blue with red, green, brown patterns, finally two oranges and three lemons; the table is covered with a blue cloth, the background yellow-green, thus six different blues and four or five yellows and oranges. (*Still Life*: 167)

Van Gogh's vivid description is rendered precisely through intense and contrasting colours, whereas Byatt's ekphrasis is concise and more abstract and stylized, reflecting a conceptual approach to art. Tellingly, 'these colour-words sang like a poem' in Alexander's mind (ibid.). Later in the novel, the fictional playwright also states that 'he liked the picture because of its stillness'. Yet, as the narrator asks, 'How could one dramatize stillness?' (ibid.).

As other critics have observed (Rippl ibid.: 529; Stewart ibid.: 66), Byatt's novel is informed by a paradox in that it frequently arrests narrative through ekphrastic descriptions while also releasing narrative impulses through characterization and sequential narrativization. Her 'verbal still lives' (Hicks 2010: 1; Stewart ibid.: 43) may produce the effect of a concretization of domestic space, enhancing the realist quality of her writing, or else bring out aspects relating to characters' states of mind and emotion. At the same time, they also interrelate with questions of cognition, sensory and visual perception, as exemplified by the passage describing the birth of Stephanie's child, William. The baby's first response to light in chapter 7, in which the colours of flowers are described as reverberating through his senses, highlights the interplay of an ongoing dialogue between visual and verbal media and cognitive science. Accordingly, the vibrant expression of colour characterizing Byatt's painterly descriptions seems to release 'an *excess* beyond the function of information' which the art critic Norman Bryson attributes to 'the realm of bodily experience' (Bryson 1988: 188).

Still Life opens up more fields of enquiry and discourse than is possible to investigate in the present chapter. More could be said, for example, on the interplay of thinking and viewing and the paradox of stillness and narrative movement embedded in the novel. Similarly, Wittgenstein's remarks on colour informing some of the arguments underlying the narrative could further expand our appreciation of the novel. More importantly, the question of ordering

Fig. 5: Vincent Van Gogh. *Still Life - Blue Enamel Coffeepot, Earthenware and Fruit.* Collection Basil P. and Elise Goulandris, Lausanne, Switzerland. Walther Ingo F. and Rainer Metzger (1989) *Vincent van* Gogh, *Sämtliche Gemälde*. Vol. 2. Köln: Benedikt Taschen Verlag. 341.

and naming the many objects of creation suggests a taxonomic approach to apprehending reality, epitomized by the juxtaposition of verbal icons, geometrical shapes or names of grasses containing their own metaphors – just as Van Gogh's sunflowers, 'which not only turned towards, but resembled the sun, the source of light' (*Still Life*: 2). These issues have already been tackled by critics in various form (Wallhead 1999: 94–96; 117–126; 153–172; Alfer 2001: 51–54; Stewart 2008; Lara-Rallo 2009; Alfer and Edwards de Campos 2010: 54–57; Stewart 2011; Hicks 2010: 1–25; Boccardi 2013: 54–55). What I have attempted in this chapter has been to bring out the theme of visuality in the novel in its interrelation with aspects of memory concerning its iconic aspects. This theme allows us to focus on another important question which remains open, i.e. that of how cognitive metaphor theory may help us understand the workings of Byatt's recurring imagery.

The subtle process of transmutation from literary culture to visuality that began to unfold in *The Virgin in the Garden* through Renaissance forms of theatricality connected with the ancient art of memory, has been the central focus of my analysis so far. As I pointed out in the introduction (v), Byatt draws on different domains of knowledge and experience to produce an increasingly rich narrative intertwined with complex imagery. In this chapter I have attempted to show how her characteristic narrative patterns operate through visualisation, fulfilling multiple functions in the novel: whether testing the power of language to describe reality or becoming historicized through the institutional context of the museum, visuality underlies the whole narrative in *Still Life*. Hence, I reflect on how subjective response to visual phenomena as well as mental pictures and poetic imagery rooted in the subliminal world of Coleridge fruitfully illustrate different modes of thought and ways of apprehending the world in the novel.

At the same time, Byatt's narrative patterns can be seen to operate through a series of narrative frames and embedded stories. These are all grafted by a process of accumulation of symbolic and semantic structures conflating single episodes as well as larger conceptual paradigms carefully woven into the narrative. In what follows, I intend to show how this narrative strategy impinges upon larger epistemological domains and becomes gradually more apparent.

3. The Swinging Sixties: *Babel Tower*

Babel Tower (1996) is the third novel in the ongoing chronicle of the Potter family, but eleven years mark the gap between the publication of *Still Life* and this third volume, during which time Byatt continued to be a prolific writer and critic, with three collections of short stories (*Sugar and Other Stories* 1987; *The Matisse Stories* 1993; *The Djinn in the Nightingale's Eye* 1994), two novellas (*Angels and Insects* 1992), a volume of essays (*Passions of the Mind* 1991) and the Booker-award-winning *Possession* (1990) on her credit. The gap marks a significant watershed in her career as a writer, evolving towards increasingly more experimental forms of narrative and a variety of genres.

Babel Tower is an expansive novel, featuring a myriad ideas and complex imagery, characters, plots and subplots, excerpts from scientific reports, newspaper articles, classics of literature, sociology and psychology, fairy tales, obscene fantasy and legal jargon – all with the same ease with which a snail wears its genetic code as an inscription on the spiral of its shell. The extraordinary mosaic of intertextual allusions mirrors an intricate symbolic network governed by the central image of a spiralling shell, which in turn connects with the idea of a tower and the biblical Babel where men and women had once shared a common tongue. Inevitably, the linguistic nature of the enterprise brings to mind Jorge Luis Borges's 'The Library of Babel' – 'an all encompassing textual universe, made up of hexagonal galleries and bottomless pits arranged around a spiralling stair without beginning or end' (Onega 2007: 58). Yet, the title of Byatt's novel deliberately echoes one of George Steiner's seminal works, *After Babel* (1975). Its focal point is language, its potential uses and abuses, its glory and decadence, its manifold traps and seductions, as well as its capacity to map unexplored areas of knowledge and revitalize human existence.[41]

While language is the dominant concern of the novel, its core idea is a metaphor governing a densely layered plot, grafted by a process of accumulation of characters and details, never-ending and spiralling, like a musical fugue or Pieter Brueghel's painting *The Tower of Babel* or, again, the genetic code of the species. On the structural as well as intellectual importance of narrative imagery, Byatt comments: 'In my experience I know what the form of a novel is when I find what I think of as the 'ruling' metaphor' (*Passions of the Mind* 1993: 9–10).

41 The title of Byatt's novel also links up with similar patterns in the narrative scheme of works by Umberto Eco, Doris Lessing and Italo Calvino (see Noble 2001: 61).

This chapter investigates how the central image of a spiralling shell underlies the structure of the novel and tries to show how a complex narrative structure interrelates with a broad social and intellectual background, mingling fiction, critical discourse and other modes of non-verbal representation.

The main character at the centre of the novel is Frederica Potter, but language is its proper subject matter, and Frederica's love of language proves as convincing as her unyielding attachment to her five-year-old son Leo. In suggesting that the capacity to generate both language and parental love is inscribed in the genetic code of the species, the novel voices some of the ideas which were shaping the intellectual history of the time in which it is set. This suggestion is voiced explicitly by one of the novel's characters, Professor Gerard Wijnnobel, a grammarian and polymath who, together with other experts in various disciplines, serves on the Steerforth Committee appointed by the government to investigate the status and teaching of the English language in British schools. Wijnnobel, who has absorbed the ideas of Noam Chomsky, is one of many minor characters that populate Byatt's novels and act as vehicles of ideas in a George Eliot-like manner.

Byatt's scrupulous efforts to incorporate current scientific observations into her work are far-reaching and sustained. In what is probably the shortest chapter in the novel (ch. VI), we are given a full picture of Wijnnobel's family history in a manner reminiscent of how Adrian Leverkühn's intellectual background was portrayed in *Doktor Faustus* or, more appropriately, of how the (self-)celebrated American professor Mortimer Cropper traced the roots of his own fame in *Possession*, giving a parallel account of both his ancestors and some crucial phases in the making of the American nation. What I wish to suggest is that such characters contribute to creating the impression of a symbolic distillation of cultural and historical processes, interlocking with the purely fictional dimension. A closer look at the text will illustrate my point:

> Gerard Wijnnobel sits in his official car and thinks about language [...] He grew up in Leiden, the son of a Protestant theologian, a Calvinist who puzzled, who agonized daily over the exact relations between virtue, pre-destination and the words of the one Book. He is not wholly and purely of Dutch Calvinist descent: his mother's father was half Jewish, a child of a Talmudic scholar and a Dutch Catholic lady who had come to believe that the Church was guilty of terrible cruelty to the Jews which had come from a misreading and misuse of the Scriptures. Gerard Wijnnobel's grandfather, in his turn, had become obsessed with the language of the Book. He had set out on a doomed attempt, part-mystical, part-historical, part- exegetical, to find the traces of the Ur-language, the original speech of God, spoken by Adam in Eden, and indeed by God, the Word himself, when he called the universe into being out of chaos, simply by naming it. (*Babel Tower* 1997: 190).

The allusion to Wijnnobel's grandfather's dream of a primeval language spoken prior to the fall of man sheds further light on the novel's thematic core and connects with other moments in the narrative evoking the idea of the origin and transformation of language. The novel's multiple beginnings in the opening chapter, for example, reflect the idea of a broken structure which can only be re-shaped partially in the form of a mosaic.

In trying to highlight *Babel Tower*'s basic concerns with language further, it is useful to return briefly to *Still Life*, which follows the destiny of Frederica's sister, Stephanie, more closely. There is a crucial moment in Stephanie's short-lived existence as a mother when, enraptured, she contemplates the formation of new words, a language, that is, preceding the awakening of consciousness, in her one-year old baby:

> He used his new voice, organising mouth and tongue round strings of primitive syllables, ba, ga, da, ma, pa, ta, varying and connecting them into chains of differently repeated patterns, bagabaga, abababa, pamatamaga, a combination of elements, abracadabra, seeds of speech. (*Still Life* ibid.: 226).

This glance at the early stage of word formation is reinforced by a description of organic growth in the garden where Stephanie sits with her baby. As nature reawakens into spring, the young mother observes her growing baby and the blooming life around her with equal wonder:

> The cats, like the nasturtiums, flourished in the light of her attention. [...] She sat on the lawn amidst tumbling cats and watched him progress towards her, three steps and a heavy descent on his backside, three steps [...] 'Fowa,' he said. 'Cat.' 'Wottit,' he said. 'Wiwottit.' She interpreted. 'Will wants it.' 'Un,' he agreed. 'Wiwottitcat.' (ibid.: 229, 230).

Time and again, the author retraces the shadowy line separating biological processes from the life of the intellect. Later in *Still Life*, the young Frederica will ask a question which prefigures the central concerns in *Babel Tower*: 'Where is the borderline between Nature and Culture' (ibid.: 265). It is no mere coincidence that both Stephanie and Frederica, who have inherited the genes of a frowning and irritable father with a Leavisite line in the teaching of English, are hypersensitive to language and the way in which it may or may not denote reality.

3.1 The Sphere of Knowledge: Two Cultures

Byatt's scientific approach to fiction combines in *Babel Tower* with a pattern of textual interconnectednes, mapping an ideal order onto an increasingly fragmenting social and cultural scene, reflected in the life of its protagonist. The 'two cultures' debate sparkled by F.R. Leavis and C.P. Snow in the years preceding those in which the novel is set, affects the intellectual climate of the novel, in which many characters are scientists. Similarly, James Watson and Francis Crick's 1953 discovery of the chemical structure of DNA fuels some of its central concerns –ethics, culture and biological determinism. As Alfer and Edwards de Campos have argued, genetics is placed at the intersection of a variety of discourses on science and the humanities, which remain current today (2010: 74). For instance, the emergence of bioethics as a new field of enquiry has considerably increased the interaction between the medical sciences and issues of communication and sociology in the last few decades. In a sense, the countercultural revolution of the 1960s and 1970s seems to have produced the appropriate terrain for these critical changes to take place.[42]

Byatt's interest in the scientific debate is further testified by her participation in various broadcasting programmes which have enabled her to interact with the scientific community. The encounter with the geneticist Steve Jones, for example, spurred her curiosity about the memory of snails, giving her the opportunity to intertwine many ideas about snail biology into the subject matter of her novel.[43] At one point in the narrative of *Babel Tower* (Byatt 1997: 463), Frederica Potter and Luk Lysgaard-Peacock discuss the hermaphrodite procreative biology of snails, bearing their genetic history as an inscription on the spiral of their shells. This leads Frederica to reflect on her predicament as a woman and mother whose marriage has broken up, which in turn raises ethical and social issues within the novel and beyond. Attracted by Lysgaard-Peacock's scientific competence and personality, Frederica ponders:

> [S]he suspects him of being another laminated being, a creature capable both of giving his entire attention to small, pearly, convoluted crawling lives, of thinking thoughts about genes and DNA of which she has no conception, and of furious, but not incapacitating sexual devotion. (*Babel Tower*: 462)

At this point in the narrative, the protagonist of *Babel Tower* is struggling to maintain her separate existential identity in the face of adversity and conjugal unhappiness. She does so by trying to work out a strategy that might enable her

42 Significantly, expert literature in the field suggests that '[Bioethics] grew and flourished in a context in which the trust, respect, and authority of every major societal institution declined. Crises of the type that led to the formation of bioethics occurred in politics, education, economics, law enforcement, and journalism' (qtd. in Wassermann and Stevenson 2014: 3).

43 The episode is described in an article by A.S. Byatt entitled 'Fiction Informed by Science' published in *Nature* 434, 17 March 2005, 2–5. See also Alfer and Edwards de Campos (ibid.: 73).

to survive her personal crisis. When confronted with letters by her husband's solicitor aimed at obtaining custody of her son Leo, she gives vent to her frustration against what she comes to recognize as a hostile and backward moral climate and cuts up the legal letters, re-arranging them in the form of 'laminations' in her personal diary. Her gesture suggests more than a passing tip of the hat to Doris Lessing's heroine in *The Golden Notebook* (1962), in which the writer Anna Wulf arranges a similar layered set of diaries recording her experiences. In much the same way, Frederica has 'the idea that she is many women in one – a mother, a wife, a lover, a watcher, and that it might be possible to construct a kind of plait of voices, with different rhythms and vocabularies' (ibid.: 462).

Tellingly, Frederica's meditations on the subject of female creativity and human behaviour further connect with the images of the Virgin Queen negotiated in the Prologue of *The Virgin in the Garden*, when the myth of the historical Elizabeth as both Virgin Queen, powerful ruler and hermaphrodite was first introduced. Gradually, it becomes clear that this is a prime instance illustrating Byatt's practice of refracting a single image into multiple references and different levels of signification, all co-existing simultaneously yet braiding together a myriad of disparate strands of narrative that make up her fiction.[44]

3.2 The Spiral Stairway of Narrative

On a formal level, the image of the spiralling double helix of the DNA worn by the snail on its shell, allows separate narrative strands to be plaited together, as the three separate beginnings in the opening chapter, preceded by a prologue, suggest:

> Or it might begin with Hugh Pink, walking in Laidley Woods in Herefordshire in the autumn of 1964. (*Babel Tower*: 2)
> Or it might begin in the crypt of St Simeon's Church, not far from King's Cross, at the same time on the same day. (ibid.: 4)
> Or it might begin with the beginning of the book that was to cause so much trouble, but was then only scribbled heaps of notes, and a swarm of scenes, imagined and re-imagined. (ibid.: 10)

Each opening corresponds to a separate section in the overall plot focusing respectively on the characters of Frederica Reiver née Potter, Daniel Orton and

44 This aspect of A.S. Byatt's work, combined with countless minute descriptions and metonymic details, is a recurrent pattern which has been emphasized by critics: Taylor 1993: 90–102; Djordjevic 1997: 44–83 ('Absorbed in the visualisation of the objects described, we do not notice – not consciously, that is – that a hefty dose of symbolism is being let in by the back door', 79).

Jude Mason. The first opening revolves around Frederica's chance encounter with an old friend, the poet Hugh Pink, here portrayed in a state of creative contemplation of the natural world as he thinks about his next poem. As Noble aptly suggests, Hugh Pink's state of self-absorbtion foregrounds the theme of memory overarching the entire Quartet (Noble 2001: 65–68). In particular, Hugh Pink's memories of their early days at Cambridge and of a younger Frederica are associated with the image of a pomegranate and the myth of Persephone, carried off by Hades or Dis into the Underworld. The myth has an obvious relevance for the circumstances in which Frederica is cast at the onset of *Babel Tower*. The second opening relates to Daniel Orton, Frederica's brother-in-law, a widowed curate whose wife, Stephanie, perishes towards the end of *Still Life*. In *Babel Tower*, we find him in the crypt of St Simeon's Church in central London engaged in answering telephone calls from people in need. One of the calls is from an anonymous person, later in the novel identified as Jude Mason. On Jude Mason, suffice it to say here that his identity remains mysterious for a large part of the narrative, though he is the author of a controversial book entitled *Babbletower*, the novel-within-the-novel of *Babel Tower*, which is part of its overall structure. The third opening contains a fragment of just this parallel narrative.

The three different openings are preceded by one more fragment, bearing no sign of a human presence and differing considerably from the lively and overpopulated scenes characterizing the Prologues to *The Virgin in the Garden* and *Still Life*.[45] Instead, we are left to contemplate a barren landscape with only a few fragments of biological and geological existence. A stone on which signs of a more remote life are carved, a few letters from a broken alphabet, ammonites, broken shells or coiled remains bearing witness to a distant past, is all that is afforded in this opener before the novel sets out to present its version of a loud swinging London in the 1960s, teeming with life, wild artistic self-expression, exciting fashions, and new challenges to morals and tradition. However, some form of life, a thrush, makes its presence felt in the raw and barren landscape of the opening pages:

> The thrush sings his limited lovely notes. He stands on the stone, which we call his anvil or altar, and repeats his song. Why does his song give us such pleasure? (*Babel Tower*: 1)

Inevitably, the silence interrupted only by the bird song reminds us of a regressive time when speech and its humanizing influence may have ceased to exist.

45 Noble (2001) offers insightful comments on the elaborate beginning of *Babel Tower*. Cf. also Onega (2007).

Yet, the thrush[46] also relates to a well-known image from 'Burnt Norton' in T.S. Eliot's *Four Quartets* (1944), which, in fact, the novel will partially incorporate in a later chapter as part of Frederica's so-called 'laminations' (ibid.: 481):

> Other echoes
> Inhabit the garden. Shall we follow?
> Quick, said the bird, find them, find them,
> Round the corner. Through the first gate,
> Into our first world, shall we follow
> The deception of the thrush? Into our first world …
>
> Go, said the bird, for the leaves were full of children,
> Hidden excitedly, containing laughter.
> Go, go, go, said the bird: human kind
> Cannot bear very much reality.
>
> (T.S. Eliot, *Four Quartets*, qtd. in *Babel Tower*: 480–81)

While the author places her quotation from Eliot's poem within a series of extracts from a complex array of different sources, all having childhood and the opposition between freedom and the need for 'a formal order' (Auden's poem 'Death's Echo', qtd. in *Babel Tower* ibid.: 482) as a common theme, the reference to T.S. Eliot is significant in the overall context of the tetralogy. In *Babel Tower*, it echoes Eliot's meditation on time and his vision of past and future, interlocking with the theme of memory underlying the whole tetralogy.[47]

46 On the symbolism of the thrush in *Babel Tower* and *A Whistling Woman*, see Jennifer Anne Johnson's insightful account (2010). Johnson suggests that Byatt intertwines the motif of the thrush with intertextual allusions to thrushes in the works of other writers, i.e. Robert Browning's 'Home Thoughts from Abroad' (1835), Thomas Hardy 'The Darkling Thrush' (1900) and J.R.R. Tolkien's *The Hobbit* (1937). Thrushes are interpreted as 'a line of wise thrushes in literature' connected with characters who speak the truth (Johnson 2010: 58).

47 Byatt has acknowledged T.S. Eliot's influence in her essay 'Still Life/*Nature Morte*' in *Passions of the Mind* (ibid.). As I noted in 1.3, Eliot's pronouncements on the dissociation of sensibility and poetic language affect the way in which Byatt revisits Renaissance patterns of birth and re-birth in *The Virgin in the Garden*. Here, however, the reference is to Eliot's musings on the nature of time: 'Time present and time past/Are both perhaps present in time future,/And time future contained in time past./If all time is eternally present/All time is unredeemable./What might have been is an abstraction/Remaining a perpetual possibility/Only in a world of speculation'. (T.S. Eliot, *Four Quartets*, 'Burnt Norton' 1944).

As will gradually become apparent, the allusion to the deceptive note of the thrush in Eliot's poem acquires a new significance in the context of the several intertexts assembled within *Babel Tower*, which in turn relate to the general discussion on violence, the responsibility that society has in preventing or generating cruelty, and its reflection in the language we speak. In raising all of these concerns, the novel hinges on the social history of the 1960s, when the so-called 'Moor Murders', capital punishment and censorship came to the foreground of public discussion. Within this social context, the reference to the deceptive note of the thrush may lead straight back to Adorno, but it also evokes George Steiner who, in his well-known collection of essays *Language and Silence* (1967), remarked: 'When the words in the city are full of savagery and lies, nothing speaks louder than the unwritten poem' (Steiner 1967: 74).[48]

The notion of savagery is explored in *Babel Tower* in the form of the dystopian fantasy entitled *Babbletower*, earlier referred to. Its author is portrayed as an obscure and eccentric young writer named Jude Mason (and modelled on Quentin Crisp), who haunts the streets of London wearing a filthy, smelly, blue-velvet frock coat hiding the manuscript of his controversial novel. Asked to comment on his own appearance, Jude Mason remarks:

> My coat is sky-blue, the colour of truth, and it is the dress at once of the Enlightenment philosophers, and the licentious beaux of the courts. My coat is sullied, as truth is sullied. My hair is nature, untended. As is my skin. (*Babel Tower* ibid.: 524)

His polemical convictions link up with a whole tradition of thought evoking much social criticism in nineteenth-century prose, in particular that of Matthew Arnold, who in *Culture and Anarchy* (1869) sharply criticized the English middle classes for their utilitarian and philistine ideas.

An accusation of obscenity levelled against the book leads to the final trial scenes which shake public opinion in much the same way as the real-life legal actions brought against such works as D.H. Lawrence's *Lady Chatterley's Lover* in 1960 or Hubert Selby's *Last Exit to Brooklyn* in 1968. The overall plot of Jude Mason's tale interrelates with the general discussion of what language is permissible in a free society and what may be termed as obscene as against

48 George Steiner seems loosely disguised in the novel as Professor Efraim Ziz (*Babel Tower*: 585), one of the characters called to give testimony in the final trial scene I shall discuss later in this chapter. Similarly, other characters taken from real life will appear in the same context: among them, Anthony Burgess, Frank Kermode, and Barbara Hardy.

having any intrinsic literary merit, as well as how free a society can be before reaching self-destruction. Ultimately, this is as an extended fable on unrestrained freedom, tyranny and violence, which generates its own metaphor of a gory tower.

Clearly, the multi-layered emplotment strategy points towards the problematic relationship between colliding narratives and fragmenting realities, mirroring the imminent breakdown of old social structures and language forms. In fact, as the vast canvas of *Babel Tower* unfolds, Frederica's language and cultural values become subject to a radical fragmentation, mirroring both the breaking up of her marriage and the crumbling of myths hitherto validated by a society that is about to change beyond recognition and, in particular, the once powerful literary tradition she so much cherishes. In the background, the cut-ups of William Burroughs subvert the literary canon.

The world in which Frederica appears in the first section of the novel is grim and confined, a wealthy country house with Gothic overtones, where a violent husband and his unsympathetic sisters provide little scope for fulfilment or inspiration. A hostile governess presides over the conservative rituals of Bran House, while the joys of motherhood or those of a highly charged sexual relationship with her husband prove insufficient or of no comfort. With the help of her old Cambridge friends, she manages to escape to London with her son and start a new life. Meanwhile, Labour wins the general election and Harold Wilson becomes Primes Minister, the environmentalists begin to cry out against pollution and the dangers of radioactivity, the Profumo scandal causes sensation and outrage, the death penalty is abolished in 1965 and the 'Moors Murders' stir up yet more sensation among the public. And while R.D. Laing and D. Cooper lead a radical intellectual campaign against conventional family structures resulting in the anti-psychiatry movement, Flower Power gains a hold on the public imagination.

The linear narrative structure that prevailed in *Babel Tower*'s account of Frederica's paralyzing confinement at Bran House is later contrasted with the 'laminations' of her renewed intellectual and social activities and her life as a single working mother. Frederica's past existence had been guided by Forster's dictum 'only connect the prose and the passion' or Lawrence's myth of the perfect unity between lovers. Both as leitmotifs and painful clichés, Forster and Lawrence haunt the narrative at every turn: when, unexpectedly, Hugh Pink, one of her old Cambridge friends mentioned earlier, runs into her in the attractive surroundings of her home, he drops a casual remark about Margaret Schlegel (*Babel Tower*: 18).

Repeatedly, Frederica's liberal and intellectual family is contrasted with the rich and conservative background of her inarticulate husband, interlocking with

Forster's famous pair of opposites in *Howards End*, the intellectual Schlegels and the philistine Wilcoxes. Also, Frederica soon recognizes that her escape into marriage in the hope to find sensual happiness and possibly overcome the grief over her sister's sudden death, was deceptive. She reflects on the nature of her choice while comparing it to Stephanie's:

> Like Lady Chatterley, walking into the woods to be annihilated, trailing little threads of quotations from Milton's blindness and Swinburne's pale Galilean and Keat's unravished bride of quietness, and Shakespeare's Proserpina, willing them all to go away, so as to lose herself and find herself in the body, in the spring. And that was our myth, Frederica thinks, carrying on her conversation with Hugh, in her head, that the body is truth. Lady Chatterley hated *words* and Nigel has no words, and I cannot do without them. (ibid.: 125–126).

Her careful study of various language forms leads subsequently to her profession as a teacher of English literature in an adult education class at an art school, as well as a reader of manuscripts on a part-time basis for a small publisher.

Preparing a lecture for her extra-mural classes on love and marriage in *Howards End* and *Women in Love*, Frederica reflects further on Forster and Lawrence until, with the same skill devoted to the cutting up of her legal letters, she turns both of their pronouncements into parodic fragments that mimic her own condition (ibid.: 382–383). Her verbal patchwork is a skilful textual 'deconstruction' of the original narratives from which those dicta are taken and an example of a thus subverted Lawrence text reads as follows:

> We are both caught up and your chin is adorable. But where everything is silent, disappointed, hurt. Even when all is perfect and one. Speech 'I love you, I love you,' it was parts. But in the perfect Oneself, of having transcended the bliss. (ibid.: 383)

Similarly, a passage from the 'restored' *Howards End* reads:

> The prose and the passion would be built and span their human love which she was never prepared to give. Only connect his obtuseness robbed of the isolation that there was no more to give.
>
> (ibid.: 383)

An implicit comic relief underlies Frederica's mocking deconstruction in her 'kind of nonsense diary' (382), a relief which has been foreshadowed in the literary reports she has been writing for the publisher Rupert Parrot, which are also incorporated into the novel. Frederica enjoys the act of writing and the 'papery' feeling it gives her because it makes her feel 'that she is herself again, and has made her body real to her, because her mind is alive' (ibid.: 155).

As she regains her freedom after her flight from Bran House, she moves through the city with increasing ease and renewed confidence, registering the cultural changes around her; she

> is an intellectual, driven by curiosity, by a pleasure in coherence, by making connections. Frederica is an intellectual at large in a world where most intellectuals are proclaiming the death of coherence, the illusory nature of orders, which are perceived to be man-made, provisional and unstable. Frederica is a woman whose life appears to be flying apart into unrelated fragments: an attempt to tear free from the life of country houses and families: a person who for two months has been a female body chemically protected from the haunting fear of conception [...]; a mind coming to grips with the fact that English literature is a structure half connected to and half cut off from a European literature which was transfigured by Nietzsche and Freud [...]; a memory containing most of Shakespeare, much of seventeenth-century poetry, much too of Forster, Lawrence, T.S. Eliot and the Romantics [...] a woman who sits at her desk and rearranges unrelated scraps of languages [...] Language rustles around her with many voices, none of them hers, all of them hers. (ibid.: 379–380)

As is apparent, her desire to make connections conflicts with the chaotic state of existence pulling her apart. While her sister Stephanie felt 'sunk in biology' (*Still Life*: 13), Frederica's 'exercises in negotiation and mediation of reality through language' (Boccardi 2013: 52) enable her to confront the formal tensions engendered by the collapse of traditional language and ideological systems, as symbolized by the 'coloured mosaic' of the stained-glass window of St Simeon's church in the opening chapter, damaged by the war and randomly re-arranged by a 'devout glazier' (Babel Tower: 7).

Critics have dwelt on the visual impact of minute details reproducing the effect of broken lines, cut-ups and laminated forms scattered throughout the narrative. Stewart, for example, has emphasized 'Byatt's flamboyantly visualized style' in his reading of the novel in terms of the art forms characteristic of the 1960s (2009: 498), while both Noble (ibid.: 69) and Alfer and Edwards de Campos (ibid.: 70) have commented on the symbolic meaning of the motley stained-glass window in St Simeon's Church. Similarly, Onega provides a perceptive reading of the narrative structure of the novel in relation to the arrangement of colours and geometrical shapes reproduced in the artistic design of fashion garments and paintings, resembling the principles of composition of fractals as postulated by Chaos theory (Onega 2007: 61) – 'the perfect combination of order and chaos' (*Babel Tower*: 331). Thus, the novel's multiple beginnings reflect the idea of a broken structure that can only be re-shaped partially in the form of a mosaic and are also subject to endless variations.

3.3 The Limits of Verbal Representation and the Realm of Dystopia

This mishmash of parodic forms, visual and verbal collage is in line with the notion of a postmodern project famously described by Linda Hutcheon in *The Politics of Postmodernism* (1989). However, it is not just her fascination for words, artistic self-expression and fiction that informs Frederica's thoughts about language. Through one more recurring metaphor, that of language operating as a net, *Babel Tower* shows with equal emphasis how language can trap and distort reality. The idea that language may be a mere web of 'words which do not describe what she feels is happening' (*Babel Tower*: 324) is in itself suggestive of Iris Murdoch's *Under the Net*. Byatt has pondered the underlying importance of this image in Iris Murdoch, who in turn derived it from Wittgenstein's *Tractatus Logico Philosophicus*. For Wittgenstein, language functions as a mesh which can blur our perception of the universe since reality can remain hidden beneath a network of concepts which fail to describe it (Byatt 1994: 11). Byatt observes that Murdoch borrows the image of the net binding both a social and philosophical significance into it. The net can be both a trap laid by society and a mesh concealing truth '*underneath* which we must creep in order to get at the precise situation' (ibid.: 10).

The novel's exploration of various language forms brings to the fore the artificial nature of textual reality and the concomitant institutions of law and marriage (Cerezo Moreno 2007: 96). Indeed, as we follow Frederica's legal battle leading to one of the two final court scenes, we become implicit witnesses of the restrictive power of language and we can detect an echo of George Steiner once more, who, in a famous essay contained in *Language and Silence*, described the decay of communicative language and the retreat of 'significant areas of truth, reality and action' (Steiner 1967: 32) from the authority of verbal language in Western civilization. Tracing the beginning of this process to the seventeenth century, he observed that truth can no longer 'be housed inside the walls of language' (ibid.: 32), and mentioned Wittgenstein to illustrate the problematic relation between word and fact. In Frederica's case, it is the judiciary language of public morals, discussed within the walls of the court, which is threatening to her because:

> It is the Swinging Sixties, but the courts are run by old men in eighteenth-century wigs, with nineteenth-century outward morals, and she will be pulped, mashed, humiliated, *destroyed*. (*Babel Tower*: 468)

However, Frederica does not stand alone in this battle against public morals since her fate is closely intertwined with that of Jude Mason. At court, both Jude and Frederica are forced 'to recite travesties of their life stories, in language they would never have chosen for themselves' (ibid.: 595).[49] Mason's *Babbletower* is put on trial because, as the discussion at court suggests, the old conservative and patriarchal morality does not allow the hidden perversions of the public school system, as experienced by both the author of *Babbletower* and his publisher Rupert Parrot, to surface openly in a book of dystopian fantasy claiming literary status:

> This book tells the truth [...] There is a gap between what many or most people now *know* about human nature and what we are allowed to say. Those of us who suffered at school - as I did, and as I can see Jude Mason did - suffered also from the little boys' normal conspiracy of silence. (ibid.: 559–560)

The novel within the novel causing so much sensation tells the story of a group of people at the time of the French Revolution, who escape the Reign of Terror to found a new community modelled on Fourier's utopia of an ideal society. Unrestrained freedom and close cooperation are meant to be their guiding principles. Unfortunately, the community leader Culvert turns out to be just another guru who is driven by his own sadomasochism to self-destruction, into which he then co-opts his followers. In a bleak atmosphere reminiscent of the castle of the Marquis de Sade, but also of the public school which Jude Mason attended as a child, this utopian community only manages to produce more misery and sexual perversion, well documented in excruciating scenes of torture evoking unspeakable sexual phantasies. The absence of order and social consensus ultimately proves self-destructive, and it is both the will to power of the leader of the Krebs people and their acquiescence which generate it.

As this utopian experiment deteriorates and the sexual language becomes increasingly more explicit and repulsive, the implicit analogies between *Babbletower* and *Babel Tower* emerge with force of clarity. A.S. Byatt introduces the metaphor of a gory tower in order to tackle, from a new perspective, the general issue of language, the claims of motherhood and happy childhood, and the need for both a social order and a private space to balance the overwhelming group pressure exerted within society. These themes will be further explored in the final volume of the tetralogy, *A Whistling Woman*, describing the counterculture in the UK as a mass phenomenon that produced fashionable trends and the conformism of cultic milieus. In both *Babel Tower* and *A Whistling Woman*,

---

49 For a discussion of the two legal cases embedded in the narrative of *Babel Tower* see Seligardi (2012).

these issues are dealt with in terms of the debates characteristic of the 1960s, such as the ethics of education, censorship and parenting, but it is language that signals the potential dangers derived from the inability of articulating speech in a society under threat (Todd 1997: 64).

Consequently, Culvert's founding speech, delivered in the so-called 'Theatre of Tongues' or 'Theatre of Speech' (*Babel Tower*: 62) provides some of the suspense, otherwise delayed in overwrought descriptions of characters and settings which slow down the rhythm of this tale. In a general atmosphere of tacit consent, he proposes to forge a new order and reinvent language, which he sees as 'a bodily product' (ibid.: 64): he claims that there are levels of experience yet unexplored which need to be described anew. Eventually, the inhabitants of 'La Tour Bruyarde' are even forced to express, or *babble*, their secret passions in public: 'For it is also my belief that what is kept secret and separate festers in body and brain, to the detriment of the individual and the community' (ibid.: 65).

Similarly, motherhood is not looked upon favourably in this community and some children are bullied or tortured in ways reminiscent of the rituals of the Swineburne School which, significantly, both Jude Mason and his publisher Rupert Parrott, as well his defendant at court and Frederica's violent husband, have attended. While the literary quality of Mason's dystopia is debated at length in the second legal case discussed at court, the reader becomes absorbed in the narrator's reflections on group psychology offered in the form of a parable. When Culvert magnetizes his audience with his visionary speech, we detect an ironic glance at the perverse complicity between charismatic leadership and the sex appeal exercised on an anonymous, submissive crowd. At first, Lady Roseace is not immune to Culvert's magnetic attraction, but when she seeks solace in solitude because of the excessive and increasingly intolerable group pressure, she is quickly forced back into the community of La Tour Bruyarde. Eventually, she perishes by means of a bizarre machine of sexual torture designed to arouse the utmost feelings of pain and pleasure (412).[50]

In a wider sense, the issues discussed in *Babbletower* and the ensuing trial also interlock with the social changes which were taking place in Britain, paving the way for the Underground movement and the counterculture of the 1960s. The Underground movement was 'the political wing of the counter-culture of the 1960s' (Martin 1981: 116), which in turn was characterized by 'the symbolism of

50 For an analysis of the theme of sacrifice and gender violence in the novel see Cerezo Moreno (2007).

anti-structure in the arts' (ibid.: 117).[51] Whether the language adopted by Jude Mason mirrors the breaking up of taboos and the sexual explicitness to be found in the cult books of the counterculture, influenced by such authors as Antonin Artaud, Jean Genet, de Sade, and William Burroughs, is also an issue debated at court. An expert on the social uses of pornography, called to contribute his assessment of *Babbletower*, explains the following:

> If anarchy is an essential precursor to the creation of an alternative society, so the deflowering of language, rendering it obscene and useless, is part of the process of structuring a new one. (ibid.: 553)

However, asked if the book in question can be seen as 'an example of the deflowering of language desiderated by the young' (ibid.: 553), the expert witness claims that it is not.

3.4 The Impact of Oppositional Culture

While the court is engaged in the highbrow discussion of such issues, *Babel Tower* captures effectively the impact of the oppositional culture in ecstatic scenes of 'happenings' and youth gatherings outside the realm of the court. In offering such a broad canvas, the novel hinges on the social history of the 1960s, related in detail in studies of history and sociology which the novel takes on board. The long list of acknowledgments placed at the end of the volume cites, for instance, a study by Bernice Martin who, in *A Sociology of Contemporary Cultural Change* (1981), argues that the cultural changes taking place in post-war England were activated by 'principles of Romanticism' rooted in Western European culture and re-enacted in the counter-culture of the 1960s (Martin 1981: 1).[52]

---

51 The theme of utopia and dystopia in *Babel Tower* and *A Whistling Woman* has been further explored by Lara-Rallo (2010), Sarah Heinz (2007: 208–223) and Sarah Heinz (2008). For a transnational analysis of how the youth protest in the 1960s has been portrayed in the novels of A.S. Byatt, Maria Corti and Uwe Johnson, see Cambiaghi (2005). For an overall historical survey of the period in Britain, France, Italy and the United States see Marwick (1998). For an illustration of the cultural forms emerging from the culture of the 1960s see Waugh (1995) and also Billi and Brownlees (2003).

52 Martin states the following: 'I see the process of cultural change in the post-war decades as a continuing working out of the principles of Romanticism which had rooted themselves in North American and Western European culture at the outset of the modern age. Like Max Weber, I am inclined to take culture seriously and to consider ideas, norms and values as powerful patterns which may facilitate, deflect, transmute and perhaps even preclude the development of possibilities which lie in the structural

Pop and abstract art have already been portrayed earlier in the novel, largely through the social climate of the art college where Frederica teaches. In a scene of performance art taking place in the subterranean hall of the Samuel Palmer School, for example, the crowd sways to the rhythm of pounding music watching a bird-man show (*Babel Tower*: 442), while the final chapter shows Frederica's intellectual friends chewing hashish in smoky atmospheres and merging their inner reality with that of a dancing group who surrender to new sensory experiences and devote themselves to art forms blurring all traditional boundaries (ibid.: 603 ff.). Even as a parodic version of alternative cultural forms, the language used in these chapters does succeed in conjuring up the vibrant rhythm of pop music and jazz poetry, while the sound and colour adjectives have a mesmerizing and psychedelic quality. It is the year 1967 and the historical and social events that accompany it are all evoked, yet, significantly, Frederica is reluctant to surrender her subjectivity and feels out of step:

> Frederica is not musical. She is not a child of her time in this. She is torn apart by the noise. By the amplification of the throb, by the howl, by the blast. […] It gives her no pleasure. (ibid.: 604)

As the mystery of *Babbletower*'s authorship and its sources are revealed, it becomes apparent that there is an implicit analogy between Frederica's nightmarish seclusion at Bran House and the torture suffered by the Lady Roseace, whereas Culvert's perversions are constructed in clear parallel to Frederica's husband's obscure sexual practices (Todd 1997: 71–72). Since pop art celebrates mass culture, even the enforced group proximity which the Lady Roseace laments in La Tour Bruyarde, can be seen to provide a grim commentary on the ecstatic abandonment and loss of self experienced by the crowd in the final chapter, ending with a happening of 'auto-destructive art' (ibid.: 611–615).[53]

Each incident in the novel is carefully placed within a framework of textual allusions spanning Blake, Auden, Mann, Nietzsche, Genet, de Sade, Leary,

---

arrangements of societies […]. In fact, I base my case on Britain – or, more accurately, England – though I believe that it has a general validity for the modern Western world and, more specifically, for North America, Protestant northern Europe and Scandinavia, where individuality and Romanticism are part of the cultural foundations of modernity' (Martin 1981: 1–2).

53 Cf. R. Hewison (1986) *Too Much: Art and Society in the Sixties*: 71–72. A.S. Byatt, who has included this volume in the list of acknowledgments in *Babel Tower*, has clearly modelled this particular scene on some of the performances held by the 'Destruction in Art Symposium' documented by Hewison.

Burroughs, McLuhan, Laing, Cooper and Norman O. Brown among others. Among them are the cult authors favoured by the youth generation of the Sixties and those whose ideas documented the radical changes affecting society at that time in a significant way. They all feed into 'the rustle of papery voices' which is *Babel Tower*, anticipated by a sample of quotations from Auden, de Sade and Nietzsche in the opening page of the novel. Tellingly, it is W.H. Auden's poem 'Circe' which provides the familiar symbolic image of the tower foreshadowing some of the events to come:

> All but a privileged Few, the elite She
> guides to Her secret citadel, the Tower
> where a laugh is forbidden and DO HARM AS
> THOU WILT IS THE LAW

By placing this short quotation from Auden's poem on the opening page of her novel, Byatt directs our reading towards the potentially disruptive forms embedded in the dissolution of all social boundaries. Auden provides one more metaphor to add to the stock of vivid imagery woven into *Babel Tower*.

Time and again, the novel displays its extraordinary collage of texts, images, social and historical discourses carefully woven into the narrative so as to suggest a parallel breakdown of unified narratives and ideological structures at the time in which the novel is set. Auden's poem, written in 1969, intimates a similar warning on the possible 'daemonic' effects engendered by the counterculture (Mendelson: 786). In turn, Patricia Waugh raises comparable remarks with regard to the therapy and psychoanalytic movement taking off in the Sixties like a new religion. In *The Harvest of the Sixties* (1995) she observes that 'in a world of moral and spiritual uncertainty, there will always be a temptation to embrace false gods or to project onto others personal desires dressed up in the impersonal languages of systematic thought' (Waugh: 68). Byatt depicts the counterculture in the U.K. in a similar vein, i.e. as a mass phenomenon generating illusory attractions and the conformism of cultic milieus.

To sum up, this chapter has brought into focus the author's use of intertextuality conflating text and the central image of a spiralling shell governing the symbolic structure of the novel. My main concern has been to show how this image proliferates, generating several interrelated images, i.e. the double helix of DNA, neurons in the brain, the Tower of Babel, the endless polyphony of voices as well as the narrative pattern structuring 'Babbletower', the fictional novel within the novel subtitled 'A Story for the Children of Our Time' (ibid.: 616). In parallel, I have sought to highlight how *Babel Tower* depicts a fractured picture of a historical moment when cultural revolution was in the air and all language forms appeared to dissolve into incoherence and fragmentation. It is a picture sparked by a colourful parody of literary and artistic styles, psychedelic culture, scientific reports and legal jargon reflecting the changing values of the age. The following chapter will further explore these issues with regard to *A Whistling Woman*.

4. A Question of Body and Mind: *A Whistling Woman*

The final volume in Byatt's ambitious project continues to explore the ways in which culture affects the individual life of the many characters in the narrative. It depicts changes in women's lives in the sixties, highlighting social attitudes to questions of gender, sexuality and woman's struggle for autonomy in the public sphere. From this perspective, *A Whistling Woman* can be considered as a storehouse of collective memories that participate in the shaping of female identity. Commenting on the germs of her *roman fleuve*, Byatt stated:

> I thought I had a perspective on time in the early sixties, with young children growing. It seemed a long time since I'd left school in 1953. Now I see that's absurd, but I wanted to write a historical novel [...] I wish I had more feeling for social patterns, because I certainly wanted to say something about English society. (Kenyon 1988: 75)

Because the novel describes a fictional microcosm embedded in a specific social and intellectual background affected by new trends in science, education, television and the counterculture of the sixties, it can be said to carry the memories of the past within it. At the same time, the author's collective memories are closely connected to a sense of history, indicating a desire to understand the past retrospectively from the viewpoint of the present, and to articulate it through imaginative re-creation.

Yet, the novel does something more than simply relate a set of stories and events in order to convey a particular sense of the past. In Byatt's fictional world, intensely personal and emotional responses that could qualify memory as a form of collective remembrance in the terms described by the French sociologist Maurice Halbwachs, become conceptualized and discussed in scientific and cognitive terms.[54] Therefore, Byatt's narrative produces a more distanced perspective on the past since emotional responses and social behaviour are frequently subject to the scrutiny of the neurosciences. The fictional interdisciplinary conference

---

54 As I noted in the introduction, Maurice Halbwachs described the ways in which social groups construct a shared past in *Les cadres sociaux de la mémoire* (1925). Cf. also Halbwachs 1950. Drawing on his views that cultural memory is always enclosed within a social group providing a framework for it, it is possible to think of women within their own social group as a distinct community of remembrance (Jansen 2000: 35).

occurring towards the end of the novel best exemplifies the author's characteristic approach to memory, turning scientific material into imaginative work. A cluster of contiguous discourses foreground scientific research in the novel, allowing a group of conference participants in ch. XXIII to discuss the mnemonic operations of the brain in humans and animals. Scientists, psychologists, geneticists and linguists who study the human brain as an apparatus animate Byatt's fictional microcosm of the sixties characterized by a formidable display of erudition.

As Jane Campbell has pointed out (2004), the novel chronicles the social advances made by women in the sixties through the lived experience of its characters. Lena Steveker (2009) has illustrated this aspect of Byatt's fiction in the light of theories of cultural memory and identity, as I have outlined in the introduction. Within the framework of cultural studies and philosophy, Sarah Heinz has further explored the interrelated issue of postmodern identity and subjectivity in her German study of Byatt's fiction (2007), while Katharina Uhsadel (2005) has firmly placed the tetralogy within the tradition of the female *Bildungsroman*, highlighting points of convergence between Byatt's novels and a genealogy of significant pre-texts. None of these critical volumes, however, does sufficiently foreground the crucial interplay between gender and the cognitive function of memory in *A Whistling Woman*, though Uhsadel shows in her close reading of the novel how these issues are woven into the plot (128–147). To my knowledge, the only study to date that does illuminate these important aspects in Byatt's fiction is Alfer and Edwards De Campos's (2010: 73–90), aside from critical essays on the interrelation of scientific, literary and religious discourses that have appeared since 2005.[55] As I shall argue, *A Whistling Woman* skilfully intertwines separate strands and theoretical discourses by conflating the two categories of gender and cognitive science, producing a series of recurring metaphors which become embedded in Byatt's narrative.

In order to address the biological dilemma of women's relation to their bodies, the author interweaves scientific and philosophical thought in her narrative. Wishing to deconstruct the old binary between woman as flesh and matter, and man as mind, the novel enacts an ancient philosophical debate interlocking

55 See Hidalgo (2005), Brown (2007) and Johnson (2010). My own early contribution on the subject is contained in an essay in an edited German volume (Cambiaghi 2006), from which the present chapter is partly derived.

with new developments in the neurosciences. Therefore, the gendered memories underlying Byatt's grand narrative of the sixties address a twofold aspect, namely memory as a framework of knowledge and acquired conventions collectively shared by women, as well as memory as a cognitive function intertwined with the feminist critique of rationality. Let us remember, moreover, that Byatt is particularly interested in questions of sense perception and experience organized as intuition, affecting the inner life of the characters in the novel, some of whom are, indeed, scientists.

In what follows, I shall sketch out a brief outline of the plot and illustrate the novel's subject matter. The second section of this chapter will examine the symbolism contained in the title and in the epigraphs introducing the novel, which succinctly translate its gender-related concerns into playful literary allusions, metaphors or puns. The third section will address the broader social and intellectual concerns underpinning the narrative by focusing on the particular kinds of community portrayed in it. While new trends in science, education, television, visual culture and the counter-culture of the sixties affect life in England during the decade, television becomes the most prominent medium for addressing public argument and discussion. Therefore, I wish to highlight how the novel chronicles a gradual transition towards visual culture, when women's issues first enter television, reflecting changes in cultural and social values. Finally, I shall illustrate how the intellectual debate of the body-mind question pervades one of the main episodes in the novel, focusing on the academic conference held at the fictional University of Northern England. At a time when many European countries were transformed into hotbeds of student activism, protests and radical culture, sexuality entered the realm of social and cultural politics, pervading much of the intellectual debate that was to be sparked off from French universities. And although Byatt's narrative captures the student protest and the counterculture in the UK as a mere mass phenomenon producing fashionable trends and the conformism of cultic milieus, it also intersects a time when feminism promised to break the dominance of conservative ideas among women.

4.1 A Fictional Microcosm Informed by Science

In *A Whistling Woman*, the plot splits and spawns endless story lines. We follow Frederica as she enters a new career in television and we become gradually more acquainted with Jacqueline Winwar, a young woman scientist who conducts research on the memory of snails. Both women are caught up with the demands imposed by their female and gendered condition while seeking to pursue work of an intellectual nature. Both have to fight their way to achieve some recognition in the public sphere, though this is still controlled by men who define the terms in which they move. In turn, the aloof and self-sufficient Agatha Mond, who shares a flat with Frederica and is, like her, a single mother, seems to lead a life of her own, whose secret is only revealed at the end of the novel. Meanwhile, student activism spreads in and outside the fictional university of Northern England in Frederica's home county, while a Quaker therapeutic community is taken over by Joshua Ramsden, a visionary and charismatic leader bearing signs of mental instability. The narrative establishes a link between his childhood experiences and his troubled mental state. Haunted by the memories of his childhood, when he witnessed his father's murder of his mother and sister, this character looks in the Book of Joshua in the Bible 'for signs of why he had been called Joshua' (*Whistling Woman*: 114). He comes to see himself as a descendant of Isaac and adopts the Christ-like name of Josh Lamb, a symbolic allusion to the idea of sacrificial offering. Consequently, he becomes involved in alternative forms of religiosity and the cult of Manichaeism, taking refuge in a parallel world which becomes increasingly more self-destructive.

Byatt immerses her fictional students' community into a climate of social malaise, showing signs of personal spiritual and mental crises. Individual traumatic memory coupled with indirect allusions to the collective traumas of twentieth-century European history become enacted in the novel through the character of Joshua Ramsden. Ramsden seems largely a constructed figure stemming from Byatt's theoretical investigation of the process of memory in all its multifaceted aspects. Thus, small-scale individual experiences of personal loss and family trauma feature in the novel, just as cultural forms of archival retrieval and symbolic representation are exemplified in the memory theatre underlying the narrative in *The Virgin in the Garden*.

Significantly, the climax of the novel occurs when the above mentioned multidisciplinary conference on the relation of body and mind taking place in 1969 at the fictional university of Northern England is abruptly interrupted by the followers of a counter-culture movement based outside the university campus. Enshrined within the same Renaissance building which had once provided the ideal setting for the staging of the verse play *Astraea* in *The Virgin in the Garden*, the academic conference is suggestive of an ideal symbolic order which is about to be disrupted by obscure forces. Leading towards this climactic moment, the novel enacts an ongoing discussion of theoretical and cultural issues through its many characters cast in a variety of situations. These range from television programmes to therapy groups and research laboratories and even include the personal correspondence of social scientists, psychologists and psychiatrists. Indeed, because introspection and creativity were focal points of the counter-culture of the sixties, the novel seeks to portray the inner picture of a seething decade. In this sense, Byatt's fictional narrative can be said to carry the memories of the past within it, a past which is as learned as it is densely organized.

A series of recurring metaphors belonging to scientific discourse provide the narrative with some internal structural cohesion, despite the many threads generated 'as though by narrative parthenogenesis' (Merkin 2003: 10). These metaphors are derived from the neurosciences and have their literary antecedents in the fiction of George Eliot. Inspired by new communication networks spreading in nineteenth-century England, Eliot assimilated many images of lines and webs into the structure of *Middlemarch* (1871–1872), establishing a visual correspondence between the fictional social microcosm of her novel and the complex systems that hold society together.[56] Similarly, Byatt nurtures her literary construct with images of nets reflecting her fascination with science. These images inform the highbrow discussion among scientists in the novel and in many ways, Byatt can be said to be translating the aims and concerns of the nineteenth-century novelist into her contemporary context – a time dominated by one computer metaphor.

Because the history of the computer interlocks with the history of close links between technology and theory, between technical apparatus and ideas relating to mathematics, logic, philosophy and linguistics, the meaning of this pervasive metaphor cannot be overemphasized in its association with the overall narrative of the novel and its subject matter. Indeed, as Douwe Draaisma has pointed out in her study of *Metaphors of Memory* (2000):

> Metaphors as literary-scientific constructs are also reflections of an age, a culture, an ambience. Metaphors express the activities and preoccupations of their authors. Without intending to, metaphors capture an intellectual climate and themselves function as a form of memory. (ibid.: 4)

4.2 Of Birds, Snakes, Mirrors and Gardens

A humorous note underlies the symbolic references contained in the title of the novel and in the subsequent epigraphs. The title itself is a playful allusion to one of Byatt's grandmother's sayings, which also provides the first of three epigraphs on the opening page:

> A Whistling Woman and a Crowing Hen/Is neither good for God nor Men

---

56 Eliot's imagery has been famously discussed by Gillian Beer in *Darwin's Plots* (1983). See also Otis (2001).

The implicit irony contained in this old proverb makes for a jocular beginning, hinting at the more lighthearted part of the novel's plot. Frederica, free from her unhappy marriage to a violent husband and the intricacies of a subsequent divorce case allowing her custody of her small son Leo, is about to embark on a new life in London as a TV journalist, after having taught in a class of adult education at an arts' college. From now on her life appears to unfold freely on a path towards emancipation from the old social constraints imposed on her gendered condition. Therefore, her whistling through the streets of London is an act of deliberate defiance to her unsympathetic grandmother's veto on her earlier behaviour, suggesting 'a sort of image of a woman walking off into the future, able to whistle' (Reynolds and Noakes 2004: 29) and having access to an unprecedented range of options.

The second epigraph consists in a longer extract from Lewis Carroll's *Alice in Wonderland*, which playfully refers to the imminent transformations affecting Frederica as she takes on a new social role, both as a single mother and as a working woman in her capacity as a TV journalist. Tellingly, the new television programme she will be asked to conduct is entitled *Through the Looking Glass* and frequently throughout the narrative, Frederica will be referred to as 'an adult Alice'. In her reading of the novel, Katharina Uhsadel has commented on the significance of these intertextual allusions (ibid.: 131–133), drawing on Byatt's introduction to the Modern Library Edition of *Alice in Wonderland* (2002) in order to highlight a similar search of identity in the tale of Lewis Carrol's adventurous clever girl and that of Frederica in *A Whistling Woman* – both are characterized by a strenuous desire to think and apprehend the world surrounding them (ibid.: 132).

The excerpt contained in this second epigraph describes a dialogue between Alice-as-serpent and the pigeon who, questioning the little girl's identity, remarks: 'I can see you're trying to invent something!' (Carrol, qtd. in *A Whistling Woman*, n. pag.). Whereupon the pigeon immediately reaches the conclusion that Alice's long neck makes her more akin to a snake than to a little girl, though Alice tries to persuade him otherwise, 'rather doubtfully, as she remembered the number of changes she had gone through that day' (ibid.). Nevertheless, the pigeon insists contemptuously: 'A likely story indeed! [...] I've seen a good many little girls in my time, but never *one* with such a neck as that! No, no! You're a serpent; and there's no use denying it' (ibid.).

This detail further highlights Byatt's endless play with analogies and multiple allusions characterizing her narrative strategy. The snake motif evokes first of all the biblical account of Adam and Eve and their consequent fall from Paradise. Thus, the pigeon's contemptuous remark is a clear reference to Milton's famous line in *Paradise Lost*: 'Out of my sight, thou Serpent!' (x, 867). Furthermore, by referring to the animal-like appearance of little Alice as a precedent for

Frederica's new glittering TV role, Byatt is symbolically incorporating the vexed question of gender and social identity into the novel, echoing a theme which has underpinned the entire tetralogy. As already noted, this concern came openly to the fore in *Still Life* when Stephanie, Frederica's sister, mused: 'Where is the borderline between nature and culture?' (ibid.: 265). Looking at both her baby uttering his first syllables and the surrounding garden reawakening into spring, the young mother had pondered the implications of organic and mental growth.

Yet, the multiple symbolism of the snake imagery needs to be unravelled further. Readers of A.S. Byatt's fiction will be familiar with the metaphor, derived from S.T. Coleridge, of a snake symbolizing the power of the imagination 'forever uncoiling' (Dusinberre 1983: 193), prominent in one of her early novels, *The Game* (1967). Here, a young fictional novelist named Julia Corbett, who even reappears as a guest in one of Frederica's TV programmes in *A Whistling Woman*, is described as being endowed with a devouring imagination which eats up reality. Time and again, the problematic dichotomy of the realm of imagination in relation to reality crops up in various ways in Byatt's writing. Tellingly, the author had made the following relevant observation in an early interview with Juliet Dusinberre (ibid.):

> The serpent is both sex and destruction, and imagination and preservation, and these two are curiously and intimately combined. Coleridge certainly knew that his serpent of the imagination was also derived from Milton's depiction of Satan. (ibid.: 193).

The dual symbolism of the snake as both a force of destruction and imaginative source is mirrored on the opening page of *A Whistling Woman* through the familiar picture of Alice, while the reference to Milton will surface again at the end of the novel. The complexity of this image is further reinforced by the notion that Milton's depiction of Satan is highly problematized through its association with the negative vagaries of the imagination and the divided nature of a mind caught in its thinking process. As Kenneth Gross reminds us: 'Satan is the only character in the poem who thinks… He is Milton's picture of what thinking looks like, an image of the mind, of subjectivity, of self-consciousness' (2005: 423).

Within the novel, Byatt brings all these motifs to bear on the various strands of the narrative, as when, for example, the expert guests of a talk show conducted by Frederica in ch.10 compare creativity to computer technology and the various 'operations of the mind' shaping consciousness (*Whistling Woman* ibid.: 153). This highbrow discussion casually refers to 'an interesting computer programme called *Pandaemonium*' (ibid.), which inevitably links up with 'the high capital Of Satan and his peers' in Milton's *Paradise Lost* (1, 756–757), i.e. the designated place where all demons assemble. Thus, the novel playfully interrelates references to cognitive and computer science, hinting at some of the ideas underlying their development in the 1960s. At the same time, it also activates its own 'mnemonic space' (Lachmann 2004: 173), accommodating countless intertextual references as well as the history of ideas characterizing a whole epoch. To use a term which appears in the first volume of the tetralogy, the narrative can be said to function as a 'memory-bank' (*The Virgin in the Garden* ibid.: 142) or, again, a memory theatre, succinctly re-inscribing part of intellectual history.

In addition to these playful allusions, the symbolic conception of thinking as self-delusion also refers to a more balanced idea about the relation between imagination and reality, described by the author in these terms: 'I see the imagination much more in a Coleridgean way as being that part of your mind which very slowly forms an adequate image of the world outside, as a mirror and a lamp' (Aragay 1994: 152).

The author clearly cherishes the old Romantic idea of a Coleridgean imagination, though she refuses to submit her rationality to the language of the body unconditionally. Therefore, her setting of the novel against the cultural turmoil of the sixties, when sexuality was forced into the realm of cultural and social politics, is all the more significant. As will be shown below, her chosen setting becomes the ideal battlefield for a renewed dialogue on the dualist nature of being, but while the dreamlike transformations of Alice are meant to symbolize Frederica's imminent change of public role and her new entry into the world of simulacra, Frederica retains her capacity to distance herself rationally from the endless and overpowering games of her new professional environment. Consequently, the metaphor of a mirror or lamp slowly shedding a warm light onto reality loses any threatening connotation, as it describes the condition of the imagination unfolding from the inner depth of a stable self.

These observations may illuminate the frequent juxtaposition of chaos and order, reason and madness, darkness and light, pervading the narrative and affecting the life of characters like Joshua Ramsden. As Boccardi aptly observes, the radical juxtaposition of these terms seems to indicate 'a failure of the imagination to encompass opposites' (53).

Finally, the third epigraph on the opening page contains an excerpt from one of Andrew Marvell's poems, 'The Garden', which refers to one of Byatt's most cherished topoi:

> Here, at the Fountains sliding foot,
> Or at some Fruit-trees mossy root,
> Casting the Bodies Vest aside,
> My soul into the boughs does glide:
> There like a Bird it sits and sings,

Then whets, and combs its silver Wings;
And, till prepar'd for longer flight,
Waves in its plumes the various Light.
(qtd. in *A Whistling Woman*, n. pag.)

Byatt has repeatedly alluded in her fiction to the archetypal motif of the garden as both a source of regenerative and creative power and as a mythical locus of paradisal bliss and love. This motif will re-emerge in *Possession*, on which the next chapter centres. As we shall see, one of the fictional intertexts contained in that novel, 'The Garden of Proserpina', hides one of the clues hinting at the yet undiscovered relation between two Victorian poets, resulting in enigmatic traces underlying their poetry and in the birth of their illegitimate child.

By contrast, the intertexual allusion to Marvell (1621–1678) in the third epigraph introducing *A Whistling Woman* excludes any glorification of sensuality and refers only to the garden as a place of inner meditation where reason rules above sense. As Frank Kermode remarks in his critical reading of Marvell's poem, 'the true ecstasy is in being rapt by intellect, not by sex' (Kermode 1980: 205). Despite the now deflated emphasis on rationality, this statement seems to fit Byatt's play with analogies as reflected in her choice of Marvell's poem as her third epigraph.

An article by A.S. Byatt, which appeared in *The Guardian* in 2004, elucidates her own reflections on the unresolved question of the relation between body and mind further, tracing developments in the neurosciences and connecting them with the literary representation of an old topos. In this article, she refers to the imagery pervading much metaphysical poetry, highlighting the inherent conflict between body and mind and setting it against T.S. Eliot's own interpretation of seventeenth-century poetry in terms of a mythical undissociation of sensibility. I have already pointed out the relevance of T.S. Eliot's views for the conception of *The Virgin in the Garden* in ch. 1 of the present study. *A Whistling Woman* continues to bear the legacy of Eliot's doctrine, albeit in a de-mythologized fashion. In the above mentioned article, Byatt refers to Marvell's poem 'A Dialogue between the Soul and the Body', where the body speaks of itself as being 'impaled' on the 'tyrannic soul' (Marvell 1985: 246).

The same imagery underlies the opening page of *A Whistling Woman*. Indeed, the singing bird with its colourful plumage, described by Marvell in his poem 'The Garden', is a well-known symbol for the disembodied soul ascending towards ecstatic contemplation and pure light. Besides, by juxtaposing the neoplatonic symbolism of a metaphysical poem to the old proverb contained in the first epigraph, expressing popular wisdom in plain language, the author plays with a double form of consciousness, both literal and allegorical. It is no coincidence that the colourful pictures of both a hen and a peacock are printed on the cover of the novel, thus rendering its embedded symbolism in visual terms.

Significantly, the novel abounds throughout with references to birds of all kinds. For example, the fairy-tale contained in the first chapter opens with a dialogue between a thrush and Artegall, one of the protagonists in the children's story which Frederica's son Leo and his friend Saskia had begun to listen to in *Babel Tower.* Furthermore, as might be remembered, the notes of a solitary thrush feature on the opening page of *Babel Tower*. If those broken notes may evoke the consoling power of the spoken word in the wasteland of modernity, the bird's colourful feathers relate to one of Byatt's favourite metaphors describing the inner workings of the mind in its attempt to re-imagine and re-construct a given picture of reality.

These metaphors form a cluster of recurring images which the author first referred to in her article on 'Memory and the Making of Fiction' (ibid.). As already noted, the author outlines two types of mental pictures in connection with the writing process as it unfolds as well as the unceasingly reconstructive activity of the mind. Because this pair of iconic images re-emerge vigorously in *A Whistling Woman*, it is useful to return to them once more and to juxtapose them to their new shape in the novel.

The first image is one of 'Feathers - being preened, until the various threads, with their tiny hooks and eyes, have been aligned and the surface is united and glossy and gleaming' ('Memory' 1998: 65). Here, the colourful picture of a glossy and bright feather has significant overtones connecting the bird symbolism of the epigraphs with the mnemonic activity of the brain and the endless ramifications of memory. In fact, the second image Byatt describes in her article is that of 'a fishing net, with links of various sizes, in which icons are caught in the mesh and drawn up into consciousness – they come up through the dark, gleaming like ghosts or fish or sparks, and are held together by the links' (ibid.). As I expounded in ch. 2, this imagery appears imbued with Coleridge's poetic diction characterizing the subliminal world of *The Rime of the Ancient Mariner* (1798). In that poem, the luminous track left behind by the fishes with all their glossy and colourful fish scales, were shown to be the product of Coleridge's elaborate use of intertextual sources (Lowes ibid.: 38 ff.). In *Still Life* these iconic elements become metamorphosed into 'feathery trails of waving light' (ibid.: 108) caught by the retina of a new born baby, and in *A Whistling Woman* this striking imagery metamorphoses further. As I shall demonstrate below, it is not just an iconic and mesmerising image describing the various operations of the brain in a literary fashion, but also a powerful analogy for the larger implications binding memory to its social and historical context. It is this aspect of the novel which I now wish to turn to.

4.3 Of Groups, TV, Culture and Communities

In an authorial aside providing a temporary suspension in the unfolding of the plot, Frederica is said to be looking back on her youth in the fifties, but her memories of that time seem to her too flimsy and elusive to be recalled with any certainty. Then, her mind had been too actively absorbed by the turmoil of living to retain any memorable impression of the time. What she remembers instead is a patchwork of semantic constructions sent down to memory in a literary shape and intertwined with random fragments describing objects and vague emotions or sense perceptions:

> Her idea of her own youth was a densely patterned carpet of mnemonics and rhythms, from T.S. Eliot, first tastes of banana, melon, whalemeat, lobster, exam questions recalled in total irrelevant detail, minor humiliations, dreadful, unfocused, unsatisfied sexual desire. The carpet of the 50s was *woven of many colours, in fine threads*, even if much of it was pastel, or fawn, or dove grey. Whereas the 60s were like *a fishing net woven horribly loose and slack* with only the odd very bright plastic object *caught in its meshes*, whilst everything else had rushed and flowed through, back into the undifferentiated ocean.
>
> (*A Whistling Woman*, ibid.: 50, emphasis added)

In seeking to portray a comprehensive image of society as recalled in her mind, Frederica can only appeal to the cultural patterns available to her as literary memory or else produce an undifferentiated list of loose objects and primary sense perceptions. On the same page, her tentative record of individual and collective memories proliferates in a longer enumeration attempting to convey her own feel of the past with only scarce references to larger historical issues. One of these is a sketchy allusion to 'the plumes of smoke and towers of flame in the rainforest in Vietnam' (ibid.: 51). And what is perhaps most striking in this sequential listing of random memories are just the two iconic symbols of a woven pattern and a fishing net, which have become accommodated into the texture of the novel.

Ultimately, Byatt gives shape in her novel to a gradual and unrelentless transition towards a visual culture permeating all facets of reality, as Frederica's old friend Edmund Wilkie – now producer of a new BBC cultural programme – will make clear to her in his preliminary instructions: 'television [...] was going to change everyone's consciousness. In large ways and small. [...] we are entering an age when language becomes subordinate to images' (*A Whistling*

Woman: 47–48). In a long passage reproducing the mesmerising and manipulative workings of television on people's consciousness, Byatt captures its transformative power and phantasmatic effects associating them with the mimetic games encountered by Alice in Lewis Carrol's *Alice in Wonderland* (1865) and its sequel, *Through the Looking Glass* (1872). Tellingly, the programme conducted by Frederica is entitled *Through the Looking-Glass*:

> *Through the Looking-Glass* was, from the beginning, a rapid and elaborate joke about the boxness of the Box. As it opened, the box appeared to contain the hot coals, or logs, the flickering flames and smouldering ash, in the hearth which had been the centre of groups in vanished rooms before the Box came. The fire in its shadowy cave was succeeded by a flat silvery mist (or swirl of smoke), in an elaborate gilded frame. The mist would then clear to reveal the interior of the Looking-Glass world. There was a revolving Janus clock, with a mathematical and a grinning face. There were duplicated mushrooms and cobwebs and windows. At the back of the box was what might have been a bay window, or a mirror reflecting a bay window. In the middle was a transparent box within a box, in which Frederica sat, into which the camera peered and intruded. All through the programme, round the edges of the contained space, from time to time, animated creatures and plants sauntered, sped, shot up and coiled. (ibid.: 134)

As we follow Frederica in the broadcasting room of a BBC television network, we are reminded of the old fireplace where previous generations had spun their tales by the only force of the spoken word, now superseded by McLuhan's 'global village'. Remarkably, different levels of meaning coexist in this striking description of a television studio seen from within, as through the eyes of Alice, who is about to enter a looking-glass world.

Thus, the virtual reality of television is compared to a world of phantasy, a reversed dimension filled with strange objects which become anthropomorphized – the 'revolving Janus clock, with a mathematical and a grinning face' (ibid.) resembling 'the very clock on the chimney-piece' which Alice sees reflected as she steps through a mirror hanging on the wall of her Victorian home in Lewis Carroll's *Through the Looking Glass* (2005: 59). Other prodigious creatures and plants appear to have a life of their own as in Alice's world, similarly inhabited by loquacious and animated characters, while the camera in the TV studio evokes the very telescope which Carroll's heroine associates with her bodily transformation as she goes through a tiny door leading to a small passage in the opening chapter of *Alice in Wonderland* (2005: 14). Furthermore, the 'flat silvery mist (or swirl of smoke)' surrounding the 'elaborate gilded frame' in the above passage relates to the 'bright silvery mist' surrounding Alice's *Looking-Glass* (ibid.: 59), just as the 'duplicated mushrooms and cobwebs and windows' in Byatt's description of the broadcasting room draw on Carroll's surreal world of magic and transmutation.[57]

In dealing with the impact of television on national and popular culture, the novelist is addressing a multiplicity of issues in her characteristic cumulative style. First of all, there is the overlapping of the fates of television and the family during the decade, when most programmes were meant for evening relaxation and entertainment. As Stuart Laing remarks in his study of 'The Television Revolution in Britain in the Sixties', programmes such as 'Coronation Street' and game-shows like 'Sunday night at the London Palladium' or 'The Black and White Minstrel Show' were 'the dominant recipe for securing and retaining the "family audience" in a decade when the single-set household was very much the norm' (Laing 1997: 174). As he further explains, this tendency presupposed the unity of the family nucleus and a shared taste. However, by the end of the decade which produced a new legislation on abortion, divorce and homosexuality and a growing awareness of feminist issues, this ideal unitary family audience no longer held. Therefore, television addressed new issues with a more focused political and social content, as well as women's issues for women's culture. Ordinary life, relationships, emotions and the politics of the personal entered the Box vigorously and Byatt's novel does capture the workings and impact of such programmes in an eloquent way. Consequently, Frederica can be said to embody the movement of British television in the sixties from the margin into the centre of culture, but since she is also a single mother, her character is meant to represent the changing condition of women in British society during the decade.

Ironically, her new professional role produces a double-edged result, since Frederica becomes transfixed into a public icon with significant ambiguities:

> She sat about dressed as a clever metaphor, in an easy-to-grasp metaphorical glass box, like a mermaid in a raree show, and posed trivial superficial questions with trivial superficial brightness.
>
> (*A Whistling Woman* ibid.: 326)

In a characteristically self-conscious manner, this description offers yet another instance of a concentrated redoubling of iconic signs and inset structures, drawing attention to both the artificiality of TV and the fabric of the novel. It also shows the transformation required of the individual, and of women in particular,

---

57 Alice eats bits of mushroom to change her appearance as she approaches the house of the March Hare in ch. 6 in *Alice in Wonderland* and there are cobwebs in Carroll's last novel in two volumes *Sylvie and Bruno* (1889) and *Sylvie and Bruno Concluded* (1893). See ch. 20, *Sylvie and Bruno Concluded* (Carroll 2005: 246).

when they take on a public role, though the novel also abounds with a variety of character-types testing alternative life patterns. Homosexual couples, singles and single parents all contribute to populate Byatt's distinctly complicated plot.

Secondly, the novel grapples with complex issues relating to the physiology of the mind and the technology of television. The TV producer Edmund Wilkie working on the programme conducted by Frederica, but controlled by him, keeps abreast of these changes. For him, all products of creativity should mirror even the most trivial facets of reality and be conceived to be seen on TV in coloured images. He maintains that 'all this can be woven together, as the technology advances, into one great living tapestry' (ibid.: 48).

The idea that television could offer an adequate representation of society and thus become truly the 'mirror' of reality ran parallel to advances in production techniques characterizing the heyday of popular television broadcast from the mid-1950s onwards. In this sense, Byatt's novel captures in the figure of the TV producer Edmund Wilkie the wave of optimism that must have affected TV professionals at the time. Yet, the notion of realism applied to television clashes with the artificial nature of the medium as a cultural artefact, since our postmodern condition has made us aware of the very fictiveness of language and of its being a cultural construct too. Consequently, the referential properties attributed to television became subject to the same questioning applied to language, as John Fiske and John Hartley expound in their classic study *Reading Television* (1978): 'television uses a constructed semiotic system to communicate culturally agreed, conventional meanings' (127). And because both oral and literate approaches govern the way television reflects reality, the question of its 'verisimilitude' depends on the interrelation of these two, problematic modes (ibid.: 97–100, 127–128).

In describing a television set as a place without clear boundaries, potentially inclined towards distorting and mirroring effects, Byatt's narrative conflates the question of the real in fiction and television discourse – both human constructs. Hence, the notion of 'a great living tapestry' (ibid.) envisaged by Frederica's colleague in connection with an evolving television technology is a fitting description for both the single artistic object and the dynamic process of culture. Furthermore, the narrative presents an effective, if highly imaginative, view of television as a spectacular site for entertainment and education, offering us a glimpse of that 'unifying synesthetic force on the sense-life' affecting literate TV viewers in the terms described by Marshall McLuhan in *Understanding Media* (1964: 343). In his classic text, McLuhan famously postulated that technological advances in communication would produce a kind of sensory harmony integrating all modes of perception.

Significantly, the fictional TV producer Wilkie seems to embody views contained in McLuhan's study. For example, when he states that 'whether we like it or not, [...] we are now going to live with light boxes full of mosaics of transmitted coloured light' (*A Whistling Woman*: 49), he echoes McLuhan's description of television as 'a mosaic mesh of light and dark spots' (McLuhan ibid.: 342). More generally, the principles outlined in McLuhan's pioneering study appear to be subsumed in the way in which a television studio is pictured as a visual and textual frame in Byatt's novel. McLuhan refers to the 'massive extensions of our central nervous systems' enveloping 'Western man in a daily session of synesthesia' (ibid.: 344), pondering that poets like Blake and Yates might have wished to attain just such a level of synaesthesia, conflating sense and imagination. Similarly, Byatt's surreal description of a television studio aims at capturing just this changing reality where images are in a state of flux and new spatio-temporal structures emerge in relation to sense perception.

The novel also describes the cultural experience of television by showing real-life characters such as Jonathan Miller and Richard Gregory who shaped the intellectual climate of the period with their versatile theatre productions and path-breaking neurological research into the workings of mind and brain. Accordingly, their contribution to Frederica's TV programme in chapter IX focuses on matters of visual perception, optical illusion and mirror games and also refers to the playful adventures of *Alice in Wonderland*, who puzzled over words, ideas, paradoxes and jokes. The virtual reality of television is therefore suggestive of a similar playing with mirrors, images, light and vision.

In weaving together this cluster of discourses, the narrative seeks to accomplish a 'great living tapestry' (ibid.). This is a metaphorical image for both the single object of creation and the dynamic process of culture envisaged by Edmund Wilkie, as I have noted above. Thus, the correspondence existing between formal and conceptual aspects underlying the whole narrative enhances the meaning of this metaphorical image.[58] We saw earlier that Byatt is fascinated by metaphors derived from scientific discourse and resembling those conceived by George Eliot in her fiction, such as, precisely, the image of a woven cloth symbolizing the social structure of the provincial world of *Middlemarch* or that of a pier-glass with random scratches on the surface which a radiant and powerful eye must order and re-shape in the act of seeing.

58 Cf. Wallhead (1999) for a first exploration of how metaphor structures Byatt's fiction. This study applies George Lakoff and Mark Johnson's theory of metaphor to a critical reading of the novels up to *Babel Tower*.

Transposing these images into her fictional world of the sixties, Byatt superimposes them on the general scientific discussion on the physiological activity of the brain engaged in visual perception. Jacqueline Winwar, for example, the young woman scientist conducting research on the memory of snails, explains her interest in neurotransmitters while referring to Donald O. Hebb, a real-life scientist who had 'seen the brain as a system of flashing lights, building electric links' (*A Whistling Woman*: 53). During the fictional interdisciplinary conference, Hodder Pinsky, an American cognitive psycholinguist with left-wing ideas reminiscent of Chomsky, speaks of metaphors engrained in the language of neurology and psychology, such as dendrite 'derived from the Greek word for a tree' (ibid.: 353) and 'the 'entry' of a sense impression into the brain' (ibid.: 354).

The metaphorical appeal of scientific language lies at the intersection of various forms of knowledge and narrative strands. Hence, the virtual reality of television in which some of these learned debates take place, evokes Alice's world of fantasy as well as Plato's famous allegory of the cave whose shadows function like images in a mirror. Indeed, Byatt's adjectival virtuosity in translating a well-known philosophical allegory into imaginative fiction conflates both levels of signification and semantic areas in a striking manner: 'The fire in its shadowy cave was succeeded by a flat silvery mist (or swirl of smoke), in an elaborate gilded frame' (ibid.: 134).

This leads me to the constant juxtaposition of light and darkness interspersed throughout the novel. As noted at the beginning of the present chapter, the novel reiterates the dichotomy of light and darkness as a fixed binary opposing reason to chaos. This is especially evident in the portrayal of the student protest and the counterculture as a dangerous and destructive force. In chapter VI, the narrator lists all the communes and historical hotbeds of student activism in 1968, i.e. Nanterre, Kommune I in Berlin, Copenhagen, Essex and the LSE in England. One of the characters emerging from these dark venues is a young anarchist named Jonty Surtees, portrayed as a rather comic figure or even as a mere caricature. He joins the legitimately elected leader of the student union, Nick Tewfell, and both move gradually into the commune located outside the college campus, which is controlled by the forces of chaos and unreason.

Similarly, the university vice-rector's wife is a rather mysterious figure with a leaning towards mysticism and the occult, while her husband, the grammarian and mathematician Gerard Wijnnobel, is a man who clearly favours the refinement of abstract thought and rationality. In his study, he has etchings of Mondrian and Rembrandt hanging on the wall, which seem the objectified emanations of his inner virtues, i.e. clear vision and the logic of rational thought. Later in the novel, he is described as 'the Architect of Babel [...] intent not upon chaos, but upon the discovery and communication of extraordinary order' (ibid.: 327). He is a polymath who sees 'the artificial invisible barriers between disciplines' (326) and recognizes that it is 'natural for the mind to erect them and to work within them – they were forms, philosophy, bio-chemistry, grammar – to which the Towers of the University gave a metaphorical solidity' (326). He also perceives that 'such towers were lookouts, from which other forms could be seen, to which other forms could be linked' (326).

A little later, the psychoanalyst Elvet Gander, loosely modelled on the real-life author of *The Divided Self* Ronald D. Laing, comments that 'ideas are stronger than individuals, so are forms of spiritual life, they twist, they pull. They mould' (328). Gander, however, is especially drawn to life in the commune at Dun Vale Hall, housing some of his patients from the psychiatric hospital at Cedar Mount, whose case history he discusses in his correspondence with his colleague and friend, Dr. Kieran Quarrell. Further expert characters involved in the analysis of group dinamics at the commune are the sociologist Brenda Pincher and her colleague and lover Avram Snitkin.

By conflating minutely described milieus with a broad social canvas, Byatt traces the inner picture of a historical epoch characterized, among other things, by a greater emphasis on introspection and creativity. Significantly, she draws on David Caute's historical study of 1968 and Charles Lindholm's anthropological investigation of cultic milieus and charisma as mental illness in order to portray potentially regressive manifestations of group culture. Joshua Ramsden, for example, loosely resembles the figure of Charles Manson, the leader of one of the most destructive cults in America, described by Charles Lindholm in *Charisma* (1990: 117–136). Conversely, the obscure forces emanating from the counterculture of the sixties are juxtaposed to Gerard Wijnnobel's ideals concerning education, reflected in his plan for the fictional University of North Yorkshire. The interdependence of art and science and the breakdown of disciplinary boundaries are meant to facilitate the 'rounding of consciousness' (Davey 1998: 1546) he calls for in education. Wijnnobel's vision is informed by patterns of rationality and coherence which find in the conference he organizes at the fictitious university of which he is vice-chancellor, their ideal scope. Striving for a 'cognitive-biological theory of everything' (26), he jostles together the discourses of linguistics, philosophy, psychology, ethology, biology, neurology, sociology, cybernetics and the humanities through the guest-speakers he invites at the conference on Body and Mind.

This polymath, who still pursues Renaissance ideals of a unified consciousness or 'undissociated sensibility', selects the cognitive psycholinguist Hodder

Pinsky as a keynote speaker for the conference he has planned.[59] Tellingly, Pinsky's paper is entitled 'Metaphors for the Matter of the Mind' and draws on the same metaphorical patterns woven into the novel. Arguing that the operations of the mind are embodied cognition and 'that brain, nervous system, and mind were the *same thing*' (*A Whistling Woman:* 353), he surveys various types of images associated with it. For example, he illustrates the etymology of 'cybernetics' and classifies the engrained metaphor– the Greek word 'kybernētēs' meaning steersman, pilot or governor – among 'mechanical images for the mind' (354), whereas he attributes various other images to different fields of knowledge, such as psychology, chemistry or electromagnetism. The notion that certain 'patterns of behaviour, or reactions to stimuli, desires or aversion' (354–355) can be defined as *hardwired* and thus suggest the image of the computer, or the idea that the atom can be compared to a solar system, with the planets rotating around the sun, are carefully elucidated in Pinsky's paper.

The second keynote speech is assigned to Theobald Eichenbaum, a controversial ethologist losely modelled on Konrad Lorenz. His paper on group behaviour and innate aggression (367) is interrupted by the student rebels, who wish to prevent him from speaking because of his reputed affiliation with Nazi ideology during the war. Earlier in the novel, we are told of his studies of imprinting in young animals and of his 'uncompromising ideas about the survival of the fittest' (29).

The juxtaposition of the two keynote speakers is strategically thought by the Vice-Chancelllor as a 'historic encounter' (29) aimed at addressing the implications of biological determinism. Both speakers share in fact 'a belief that certain biological structures were innate, but differed as to what these were, and as to the nature of the learning process, and the growth-patterns of human and other societies' (29).

The novel demonstrably interrelates various fields of knowledge and narrative discourses by networking through metaphors. Operating on several levels, it conflates different narrative threads, conceptual images and areas of inquiry. Byatt has openly declared in her essay on 'Fiction informed by science' (2005) that she has derived some of her ideas for *A Whistling Woman* from Jean-Pierre Dupuy's volume *The Mechanization of the Mind* (1994) on the relation

59 His name is a combination of Noam Chomsky and Steven Pinker, as A. S. Byatt suggests in 'Fiction Informed by Science' (2005). It may also link up with Marvin Minsky, the founding father of artificial intelligence, as Alistair Brown points out (Brown 2007: 60).

between artificial intelligence and the brain.[60] But clearly the novel explores different epistemic spheres and is indebted to more than one scientific study, as the acknowledgements placed on the final page make clear.

Hence, in the wake of evolutionary theory and its neo-Darwinian development, the conference also presents the ideas of Luk Lysgaard-Peacock, a geneticist who seeks to explain the reasons for male redundancy in any species.[61] He argues provocatively that parthenogenesis would be a more effective way for women to reproduce their genes but, ironically, the object of his research provides some commentary on his private life, since he is portrayed as agonizing over unrequited love for Jacqueline Winwar, the young researcher involved in the study of the physiology of memory. Indeed, many characters in the novel are cast as both scientists and sexual beings engaged in problems of finding a suitable partner or of parental existence. Even the Vice-Chancellor does not escape the tension between private and public life, since his reputed wisdom and rational mind are matched by the mental instability of his enigmatic wife.[62]

The question of the constant opposition between light and darkness in the novel therefore relates to patterns of fixed binaries traditionally associated with ideas of truth and rationality as well as platonic conceptions of archetypal forms and intelligible light. A gender-sensitive awareness, however, will be clearly suspicious of such fixed binaries, a point which Lena Steveker, drawing on Byatt's observations regarding the neo-platonic distinction between mind (*logos*) and body (*materia*), has raised in her study of Byatt's fiction (Steveker 2009: 65–73).[63]

Indeed, the idea that objectivity and reason may be characterized as male and subjectivity and feeling as female has long been questioned by theorists

---

60 Here, I am reminded of an early essay by Italo Calvino (1967) on the permutational aspects of narrative, bearing a close relation to some of the ideas explored in *A Whistling Woman*. See 'Cibernetica e fantasmi: appunti sulla narrativa come processo combinatorio' in Calvino (1980) [tr. 'Cybernetics and Ghosts' in Calvino, *The Uses of Literature* (1986)].

61 Names have often a metaphorical relevance in Byatt's fictional characters. The colourful plumage of the male peacock is a fitting illustration for the ideas Luk Lysgaard-Peacock expounds. For more explanatory details on his name see Byatt (2005).

62 Drawing on further clues placed in *Babel Tower*, Uhsadel correctly associates the character of Lady Eva Wijnnobel with that of Bertha Rochester in *Jane Eyre*, teasing out in her reading the implications generated by the comparison between the two figures (Uhsadel 2005: 142–143).

63 The first critical study of Byatt's fiction in relation to questions of gender, art and creativity is to be found in Franken (2001). Franken, however, deals with Byatt's early novels and *Possession*, but does not discuss the novels' quartet.

of feminist and gender studies. In the realm of science, the contribution of the physicist Evelyn Fox Keller paved the way towards a feminist critique of rationality and the possibilities of a gender-free science. In *Reflections on Gender and Science* (1985), she surveys the 'roots, dynamics and consequences' (8) of a prevailing 'network of associations and disjunctions' (ibid.) underlying the structure of scientific discourse. Taking her lead from Plato's epistemology, she redresses the historical division between mind and nature.

Similarly, the feminist philosopher Luce Irigaray hints at the negative imagery embedded in the dark symbolysm of Plato's cave relying on masculine definitions of concepts of truth and rationality. In her *Speculum of the Other Woman* (1985), Irigaray sees the cave in Plato's allegory as representing the woman's womb; therefore 'breaking out of the womb means breaking into truth and knowledge', as Susan J. Hekman notes in *Gender and Knowledge* (1990: 34). By the same token, the earth seems to be defined in terms of dark holes threatening the light of reason, a dichotomy which, significantly, also colours Byatt's symbolism in *A Whistling Woman.*

Byatt does not seem to question this rigid dichotomy, but rather to reinforce it. The novel does truly celebrate the life of the mind, including the minds of women, but it does not seem to replace the phallocratic language of rational thinking. However, Byatt's solution out of the impasse caused by this standard binary lies elsewhere, namely in an alternative conception of rationality which points both towards George Eliot's idea of an incarnated mind and to the work of the contemporary neuroscientist Antonio Damasio.

As we have seen, science features prominently in *A Whistling Woman.* Many of its characters are scientists and its climax provides scope for an imaginative survey of both gender-related and philosophical issues. Though the fictional academic conference is interrupted by the turmoil following 1968, the novel as a whole is a celebration of the life of the mind and of the complexities it generates. Not only are the chief concerns of cognitive science intertwined with the question of the construction of female identity, but an attempt is made to bridge the rift between the two cultures of science and the arts, as well as emotion and intellect, though the means by which this aim is pursued may at first seem paradoxical.

4.4. The Feeling Brain

In the concluding page of *A Whistling Woman*, the author acknowledges the work of Antonio Damasio, an influential Portuguese-American neuroscientist currently heading the Brain and Creativity Institute at the University of Southern California, who has achieved great international acclaim thanks to his work on the neurology of emotion, memory and language. In *The Feeling of What Happens* (1999), he describes in detail the process by which consciousness arises in the mind, while in *Looking for Spinoza* (2003) he suggests that human experience is founded in 'feelings of myriad emotional and related states, the continuous musical line of our minds, the unstoppable humming of the most universal of melodies' (3). In a way whose appeal to Byatt can easily be recognized, he investigates the biological structure underlying emotional processes which are the basis for feeling, and sketches a very clear distinction between feeling and emotion,[64] pointing out that the original Latin word *affectus* did not divorce emotion from feeling and questioning 'the Cartesian idea of a disembodied mind' (Damasio 1994: 250).

Persistently, he reiterates the idea that feeling is the mental representation of the change affecting the body and causing emotion. In other words, he makes it clear that a state of emotion is triggered off by an external object and is rooted in the body. Since a whole philosophical tradition has placed emotion at the opposite end of reason, Damasio significantly alters a pattern that has long been validated by discursive and social practice. Because the brain's regulatory operations depend on the creation of mental images in the process called mind, the mind is the idea of the body. Damasio claims in *The Feeling of What Happens* that the 'mind's pervasive aboutness is rooted in the brain's storytelling attitude' (1994: 189).

Byatt seems to acknowledge and even appropriate this line of thought.[65] Her persistent attempt to capture the sensuous movement of consciousness in its interrelation with biological and cognitive processes suggests that, rather than subscribing to the idea of a mind which subjugates the body, the novelist pays close attention to the narrative rhythm of the feeling brain rooted in the body and immersed in a social environment. Her overlapping interest for both the scientific metaphors generated by George Eliot in *Middlemarch* and cognitive science provide the terrain on which to map a densely layered fiction, eschewing strict boundaries and challenging the reader with new viewpoints.

Admittedly, many images derived from contemporary science, such as brain scans or the double helix of the DNA, have meanwhile become common place

64 Damasio suggests that the very etymology of the word 'emotion' describes the physiological process involved in emotional states: Lat. *exmovere*: to move away, to stir up. Cf. Damasio 1999: 35–42, 50–56.

65 Significantly, Byatt reviewed Damasio's *Looking for Spinoza*. See 'The Feeling Brain.' rev. of *Looking for Spinoza*, by Antonio Damasio, *Prospect* 87 (2003): 73–74.

icons in advertising and popular culture. At best they may turn into what biologist Stephen Jay Gould has defined as 'loci for modes of thought' (qtd. in Ede 2005: 4) and artists have productively engaged with such images offering alternative or multiple ways of seeing and 'interpreting what it feels like to be human' (Ede 2005: 4).

In the introduction to the present study, I referred to how Wolfgang Iser compared the workings of cultural memory to the shape of neural networks active in the brain, an idea replete with allusions to the ongoing developments in cognitive science and the media. The very notion of intertextuality was described by Iser (1997) as a connective tissue in a densely layered fiction by means of this conceptual metaphor, which has meanwhile become pervasive. These allusions adequately refer us back to George Eliot, whose scientific metaphors in *Middlemarch* gained such a hold on Byatt's imagination. In *Passions of the Mind*, Byatt devotes a chapter to George Eliot's essays. She quotes from her correspondence with Frederic Harrison in order to highlight 'one of Eliot's best-known artistic statements of intent' (Byatt 1993: 97), namely the notion that her work should 'make certain ideas thoroughly incarnate, as if they had revealed themselves to me first in the flesh and not in the spirit' (ibid.: 98). What fascinates Byatt is precisely Eliot's capacity to make '*incarnate certain ideas* that she apprehended in the flesh, i.e. sensuously, materially, through feeling' (ibid.: 98). *A Whistling Woman* shows the extent of this kindred affinity in Byatt's work. The fictional conference portrayed at the end of the novel makes it even more explicit: 'There were various literary and historical papers, including one on George Eliot's metaphors from anatomy, perception, tissue study and webs in *Middlemarch*' (*A Whistling Woman*: 363).

For Byatt the creative process is best described as the activation of synaptic connection in the brain, an idea which she has expressed both in critical essays and in her fiction. When Hodder Pinsky remarks in *A Whistling Woman* that human beings cannot think without metaphors, we enter the realm of cognitive science and the constructivist theories of memory that animate the fictional academic conference. The germs of this lively discussion, however, can be traced back to *Still Life*, where the narrator claims that 'we cannot resist the connecting and comparing habit of the mind' (*Still Life*: 236) since 'knowledge had its own sensuous pleasure' (ibid.: 153).

Thus, in rendering the aesthetic appreciation involved when discovering a new form and order, the author hints at the emotional and sensuous responses that inform the life of the mind. Concurring with the findings of cognitive science, Byatt aims at conveying the pleasure underpinning the creative process, shifting the free flow of mental processes described by the neurosciences to the realm of the literary imagination. And if the 'mind's pervasive aboutness is rooted in the brain's storytelling attitude', as Damasio observes in *The Feeling of What Happens* (ibid.: 189), Byatt is simply making these processes more manifest by reinscribing the sensuous realm of the body onto the written page, translating complex theoretical notions into imaginative fiction.

The interplay between embodied cognition and fiction has meanwhile become a widespread theme in literary studies. This need not surprise us, especially if we accept the claim made by the neurobiologist Semir Zeki that artists are after all 'unintentional neurologists, exercising to capacity all aspects of the visual brain, thereby demonstrating how well it works' (qtd. in Ede 2005: 103). This observation is made in the context of the visual arts, but we need not restrict it solely to this realm, especially in the case of a writer like A.S. Byatt who has so actively engaged with these issues.

Yet, there is one more reason why we need not be taken aback when surveying the pervasive interest that cognitive science has generated in literature and the arts. Ever since Maurice Merleau-Ponty's investigation into phenomenological processes affecting the body appeared in 1945 (*Phénoménologie de la perception*), the rigid dichotomy of mind and body started to be questioned, paving the way for subsequent studies on gender and cognition. A direct quotation from Merleau-Ponty's landmark contribution to phenomenology seems to shed light on much that was to follow regarding the interplay of mental and physical processes:

> Everything is both manufactured and natural in man, as it were, in the sense that there is not a word, not a form of behaviour which does not owe something to purely biological being–and which at the same time does not elude the simplicity of animal life and cause forms of vital behaviour to deviate from their pre-ordained direction through a sort of leakage and through a genius for ambiguity which might serve to define man.
>
> (Merleau-Ponty 2002: 220)

Byatt may not have added any new insights to the theoretical debate regarding such issues, but she has intuitively rendered them more manifest and widespread through narrative, drawing on a tradition that looks back on her predecessor George Eliot and looks forward to the future of science in its dialogue with literature and the humanities.

This chapter has displayed how the cognitive processes of memory and the persistent reference to cultural memory in its ongoing dialogue with the literary canon have continued to engage the author's imaginative world. Interrelating her textual strategies with the cognitive processes of the mind, Byatt touches upon a complex nexus of theoretical issues which problematize the body-mind question. Hence, she deploys Damasio's exploration of the biological structure underlying emotional processes to nurture some of the topics discussed, providing an adequate backdrop for the fictional academic conference on Body and Mind. This is not the only reference to neuroscience contained in the novel. Indeed, any attempt at uncovering the dense cluster of ideas woven in Byatt's narrative will have to reckon with a wide selection of scientific discourses. The long list of acknowledgements placed at the end of this as well as other novels in the series demonstrate the scope of Byatt's interest in science. In addition, her own contributions to scientific journals or public discussions demonstrate her attempt to maintain a dialogue between science and the humanities.[66] My own analysis, therefore, has attempted to survey a broad terrain of contiguous ideas to map out the social and intellectual themes underpinning Byatt's fictional recreation of the sixties and illuminate the point of convergence for many of the incidents described in the novel.

66 In her contribution to *Nature* Byatt comments at length on the scientific ideas underpinning her fiction (see Byatt 2005). Meanwhile, several articles have appeared dwelling on the intermingling of science and literature in her novels. See Hidalgo (ibid.), Brown (ibid.) Lara-Rallo (2011) and Walezak (2018).

5. (Dis)Possessing *Possession: A Romance*

The present chapter examines the range of textual and contextual references that define the cultural scope of *Possession* (1990), Byatt's best-known novel which earned her vast international acclaim owing to its receiving of the Booker Prize in 1990, which marked a watershed in her writing career. The novel owes much to its author's profound knowledge of the English literary tradition and to a process of reworking the great writing of the past. It is an extraordinary kaleidoscope of metaphors and narrative styles, arising from the subtle interweaving of genres, disciplines of learning and fervent imagination that produce a perfectly orchestrated polyphony of voices across two different epochs – the mid-nineteenth century and the 1980s. As mentioned in the introduction (ii), the novel becomes in effect transformed into a papery museum or favourite textual location for Victorian culture (Lara-Rallo 2009; Steveker 2009), generating a number of echoes in the context of the twentieth-century plot. As such, it is frequently mentioned as a paradigmatic example of intertextual narrative.

In the ongoing process structuring the formation of culture, intertextuality can be seen as 'an act of memory' (Lachmann 1997: 15). The mnemonic function of literature involves in fact 'the representation and transmission of knowledge' (Lachmann 2008: 306), so that the memory of a text coincides in practice with its intertextuality (Lachmann 2004: 173). These general concepts have been reiterated in several contributions to the burgeoning field of cultural memory studies since the late 1980s, as I have already expounded in the introduction to this volume. In their contribution to *Literature and Memory*, for example, Erll and Nünning state that '[t]he memory of literature is based on a resemiotisation of signs, on a process which re-charges elements of old texts with meaning' (Nünning, Gymnich and Sommer 2006: 15) – which corresponds in practice to a mode of intertextual writing. Hence, the interplay between memory and intertextuality proves particularly fruitful to a critical reading of *Possession*.

A more recent study by Kate Mitchell (2010) reiterates further that the novel 'engages the idea of the past as a possession in order to re-centre the literary text as *a medium for cultural memory*' (94, *emphasis* added). The same idea underlies also Lena Steveker's analysis of Byatt's fiction (2009).

Notwithstanding the spectacular proliferation of intertextual writings and narrative genres in the fabric of *Possession*, we should bear in mind that the mnemonic function of literature has been inscribed in Byatt's *œuvre* since the conception of her early novels. As I noted in Ch. 1, *The Virgin in the Garden* includes significant reflections on cultural memory as a process generating different approaches to educational practices and changing mental habits, and a specific reference is made in that novel to the notion that works of art are 'themselves memory-banks' (*The Virgin in the Garden* 1994: 142).

The following sections are designed to bring out the polyphony of intertextual voices underpinning the different temporal planes in *Possession*. Beginning with a preliminary discussion of the ideas underlying the genesis of the novel, the chapter illustrates its plot and structure before examining the different layers of intertextual traces disseminated in the novel.

5.1 The Title

Although *Possession* was written in a relatively short space of time, two years, we know that its period of gestation was much longer (Wachtel 1994: 79; Tredell 1994: 59; Todd 1997: 24). The original idea for the novel came out of the author's work as a critic. In 1970 she published a critical study of the poets William Wordsworth and Samuel Taylor Coleridge (*Wordsworth and Coleridge in Their Time*), later republished with the title *Unruly Times* (1989). Byatt researched her volume on the Romantics in the British Library; some years later, she was able to watch a fellow expert on Coleridge, the Canadian critic Kathleen Coburn, at work in just the same place. The decision to call her novel *Possession* came as a direct result of this chance observation, as Byatt herself has explained:

> It really came out of my passion for that great Toronto scholar, Kathleen Coburn, who was working on Coleridge in the British Library when I was working there. I looked at her one day, walking around, making notes on Coleridge's notebooks, and I thought, she can't have thought a thought for the last thirty years that isn't in some sense *his* thought, and then I thought, everything I know about his thought has been put together for me by her. And I thought, you could write a wonderful novel called *Possession* about the relationship between a dead poet and a living scholar, who really, as it were, was in possession or was possessed.
>
> (qtd. in Wachtel ibid.: 78–79)

The idea of possession in the spiritual or intellectual sense soon began to overlap with a series of other, hidden meanings which seemed merely to await discovery and emphasis. One such which immediately came to the fore was the material possession of research items or documents, in part because the Coleridge scholar Byatt had seen at work in the British Library apparently did actually remove Coleridge manuscripts from British soil, smuggling them to North America:

> so I thought one could have a sort of transatlantic scholar trying to get possession of these letters in a purely physical and also financial sense. (ibid.: 79)

These two different meanings of the term 'possession' were joined by that of 'demoniacal possession', as of someone experiencing a state of being pervaded by contact with extra-sensory or supernatural reality. This led the author to explore aspects of Victorian culture which were in a sense the converse of its characteristic enthusiasm for scientific discovery and faith in progress. Spiritualism and the use of mediums to communicate with the souls of the dead not only provided material for this next level of meaning, but also offered a literary connection, inasmuch as there was one Victorian poet, a favourite of Byatt's, who had served as a medium by giving a voice to many a personage from the past: Robert Browning.

> And I thought that you could compare the spiritualist séance with Browning's poems as a way in which the voices of the dead speak through the living. (ibid.: 79)

All that was now needed was to create a couple of poets, each in love with the other, in order to acquire the final meaning of the term, that of loving and sexual possession. Another couple of writers could possess themselves of the lives and works of their Victorian forbears and, finally, take possession of each other.

In recalling that the characters of her novel were shaped by her love for Victorian poetry, Byatt has emphasised that the inspiration for *Possession* was governed by completely different mechanisms from those which lay behind her previous novels. This time, what had led her to *Possession* was 'a witty concept, an idea' (Tredell ibid.: 58).

5.2 The Plot

The unexpected discovery of a number of letters written by the Victorian poet Randolph Henry Ash to an unidentified lady is the catalyst for a momentous series of events, whose final consequences the young scholar Roland Michell, assistant to Professor James Blackadder of Prince Albert College, cannot as yet suspect. He does, however, guess at the importance of what appear to be genuine papers, left behind in an old and dusty edition of Giambattista Vico's *Principii di una scienza nuova*, which once belonged to the poet and now has its place on the shelves of the London Library. The book, consulted by Roland one September day in 1986, has remained undisturbed for years. We are in St. James's Square in the heart of London, so the spirit of Randolph Henry Ash, who lived nearby in Great Russell Street, still haunts the place. Roland is well aware that the corridors he walks through were once frequented by Carlyle and George Eliot (chapter I). All the same he cannot resist the temptation to smuggle out the fragments of the letters, which seem to cast light on a hitherto unknown aspect of the Victorian writer's life. Who is the mysterious female figure to whom Randolph Henry Ash addresses the pressing attentions revealed by the letters? From its very first pages, *Possession* is thus characterised as a quest, a search which promises suspense, surprises and the pleasure of following clues, in the manner of a thriller.

With the help of Maud Bailey, a teacher at Lincoln University and director of its Women's Resource Centre, he identifies the mysterious recipient of Ash's letters as the poetess Christabel La Motte, of whom Bailey is a specialist. In the novel, Christabel La Motte is portrayed as the latest icon for feminist academic circles, with her warmest supporters being found, of course, in France and the United States. Amid all kinds of difficulties, exacerbated by the machinations of a horde of rival scholars, Roland and Maud follow clues which gradually reveal the previously unsuspected love affair between Randolph Henry Ash and Christabel La Motte. The male writer's persona had been handed down to posterity as the very epitome of well-regulated decorum, the perfect picture of Victorian family life, lovingly preserved by his wife Ellen. As for Christabel, feminist critical theory – as personified in the figure of Leonora Stern of Tallahassee University in the U.S. – had lauded her total dedication to her creative output, in an age in which women's representation of self suffered the constraints of the patriarchal society so strenuously propounded by Victorian values. Until now it had been thought that Christabel, author of a poetic fragment centred on the figure of the fairy Melusina, had shared her whole life with the painter Blanche Glover in their Richmond home, Bethany Cottage, the almost sacred locus (in feminist eyes) of an illicit relationship between two women artists ignored by traditional culture.

Certain clues lead to Seal Court, near Lincoln, the gothic country home of Sir George and Lady Joan Bailey, who are the unwitting owners of a part of the Ash-La Motte correspondence, concealed in an old porcelain doll. Under the watchful eyes of its current owners, this Victorian antique, once the property of Christabel La Motte, is found by Roland and Maud in the room where she spent her last years in solitude. Sir George and Lady Joan are descended from her sister, Lady Sophie Bailey, while Maud Bailey herself belongs to another branch of what seems to be the same family.

For Roland, who continues to share a modest basement flat in a decaying house in Putney with Val, his former fellow student, this initial discovery is not merely an academic event which upsets all previous scholarly opinions on Ash and La Motte, but also brings upheaval in the private lives of the protagonists. In a latter day re-evocation of a semi-gothic mood, Roland and Maud live out old emotions. Following in the footsteps of their Victorian counterparts, the two of them reincarnate the nineteenth century love affair which originates in the centre of London, comes into being during a trip to Yorkshire and finds its *dénouement* in Brittany; the epilogue takes them once again to the hills and moors of the north. The apparent order of the symmetrically arranged couples, distributed across two levels of narrative and time which continually intersect, is dramatically overturned by the suicide of Blanche and the happier change in the life of Val, who finds a new partner in the shape of the successful solicitor Euan MacIntyre.

The complex weave of the plot is complicated further by a number of secondary characters that are equally desirous of getting their hands on the solution to the mystery, which itself is only finally and fully unveiled in the gothic setting of the poet Ash's burial place at night, complete with a raging storm. The last clue, which reveals the fate of Maia, the love child born from Randolph and Christabel's secret affair, is contained in a letter sent by Christabel to Randolph and intercepted by his wife Ellen. The letter, which never reached its addressee in his lifetime, is buried together with the poet's corpse in Hodershall cemetery, where the villain of the piece, the arrogant professor Mortimer Cropper from Robert Dale Owen University in the USA, a collector of Randolph Ash memorabilia, tries in vain to obtain possession of it. Cropper is the sworn enemy of British academics and of the doyen of Ash experts, James Blackadder. They all meet in the so-called *Ash Factory*, sited in the labyrinthine basement of the British Museum. Beatrice Nest, on the other hand, is the editor of the diaries of Ellen Ash, a research subject forced upon her in the days when British Academia was a male-dominated preserve, at the expense of her preferred subject, the poetry of Randolph Henry Ash (see Ch. XII).

All the characters involved in the quest concur in the end that Maud is not only a direct descendent of Maia Bailey – who was brought up by Christabel's sister and mistakenly believed to be her own daughter – but is also the legitimate owner of the letters which had so laboriously been tracked down. Nonetheless, what the characters in the twentieth-century plot can never know, since thanks to a *coup de grâce* unleashed by the omniscient narrator in a postscript, it is revealed only to the external reader, is that Ash – who it was thought had never known of the existence of his daughter – did in fact meet the young Maia in a mythical flower garden. He gave the girl a message for Christabel, to mark his recognition of the child, but Maia, in her innocence, forgot to pass it on.

5.3 The Structure of the Novel

Even as briefly summarised above, the tangled web of the story already gives an impression of the complexity of a composite, multi-layered work which seems to accumulate characters, symbols and narrative genres as it progresses. Indeed each character hides another, projected onto a different temporal plane and often connected by an implicit analogy or else by a further, linking dimension, expressed through myth or fairy tale or else through letters and diaries. In similar fashion, each metaphor contains another, in an upwardly spiralling play of echoes and allusions that allures and entraps the reader.

This creative exuberance is typical of much of Byatt's fiction, with *Babel Tower* perhaps the most conspicuous example. For *Possession*, however, she uses a well-jointed palimpsest that enables judicious distribution of the complex plot over two periods, the Victorian nineteenth century and the 1980s. Maud Bailey and Roland Michell reflect the image of Christabel La Motte and Randolph Henry Ash; there seems to be an arcane correspondence between Beatrice Nest and Ellen Ash. The recent feminist critics provide a pretext for a modern caricature of the outcast witches of yesteryear, as sketched out in the figure of Christabel: her life after the birth of her daughter was spent in the gothic tower of Seal Court. After giving birth to Maia in mysterious circumstances, the pale poetess cut off her blonde locks, giving herself the appearance of a witch. In contrast, in the twentieth century, tragedy is no part of the fate of women such as the feminist scholars Maud Bailey and Leonora Stern, who are amusingly parodied in ch. XVIII:

> Maud and Leonora, coming out of a shop in Lincoln, were almost killed by a large car, reversing at great and silent speed. They were carrying hobby-horses, with velvet heads on solid broomsticks, beautifully made with flowing silken manes and wicked embroidered eyes. Leonora wanted them for various godchildren and said they looked English and magical. (Byatt 1991: 318–319)

The broomsticks are a comic detail missing from the corresponding description of Christabel in the Victorian period. The latter lives out her own tragedy in solitude, while her lover, Randolph Henry Ash, perhaps expresses a presentiment of her destiny when entitling a poem *The Incarcerated Sorceress* (ibid.: 68).

This play of mirrors between past and present-day characters is dominated by the central pair of couples, Ash-La Motte and Michell-Bailey. In addition, the novel is enriched by elements which both fill out its structure and complicate it from within. The passionate correspondence that reveals the unknown love affair between Randolph and Christabel branches out from the main narrative axis and takes on a fundamental role in the organisation of the novel's material. The letters themselves, with the exception of the few fragments whose discovery sparks off the story and of those which are found at its end, take up an entire chapter, the tenth, underlining their crucial importance. The correspondence allows the external reader to concentrate exclusively on the lives of the Victorian characters. Like an epistolary novel in miniature, the sequence shifts the reader's awareness entirely to the historical period of their story, without further distractions. The religious doubts and scientific interests of Randolph Ash, the Spiritualism, literary and artistic enthusiasms of the two poets all duly appear in the letters, which thus reflect the deep minds of the correspondents. The papers add to the fascination of the novel for the reader, and an explication of this fascination lies partly in their breathless pace expressing the lovers' typical impatience. They are also interesting formally since they provide an interpolated frame narrative allowing the reader 'to experience the fictional world from within' (Fludernik 1996: 48), adopting the characters' consciousness.[67]

We should not however overlook that further sets of letters follow the one just mentioned, namely those written by Ash to his wife Ellen; those exchanged between the scholars interested in the poetry of Ash and La Motte; and there are also a series of other letters by minor characters or from major to minor characters (in chapter XX, for instance, is a letter from Christabel to Priscilla Penny Cropper, whose part in the labyrinthine plot is to be a distant forbear of Mortimer Cropper, the American rival of the British researchers).

This initial grafting of one genre onto another is joined by a substantial number of lyrics and poems written in Ash's and La Motte's voices. Outstanding among these are the dramatic monologues modelled on Robert Browning; the epic which recalls the Norse sagas of William Morris; the poetry inspired by the

67 Fludernik's seminal study introduces the term 'experientiality' to denote narrative's 'quasi-mimetic evocation of "real-life" experience' (ibid.: 12). She refers to figural narrative to indicate the way in which writers may portray consciousness, and points out that 'epistolary narrative participates in this emphasis on consciousness' (1996: 48). For a related discussion of Byatt's use of interpolated frame narratives, including fairy-tales and 'collage-like structures', see Harries (2008), for whom 'Byatt's juxtapositions and framing structures suggest her continuing interest in alternative narrative possibilities' (91). Cf. also Byatt's essay 'Old Tales, New Forms' in her collection *On Histories and Stories* (2000: 123–150), where she reflects on different forms of patterned narratives in novels by European authors.

figure of the fairy Melusina; a collection of mysterious love poems, entitled *Ask to Embla*, which is the secret vehicle for the sublime expression of Ash's love for Christabel; lastly, lyrics of a more intimate character that reflect a certain Victorian manner, for instance that of Elizabeth Barrett Browning or Christina Rossetti. The fragmentary intensity of some of Christabel's poems evokes the poetry of Emily Dickinson, whose reclusive life was also a major inspiration for Christabel's biography. All these poems are an integral part of the text; practically every chapter begins with a poem by Ash or La Motte.

In an interview with Nicolas Tredell, Byatt had this to say on the density of embedded poetic flashes in the narrative:

> The poems are part of the text, in the sense that they were all written at the place where they came in the text [...] each poem should be read in its place and it's part of the metaphorical structure of the place it's in. (ibid.: 63)

We will return to this aspect in more depth later, with reference to certain moments when the symbolism of the poems summarises the condition of the characters or anticipates a further development in their story.

In addition to the poems there are the diaries of Ellen Ash, Blanche Glover and Sabine Lucrèce Charlotte de Kercoz. These naturalistic glimpses of inner lives that would otherwise be absent from the narrative add to its realism overall. The confessional tone of the diaries, which document the fictional historicity of the events, allows constant variation of the narration in several directions, according to their attribution to the various narrative voices. The plot is also further complicated thereby, raising the level of suspense with the continual and sudden revelations of the letters and diaries.

The fictional documentation of the events is also carried forward by the contributions from the various imaginary scholars active in the twentieth-century plot of *Possession*. Extracts from critical studies on the Victorian figures, written by Mortimer Cropper, James Blackadder and Leonora Stern, are alternated with quotations from real publications, such as the essay by the Italian scholar Silvia Vegetti Finzi entitled 'Melusina, malia e fobia del femminile', published in the volume *Melusina. Mito e leggenda di una donna serpente*, which Byatt cites by name, alongside other genuine works by Jacques Lacan and Sigmund Freud.[68] The superimposition of real items and fictional narrative brings us to a crucial aspect of A.S. Byatt's work, in which the juxtaposition of fact and fiction has been a

68 See the note of thanks in the introduction to the novel. Vegetti Finzi's essay appeared in *Melusina. Mito e leggenda di una donna serpente*. Eds. A. Barina et al. (Roma: Utopia, 1986).

recurrent theme from her early novels and short stories.[69] It is developed still further in *Possession*, placing the novel in a postmodern framework. In parallel with the genuine references, a corpus of extracts from criticism is built up, parodying typical academic productions. One memorable instance is the autobiography of the self-assured Professor Cropper, who considers himself the world's leading expert on Randolph Henry Ash (Ch. VI). There is an equally humorous portrayal of the feminist critical clique, most egregiously personified by Leonora Stern. Running through the chapter headings in her *Motif and Matrix in the Poems of La Motte*, the satirical intent emerges clearly: 'From Venus Mount to the Barren Heath', 'Female Landscapes and Unbroken Waters', 'Impenetrable Surfaces', 'From the Fountain of Thirst to the Armorican Ocean-Skin' (Ch. XIII, 243).

Lastly, we also find a great deal of material from fairy tales and mythology, grafted onto the narrative in the form of poetry or storytelling and lending it a new, atemporal dimension, one in which lie hidden both the deeper significance of the events and the meaning of the quest that involves both characters and readers. In addition to the poetic content, centred on the figure of the fairy Melusina, and the material inspired by the legend of the drowned city of Is, three fairy tales – which will be discussed in more detail later – are woven into the plot of *Possession*: 'The Glass Coffin', 'The Threshold' and 'Gode's Story'. Christabel's trip to Brittany, where she takes refuge with her relatives Raoul and Sabine de Kercoz, concealing her pregnancy from everyone, creates a pretext for the introduction of many mythological themes, which in turn allow comparison between traditions of pagan and Christian origin. The marvellous and the magical also enter the narrative through this channel, in particular through Christabel herself, with her special interest in the fairy Melusina, and the Breton side of her family, represented by her uncle, Raoul, and cousin, Sabine. Nor is it a mere coincidence that her father, Isidore La Motte, was the author of an important collection of myths, consigned to history (in *Possession*) like a third Grimm. Raoul is his double.

---

69 See, for example, the autobiographical short story 'Sugar' in the homonymous collection *Sugar and Other Stories* (1987), affording an interesting insight into the formation of narrative patterns and imaginative fiction out of real-life memories. The author acknowledged its autobiographical quality in her introduction to the French translation, later included in *Passions of the Mind* as 'Sugar/Le Sucre' (21–25). Similarly, 'Precipice-Encurled' in the same collection of short stories deals with the complex interplay of fact and fiction, drawing on the life of Robert Browning and the attempts of reconstructing some of its episodes at the hands of a twentieth-century (real) scholar. As Campbell has perceptively shown, the short story highlights 'the hazards of creativity' (2004: 97).

Furthermore, as is made clear only later, several of the novel's central metaphors, also recurrent in the poetry of Ash, carry the hidden meaning of the quest, which goes well beyond the intent of an entertainment in literary detection. These metaphors are taken from classical and Norse mythology and involve the myth of Proserpine, evoked in a poem by Ash which heads the first chapter, and the creation myth described in the epic poem Ragnarök, which opens chapter XIII.

The centre of *Possession*, which has twenty-eight chapters, plus a postscript and quotations from Hawthorne and Browning preceding the narrative, is built around a trip to Yorkshire by the two Victorian poets, for whom the journey is a celebration of their love and their spiritual and physical union. The trip takes place in June 1859 and is repeated a century later by Roland Michell and Maud Bailey. Following in the footsteps of Ash and La Motte, the two young scholars eventually share their predecessors' destiny as lovers.

Possession is thus an amalgam of heterogeneous materials whose equilibrium derives from a complex structure, itself sustained by a solid temporal axis which orientates the reader in the constant shifts between the two worlds being compared. This axis leads to a proliferation of texts, whose insertion into the overall pattern provides the other principle by which the structure of the novel is regulated. Within this architecture, certain events (the journeys to Yorkshire and to Brittany) also play a primary role in the novel's structural organization, because of their importance in developing the plot. The labyrinthine play of mirrors and symmetrical juxtaposition, requiring careful reading and observation of the characters and events described, constitute a further principle by which the structure of *Possession* is determined.

5.4 The Victorian World

As we have seen, the depiction of the Victorian world is achieved in part by a meticulous intertextual process which documents the life of the pair of Victorian poets in their own epoch. This is further enhanced by a series of tiny details which build up into a kind of literary scenography within *Possession*. One clear example of this is provided by the names chosen for the various characters, which are woven into a subtle and seductive web of relations, both internal and external to the novel itself. The name Christabel evokes several associations, most obviously S.T. Coleridge's unfinished poem *Christabel*, 1816, in which the heroine succumbs to a curse placed on her by Geraldine and loses the love of her father, Sir Leoline. The theme of the seduction and presumed loss of innocence of the heroine of the poem, written in the form of a traditional romance, is thus connected to the tragic destiny of Christabel La Motte. Her name also alludes, however, to another thematic reference, this time to a historical personage, the suffragette Christabel Pankhurst (1880–1958). The allusion reflects the innovative side of this female character, who despite the typical social conditioning of her age presents a strong-willed temperament and an individuality that justify her being singled out by later feminist critics as an icon of a new kind of woman. One instance of this is the way Christabel is seen by her cousin Sabine during her stay in Brittany:

> She is quick and razor-sharp and witty. (372)

and

> she has us all under some spell, for no one of us dare to take her to task. (372)

On the other hand, her surname of La Motte conceals a further, important symbolic reference, evoking another genuine historical figure, Friedrich, Baron de La Motte Fouqué (1777–1843). He was the author of a fairy tale, *Undine*, based on a story by Paracelsus (Harf-Lancner 1989: 488 and 494n49). The nymph Undine is a personification of the element of water,[70] and her story is connected to the figure of the fairy Melusina, half woman, half serpent, whose interpretation by A.S. Byatt as it appears in *Possession* will be discussed in more detail below.

One further allusion links up with the contemporary, meta-literary dimension, since the figure of Christabel pays homage indirectly to an academic colleague much admired by Byatt, Isobel Armstrong. Armstrong is not only the dedicatee of *Possession*, but has also been cited by the novelist as 'the best living Browning scholar' and a feminist expert in nineteenth-century women's fiction and poetry. Indeed, Byatt has observed that she 'seemed thoroughly the right person to dedicate *Possession* to' (qtd. in Franken 2001: 134 n11). This accumulation of semantic allusions highlights the author's liking for using encoded language that invites the reader to play a game of discovery, seeking further truths. It also has the function of placing the narrative in a specific ambience.

The name of Randolph Henry Ash is also rich in associations, albeit less openly connected to other literary figures, whether real or imaginary. The allusions here are veiled. Perhaps the first meaning to reflect on is the immediate one of the word ash itself, which via the sense of 'ashes' alludes to the basic idea for the novel: the involvement of living people in the lives and experiences of dead characters. Ash himself

---

70 In her study of mythological representations of the female, Anna Maria Stuby explores the double nature of these figures, showing how the blending of nymphs and witches is indicative in myth of a boundary area between civilisation and nature. In other words, the female is represented like the two-faced Janus and Melusine, too, so beloved of Christabel, is a similar dual characterisation (Stuby 1992: 49–74).

had given voice to the dead by evoking them in dramatic monologues, the literary form which made his name with the public and critics of his time. This aspect is of course derived from the biography of a real Victorian poet, Robert Browning. It is not by chance that the novel is introduced by an excerpt from Browning's 'Mr. Sludge, "the Medium"', from his collection *Dramatis Personae* (1864), together with another extract from Nathaniel Hawthorne's preface to *The House of the Seven Gables* (1851).[71] *Possession* is interspersed with several dramatic monologues, invented by Byatt for the pen of Randolph Henry Ash. One such is the portrait of 'Swammerdamm', a seventeenth-century Dutch naturalist, brought to life by Byatt through the poetic voice of Ash, in a clever imitation of Browning (Ch. XI). Another is 'Mummy Possest' (Ch. XXI), a portrayal of a woman with psychic powers that links directly to Mr. Sludge, Browning's own medium. A further allusion is thus created to the idea of an inaccessible truth, in the ceaseless interplay of fact and fiction.

The second basic meaning of the word *ash* is of course the tree whose magical vitality made it the cosmic tree of life in Norse mythology and the sagas. The myths tell of the apocalyptic havoc wrought when the tree of life is uprooted, an idea which is parodied in Ch. XXVIII when the American Mortimer Cropper forces his way into the cemetery where Ash is buried, desecrating his tomb, as it were, in order to obtain his final secret (Fountain 1994: 205).[72] It is therefore no coincidence that Ash is also the author of a mythological poem entitled *Ragnarök*, centred on the Norse creation myths (the *Eddas*). This aspect makes him seem very close to another genuine Victorian literary figure, William Morris. After visiting Iceland in 1871, Morris wrote an epic modelled on the sagas called *Sigurd the Volsung* (1876).

It is clear at this point that Randolph Henry Ash and Christabel La Motte are archetypal figures featuring a series of textual references that place their experiences in a kind of literary 'cartography' that maps out Victorian culture (Yelin 1992). Indeed, the precious collection of letters recording their love affair is not only pivotal to the novel's plot but also recalls the correspondence between Robert Browning and Elizabeth Barrett, the real-life protagonists of another poetic affair. Certain implicit references also point in the direction of yet another celebrated literary love story, the union of George Eliot and George

71 The extract from Hawthorne will receive more attention in discussing the formal aspects of *Possession* in relation to the romance.

72 Fountain also illustrates the precise references to Yggdrasil, the Norse tree of life, which grows at the centre of the universe where the origin and end of the world merge together. At the end of the world, Yggdrasil trembles, suffers and dies, alluding to the permanent cycle of life and the possibility of being born again (208n30).

Henry Lewes, who lived under the same roof for years without marrying since Lewes was unable to obtain a divorce from his wife.

If these are the horizons set for the identity of the two main Victorian characters, their inner being is reconstructed mainly thanks to their letters and the trip they take together to Yorkshire, again reflecting the typical tendencies and preoccupations of their time and culture. From their first meeting at the breakfast table of Crabb Robinson – as is deduced from two drafts of letters found in the London Library and from Crabb Robinson's own diary, carefully combed through by Roland Michell (Ch. III) – their correspondence is a crescendo of pace and tone until their second encounter. This takes place in Richmond Park under windy, leaden skies, as is recorded in their letters (Ch. X: 190–191).

It is interesting to note that Crabb Robinson is another real-life character, plucked by the novelist from contemporary accounts of the London cultural scene against which the plot of *Possession* is set. Henry Crabb Robinson (1775–1867) was a friend of celebrated poets and writers such as Wordsworth, Coleridge, Lamb and Carlyle, often attending their lectures. He was also one of the founders of University College London,[73] which provided the model for the novel's fictitious Prince Albert College. We have already recalled that A.S. Byatt had written a biography of Wordsworth and Coleridge, and it was here that the novelist first portrayed the figure of Crabb Robinson (Byatt 1970: 45–46), underscoring his role as a careful observer of London literary life, whose outstanding moments he recorded in his diary and personal correspondence. From the very first pages it is thus possible to grasp what will be the typical narrative procedure of the novelist in her work: one based on an intricate web of textual references and historical data, blended with pure invention. The points of intersection between these two kinds of material are often seamless – the reader of the nineteenth century plot of *Possession* may well be entirely unaware of who Crabb Robinson was, without detriment to his or her enjoyment. Conversely, so far as the part of the plot set in the present day is concerned, the seams between real data, textual references and pure fiction are clearly visible, as will be shown below.

In their love letters, the poets Ash and La Motte offer each other their respective images of self, allowing the external reader a close-up view of their lives, as if in a filmed sequence. Given that their first meeting did no more than spur them on to know each other better, this greater intimacy is achieved through their exchange of letters. Ash writes of himself:

---

73 See Drabble (1985: 836).

> For all I am is a nineteenth-century gentleman plumb in the midst of smoky London – and what is peculiar to him is to know just how much stretches away from his vanishing pin-point of observation – before and around and after – whilst all the time he is what he is, with his whiskered visage and his shelves full of Plato and Feuerbach, St. Augustine and John Stuart Mill. (158)

This cultured gentleman, dedicating himself to the understanding of the ideas of his time and of those that shaped the mindset of his predecessors, is an archetype of the Victorian intellectual, poised between the new knowledge of science and liberal thought and the doubts instilled by the wavering of his religious beliefs. He claims he loves the company of 'other imagined minds' (158), to which he gives new life and physical form in poetry, in the spirit of the 'great ventriloquist', the name given to him by his American biographer, Mortimer Cropper (107).[74] It has already been pointed out that this habit of giving voice to real or imagined characters in history is a trait of Robert Browning, the author of the true literary precedents for such poems by Ash as 'Swammerdamm' and 'Mummy Possest'. Like Swammerdamm, the seventeenth-century Dutch scientist who invented the microscope, Ash is interested in life in all its manifestations, great and small: he states his intention of writing a poem on insects (158), while at the same time devoting himself to the study of mythology, the origin of the species and the relationship between science and religion. We learn that he is a friend of Michelet (249), the French historian (1798–1874) who genuinely proposed to recreate the past in its entirety, taking into account the influence of ethnic and geographical factors on the formation of the minds of men who had played an active part in history. This historical figure had mapped his romantic impressions of nature and life in books on the four elements of water, air, earth and fire, with which Ash's naturalistic poems – like the paintings of J.M.W. Turner – seem to have particular affinity (212).

Other similar digressions combine to recreate in the novel the cultural ambience of its chosen epoch, placing Ash against a fully realistic background. Ash's own interests extend to include other fields, such as geology, science and its rapport with religion and poetry. His interest in fossils and the origin of life reflects the spirit of an age which was profoundly shaken by the theories of Charles Darwin, who published *On the Origin of Species* in 1859, and those of Charles Lyell, put forward in his *Principles of Geology* (1830).

74 The name is the title of the biography of Ash published by Mortimer Cropper in 1969. In the novel we learn that the sobriquet was coined by the poet in a monologue-caricature of himself.

The letters of Ash and La Motte also reveal their literary enthusiasms, since both authors submit their own writings to the other's judgement. We learn that *Ragnarök*, the epic poem in which, as we have seen, Ash narrates the genesis of the world in accordance with a pagan tradition found in Norse mythology, has deeply disturbed Christabel's conscience. In her reply she writes:

> you are to know then [...] that your great poem Ragnarök was the occasion of quite the worst crisis in the life of *my simple religious faith*, that I have ever experienced, or hope to experience. It was not that anywhere in that poem you attacked the Christian religion – which indeed was not made mention of with complete Poetic Propriety – and moreover you speak never, in your poetry, with your own voice, or from your own heart directly. [...] I digress wildly from Ragnarök and its pagan Day of Judgment and its pagan interpretation of the mystery of the Resurrection, and the New Heaven and the New Earth. [...] It seemed to me you made Holy Scripture no more than another Wonder Tale – by dint of such writing, such force of imagining. (160)[75]

Christabel, who at the time of her correspondence with Ash is still living a reclusive existence with the painter Blanche Glover in their Richmond home, is fearful of tackling themes which range beyond the confines of biblical certitude. In the mythology handed down by the Eddas, *Ragnarök* is the Norse term for the Twilight of the Gods, the apocalyptic ending of the universe before a new cycle of life. The concept shakes Christabel's conscience, while Ash's speculative intelligence unhesitatingly explores every field of knowledge, his powerful imagination sustaining him even where his reason wavers, shored up by long-standing convictions. Like another great Victorian poet, Alfred, Lord Tennyson, whose composition *In Memoriam* (1850) reflected the sensibilities of the age in its combination of poetry and scientific thought, Ash embraces the full range of knowledge made accessible in his time. In secret, he also examines the signs of a hypothetical circularity of time, as may be deduced from his reading of Giambattista Vico's *Principii di una scienza nuova*, the work that the young Roland Michell consults in the London Library, using Ash's own edition (Ch. I). This casts a different light on Ash's interest in themes such as the biblical accounts of the resurrection and the figure of Lazarus: the latter he also makes the subject of a poem, *Déjà-vu, or The Second Sight*, whose title Christabel is keen to understand in depth (166). Indeed, it is her poetic intuition which reveals the ulterior meanings of the poem, which is not included in the novel itself, as she explores the concepts of 'eternity' and 'prophecy' contained in the work. The ending of the novel makes clear the sense of these abundant references, behind

75 *Emphasis* added.

which is hidden a broader design, incarnated in the destiny of the two lovers and which may only be guessed at by the reader beforehand.

Christabel's physical existence may be restricted to the confines of her home, but this does not prevent her mind from roaming freely through the world of imagination and poetry, in an atmosphere which recalls the figure of Emily Dickinson, as has been noted above. In one of her first letters to Ash, Christabel La Motte offers this self-portrait:

> I live circumscribed and self-communing – 'tis best so – not like a Princess in a thicket, by no means, but more *like a very fat and self-satisfied Spider in the centre of her shining Web*, if you will forgive me the slightly disagreeable Analogy. Arachne is a lady I am greatly sympathetic to, an honest craftswoman, who makes perfect patterns, but is a little inclined to take unorthodox snaps at visiting or trespassing strangers, not perceiving the distinction between the two, it may be, often until too late. [...] *I am a creature of my Pen*. Mr. Ash, my Pen is the best of me, and I enclose a Poem, in earnest of my great goodwill towards you. (87)[76]

The metaphor of the spider earnestly spinning its great web is a recurrent image in the novel, symbolising female creativity and providing the inspirational motif for one of the poems that Christabel sends to Ash ('Metamorphosis', 161). The trope also seems to overlap with the archetypal image of the spider as emblem of seduction and amorous entrapment. The centrality of Christabel in the affair with Ash is thus made explicit: it is he who will visit her secretly in Richmond Park, attracted by the charm of the poetess on paper.

A poem on the figure of the fairy Melusina, from Breton legend, is one of the projects which occupy Christabel's imagination. She also feels the influence of the spirit of her age, writing poetry on ants and insects. In 'Psyche', the natural world inspires her to a reflection on the human condition:

> The Ants toil for no Master
> Sufficient to their Need
> The daily commerce of the Nest
> The storage of their Seed
> They meet – and exchange Messages –
> But none to none – bows down
> They – like God's thoughts – speak each to each –
> Without – external – crown (162)

76 *Emphasis* added.

If the spider's web stands for artistic creation, the independence of the ant is a reflection of Christabel's proud solitude. In addition to scientific commentaries, the correspondence between the two poets also turns to such themes as Spiritualism, taking its cue from the curiosity of Christabel, which leads her to the lectures on the subject that were so typical of Victorian cultural life (169–170), and the British national character as compared to that of the Americans (170).

Christabel's letters give a detailed picture of her life with Blanche, reconstructing the story of their relationship and their shared plans for the future, which came out of a meeting at a lecture by Ruskin on the dignity of craftsmanship and individual labour. 'We were two who wished to live the life of the Mind' (187) states Christabel, reminding us of how unconventional a choice it was for the period, for two women to dedicate their individual selves to art, rather than to marriage and the keeping of a household. The parallel with the *Lady of Shalott*, encouraged by Christabel herself (187), further underlines the prerogative of exclusively female creativity which she and Blanche are determined not to forego. This creativity is also expressed in the recurrent symbol of Melusina, a creature half woman, half serpent with whom Christabel feels affinity and which we will deal with below.

The figure of the *Lady of Shalott* became well-known in Tennyson's poem of the same name, the story of a woman shut up in a tower, where she spends her days weaving a carpet (actually a 'web' in the original text). She is forbidden to view the world outside – the legendary city of Camelot – except through a mirror, whose reflected images provide her with the subjects for her weaving. The arrival of Lancelot, however, distracts her attention to the point where she gazes on him and the real Camelot; as a result, the carpet falls from the tower window and the mirror cracks, casting a curse upon her. When Christabel takes over the image as an emblem of her art, she cannot yet know that even greater solitude awaits her in her own life, in the tower of Seal Court, following the birth of her daughter Maia from her relationship with Ash. Long before those events, Christabel portrays her solitary existence within the walls of Bethany Cottage as follows:

> What is a House? So strong – so square
> Making a Warmth inside the Winds
> We walk with lowered eyelids there
> And silent go – behind the blinds
>
> Yet hearts may tap like loaded bombs
> Yet brains may shrill in carpet-hush
> And windows fly from silent rooms
> And walls break outwards – with a rush – (210)

Beneath the seeming layer of silence and domestic quiet may lurk the soul's dismay, and the gothic intimacy of a home may be transformed into explosive power, with windows bursting and walls suddenly collapsing.[77]

If Christabel's life is wholly taken up by poetry, the existence of Randolph Ash's wife Ellen is entirely dedicated to good housekeeping and the running of a respectable family, based on traditional values and a presumed spiritual order of things, but utterly lacking a physical and carnal dimension.[78] Ellen, who venerates her husband's learning and poetic aura, does not allow even Blanche Glover to break up this illusion of order, minutely described in her diary (Ch. XII), preferring to keep to herself the secret of Ash's affair with Christabel after she discovers it. The Victorian values that Ellen so tenaciously defends are given greater resonance by the description of her family background, in particular of her mother, who preferred to punish her servants personally. Ellen is unstinting in her support of Ash, whom she helps in every way she can: when Randolph writes to her from Yorkshire, reporting on his scientific discoveries and the fossils he has found, and asking her to attend professor T.H. Huxley's lectures in his stead (214), we can intuit her readiness to perform any task her husband requires of her. At the time Randolph writes his fulsome letters to his wife, complete with a jet

---

77 A.S. Byatt has stated that she drew directly on the poetry of Emily Dickinson for inspiration in creating the verses by Christabel. Her comments on the subject are particularly significant: 'I couldn't use Christina Rossetti because Christina has a kind of Christian piety which I'm quite unable to reproduce, not being a Christian. [...] so I turned to someone who I think is the greatest woman poet of all, Emily Dickinson. I read and reread her poems and her very strange letters and picked up hints from her style, out of which I made an English version of her. Then I realised that my Christabel had a kind of sexual frankness which almost no English women, except George Eliot, had in those days, so I made her part French, and that brought with it all the Breton mythology which comes into her poetry. So she's a kind of Emily Dickinson, who was a disciple of Keats and loved reading sixteenth-century poetry' (qtd. in Wachtel ibid.: 80).

78 The novel allows the reader to intuit that Ellen and Randolph's marriage was never consummated. The author's own comments on the characterisation of Ellen are significant in this context: 'She's in a sense the archetypal Victorian case of the woman who was told nothing about sex. She's also a bit like Tennyson's wife, who was required to wait so long to be married that it must have become very frightening. She might not have been frightened when she was a girl, but when she's lost her beauty... The other person I think of in this context is Jane Carlyle, who was examined just before her death when she had her accident and was found to be virgo intacta. The whole of the Carlyles' marriage had existed without any sexual relationship. Of course, the theory everybody has formed is that Carlyle was impotent, but *my* theory, or at least a possible theory, is that Jane Carlyle simply couldn't face it' (qtd. in Aragay 1994: 163).

brooch in the form of a garland as a mark of his affection, he is already accompanied by Christabel. At this point of the narrative, Ellen prefers to ignore the special circumstances which bring Randolph and Christabel together; the Victorian morals survive intact the upset of the Yorkshire trip, which ironically takes place in the same year that Darwin published *On the Origin of Species* (212).[79]

The relationship between Christabel and Blanche is also sustained by an apparent order, which wavers and then collapses when Ash enters their lives. The quiet harmony which previously characterised their existence is described in Blanche Glover's diary (Ch. IV, 43–47). It reproduces an atmosphere of gothic intimacy not unlike that depicted by Christina Rossetti in her narrative poem *Goblin Market* (1862), centred on the love of two sisters.[80] Blanche's painting is inspired by the mediaeval legends which Victorian literature also frequently drew on: 'Merlin and Viviane' (172) and 'Christabel before Sir Leoline' (45), taken respectively from Tennyson's *Morte d'Arthur* and from Coleridge's fragment *Christabel*. The liking for mediaeval subject matter reflects the aesthetics of her contemporaries, the Pre-Raphaelites, but the delicacy and soft tones of her paintings reveal a lack of vitality that Blanche herself recognises:

> I paint so thinly, as though my work were unlit stained glass that requires a flood of light from beyond and behind to illuminate and enliven it, and there is no beyond and behind. Oh, I want *Force*. (45)

After Christabel leaves her to follow Randolph Ash, Blanche's already isolated existence becomes a burden of solitude that is too much for her to bear, and she kills herself. Her suicide is recorded in the novel by a newspaper cutting (309). The celebration of this wide-ranging picture of the Victorian world reaches its peak in Chapter XV when, in June 1859, Christabel and Randolph make their journey to Yorkshire. The omniscient narrator describes the couple in the carriage at length, giving us at last a detailed physical description. The sensation is that of a long-awaited close-up view of the two characters. Their appearance is minutely portrayed, with special emphasis being given to a number of traits in Christabel's looks which prefigure those of her descendant Maud Bailey. The description of Randolph and Christabel's journey by carriage recalls another

79 Ellen's diary also records Randolph's absence (222).

80 The following lines from *Goblin Market* emanate the atmosphere of particular intimacy which seems to mark the relationship between Blanche and Christabel: 'Golden head by golden head,/Like two pigeons in one nest/Folded in each other's wings,/They lay down in their curtained bed [...]/Cheek to cheek and breast to breast/Locked together in one nest' (Rossetti 1970: 18).

well-known literary coach journey set in the Victorian period, in John Fowles' *The French Lieutenant's Woman*. In *Possession*, however, the omniscient narrator does not interfere in the events being described: Christabel and Randolph sit facing each other as the Yorkshire landscape rolls past before their distracted gaze. In Fowles' novel, on the other hand, the narrator, bearded and wearing a top hat, suddenly appeared in the scene of Charles' journey by carriage, taking advantage of his protagonist's being momentarily asleep to address the external reader and openly reveal his own narrating identity.

The coast and the open Yorkshire countryside inland are the backdrop and the culmination of Randolph and Christabel's love story: at last they have left behind the confined spaces of domestic and city life. A feeling of freedom and of the natural flow of life imbues these pages, in which descriptions of the sea and the long, windswept beaches are interwoven with the account of their physical lovemaking. Ash, who has brought with him a copy of Lyell's *Principles of Geology*, perceives the connection between his unrepeatable individual experience and a vaster, transcendental dimension. He is struck by the image of Christabel standing out against the grey slate rocks of the seashore:

> Most of all, he saw her waist, just where it narrowed, before the skirts spread. [...] He thought of her momentarily as an hour-glass, containing time, which was caught in her like a thread of sand, of stone, of specks of life, of things that had lived and would live. She held his time, she contained his past and his future, both now cramped together, with such ferocity and such gentleness, into this small circumference. (287)

This is a turning point in the narration, insofar as we may assume that at this point Christabel is already pregnant with Maia, a consequence which is not yet openly stated in the narrative but which will emerge more fully subsequently. In making this moment on the seashore the epicentre of her narrative, A.S. Byatt superimposes the image of the hour-glass on Christabel's silhouette and thus unites the biographical data of the poets' love affair with the wider themes of the circularity of time, the origin of the species and the pagan and Christian accounts of the genesis of the universe, all of which abound in Ash's poetic works. Furthermore, the hour-glass is a metaphor which also sheds light indirectly on one of the themes which inspired the novel, the relationship between past and present, as well as linking to the author's reflections on the relations between individual, culture and society, as expressed symbolically in her idea of a 'knot' tying together infinite variables to which I shall return later.

Lastly, the external reader of the novel may guess at something which the twentieth-century characters interested in the work of the two Victorian poets cannot yet know, namely that the muse who inspired Ash's mysterious love poems entitled *Ask to Embla* was not Ellen, but Christabel:

> They say that women change: 'tis so: but you
> Are ever-constant in your changefulness,
> Like that still thread of falling river, one
> From source to last embrace in the still pool
> Ever-renewed and ever-moving on
> From first to last a myriad water-drops
> And you – I love you for it – are the *force*
> That moves and holds the form.
>
> R.H. Ash, *Ask to Embla*, XIII (262)

Since the modern critics in *Possession* are unaware of the affair between Christabel and Randolph, they inevitably misread the hidden truths contained in their works, but their misinterpretations will be discussed in more detail below in the section dealing with the novel's contemporary setting. Ash is powerfully attracted by the woman poet's marked individuality and, in the poem quoted above, secretly compares her to the 'thread of falling river' that rises from its source and joins with the pool below, changing in shape but always the same as itself. Otherness from and fusion with the beloved are both celebrated in the lines. It is worth noting here that the names given to the lovers in the poems also occur in Ash's epic *Ragnarök* (Ch. XIII, 241). In both Ash's poem and the original *Poetic Edda*, Ask and Embla are the names given to the first men, created by the Norse gods from two tree trunks, an ash and an elm. These references thus reveal the inmost meaning of Ash's poems: like Ask and Embla, or Adam and Eve, Randolph and Christabel come to life again after their union, which is equivalent to a new genesis, a new cycle of life which brings with it Maia, but also the new poetry of Ash and La Motte.

The great tapestry of Victorian life and letters woven into *Possession* by A.S. Byatt is based on an effort of philological reconstruction so meticulous, and so felicitously combined with pure fiction, that it is virtually impossible to do justice either to the scope and scale of scholarly research it represents, or to the fascination of its resulting literary attractions.

5.5 The Contemporary Setting

The contemporary frame for the nineteenth century core narrative of *Possession* is the scene for the intrigues of a group of academics, all obsessed by the discovery of a literary secret destined to bring about a revolution in studies of the Victorian poets Ash and La Motte. The typical settings and themes of academia make this part of the work reminiscent of the campus novel, a genre whose best-known exponents are Kingsley Amis (*Lucky Jim*, 1954), Malcolm Bradbury (*The History Man*, 1975) and David Lodge (*Changing Places*, 1975). Byatt herself, however, has stressed that *Possession*'s links with the genre are only tenuous, given that her depiction of the university ambience is quite different from the typical campus portrayal:

> In most academic novels the one thing nobody ever does is read a book, let alone *think* about what they've read as though it mattered. [...] Yet in a sense *Possession* is an academic novel, because all of the academic characters are slightly caricatured in a way the Victorian characters are not. [...] I think if it is an academic novel, it's trying to correct the usual one which is about people's sexual behaviour and about power struggles in departments. It is about those things, but it's really saying that *reading* ought to be *at the centre* of studying literature or why bother.
>
> (qtd. in Aragay ibid.: 156, *emphasis* added)

Reading is indeed the motivating force for Byatt's twentieth-century characters, as they compete fiercely in the race to wrest the final secret from the Victorian poets' letters. As in a chivalric romance, complete with quest – in this case a search for hidden treasure, the clutch of respectable professors follow the tracks that lead to the tomb of Randolph Henry Ash. Their distinguishing marks are their school of thought and focus of reading, since each represents a particular branch of literary studies. This is the aspect in which Byatt gives herself free rein to parody the mores of her twentieth-century academics and the disciplines they represent. While Christabel and Randolph find their reason for living in poetry and creativity, the modern protagonists seem pale individuals by comparison, feeding on the lives of others as consigned to literary history. The youngest of them, Roland Michell, is perhaps the most sympathetic to the reader, not least because, at the end of the quest, he, too, finds himself to be a poet.

Like their Victorian counterparts, the names of the modern couple of protagonists are replete with literary echoes that make them true textual products of particular cultural and historical circumstances. The name Roland carries an allusion to Robert Browning's poem 'Childe Roland to the Dark Tower Came', from the collection *Men and Women* (1855), in which a roving knight crosses hostile country to reach the dark tower from whose summit he will sound his horn. The allusion is polyvalent, as always, since it brings with it a connection to the legendary feats of Roland, as told in the *Chanson de Roland*, and to his later incarnation as Orlando in the epic poems by Ariosto and Boiardo. The image of the knight reaching his goal provides Byatt with a metaphor for the success of Roland's researches, since the young man not only discovers his own poetic vocation but also receives his first serious offers of employment. He is thus catapulted from a marginal and precarious existence on a short-term research contract to the centre stage of academic life, a transformation which enables him to conquer even the icy Maud, prising her out of her self-regarding cocoon of feminist critical theory.

Roland's previous self-image was rather grey and listless. 'He's not forceful. It's his major failing', was the judgement of his tutor, professor James Blackadder, while Roland viewed himself as a latecomer and a failure (Ch. II, 10–11). Like Maud Bailey, the researcher from the Lincoln University Women's Resource Centre with whom he shares the results of his work, Roland relativizes the world around him. Not believing in the existence of a unitary ego, his life seems incoherent and rather shapeless:

> Roland had learned to see himself, theoretically, as a crossing-place for a number of systems, all loosely connected. He had been trained to see his idea of his 'self' as an illusion, to be replaced by a discontinuous machinery and electrical message-network of various desires, ideological beliefs and responses, language forms and hormones and pheromones. Mostly he liked this. He had no desire for any strenuous Romantic self-assertion. (424)

This kind of characterisation, polarised in the figures of Roland and Maud, provides the pegs on which Byatt hangs her ideas on culture, theory and literary practice in the present, constantly contrasting them with those of her predecessors in the Victorian period. Roland and Maud are archetypes of present-day culture insofar as their mindset belongs to a context which is orientated towards postmodern deconstruction of the subject. In accordance with the dictates of current literary theory, the two young researchers have learned that writing conceals the traces of a system of signs that reduce the authorial voice to a passive element as the receptacle of that complex semiotic system. The cultural environment to which (s)he belongs is the true authorial subject, not the writer: through such observations, interspersed in the present-day plot, the novelist expresses views with which she wishes to take issue. This is why Roland thinks of his idea of self as mere illusion, making him diffident about the prospect of a relationship with Maud, even when all the signs point in that direction:

> All *that* was the plot of a Romance. He was in a Romance, a vulgar and a high Romance simultaneously, a Romance was one of the systems that controlled him, as the expectations of Romance control almost everyone in the Western world, for better or worse, at some point or another. He supposed that Romance must give way to social realism, even if the aesthetic temper of the time was against it. (425)

Roland's extreme awareness of the cultural phenomena that dominate individuals and their subjectivity makes him mistrustful of feelings, especially when he recognises their cause and the context in which they arise. We may certainly assume that he will have read Roland Barthes (indeed, their being namesakes is quite likely not a coincidence), who famously argued that every cultural phenomenon is the expression of a system of signs, and that every act of writing is the result of a proliferation of preceding texts, a fact which places the writer in a dialogue with his/her forerunners, while only the reader is in a position to receive the full plurality of all the echoes created.[81]

Maud, too, shares his doubts and theoretical premises, which lead her to this reflection:

> Narcissism, the unstable self, the fractured ego, Maud thought, who am I? A matrix for a susurration of texts and codes? It was both a pleasant and an unpleasant idea, this requirement that she think of herself as intermittent and partial. (251)

Maud has these thoughts during her trip to Yorkshire with Roland, after reading Mortimer Cropper's biography of Randolph Henry Ash. Reflecting on the particular type of subjectivity that characterises the author of the study and his subject, Maud poses a series of questions that are at one and the same time both purely literary and also psychoanalytical, amplifying the literary self-awareness of the writing of *Possession*:

> Was Ash subject to Cropper's research methods and laws of thought? Whose subjectivity was being studied? Who was the subject of the sentences of the text, and how did Cropper and Ash fit into Lacan's perception that the grammatical subject of a statement differs from the subject, the 'I', who is the object discussed by that statement? (250)

Observations of this kind serve to characterise Maud as representing a particular school of thought, steeped in current feminist critical theory. But Maud's observations also perform the function of discussing the role of writing in the light of the mechanisms which govern it, giving the novel a meta-literary and self-referential dimension.

In contrast to Maud, Roland belongs to a more dated and less fashionable field of research, whose methods are carried on by James Blackadder in the tradition of F.R. Leavis, although, as has been seen, Roland is not unaware of the existence

81 Cf. Roland Barthes, *Le Degré zéro de l'écriture* (Paris: Le Seuil, 1953) publ. in English as *Writing Degree Zero* (New York: Hill and Wang, 1968). See also 'The Death of the Author' (Barthes 1977: 142–148), in which text is defined as follows: 'a *multidimensional space* in which a variety of writings, none of them original, blend and clash. The text is *a tissue of quotations* drawn from the innumerable centres of culture' (148). My *emphasis*.

of other theoretical approaches.[82] It is he who recognises that all the scholars caught up in the quest are prisoners of a metaphor, unable to see things for what they are (253–254). Covertly, Byatt has Roland utter thoughts which are in fact her own, regarding the role of criticism and literary theory, and their relationship with the literary text. Statements made by the novelist on numerous occasions allow us to verify, as will be demonstrated in the following sections, that Roland's views on creative writing and its rapport with literary criticism coincide with her own.

While Maud reads the essays of the American Cropper during the trip to Yorkshire, Roland reads Leonora Stern's work on the poetry of Christabel La Motte. He is especially irritated by the American critic's insistence on interpretations based exclusively on human sexuality. 'It isn't a matter of her gender and my gender' (254), he observes, although he must recognise in spite of himself that Maud's work also fits into the psychoanalytical, feminist trend of literary criticism.

Maud Bailey and Leonora Stern, though they share a critical focus on the same Victorian woman poet, are really opposite personalities, whose peculiarities are amplified by their nationalities, one British, the other American. Maud is a young, attractive and already successful scholar, author of a study on the spatial fantasies of Victorian women, entitled *Marginal Beings and Liminal Poetry* (54). Her name, like that of Roland, is replete with literary echoes, the strongest being the title of Tennyson's *Maud – A Monodrama* (1885), in which a male voice expresses his love for the eponymous heroine, beginning one lyric with the celebrated line, 'Come into the garden, Maud'. If we remember that Roland finds his own poetic vocation for the first time in the garden of his home in Putney, to which he was previously forbidden access by the cantankerous Mrs. Irving (see Ch. XXVI), the symbolic significance of this particular reference becomes clear. His creativity flowers in a garden, the fair setting for the satisfaction of all his drives, given that he has also won the beautiful Maud. The garden is also a kind of *Leitmotif* that takes us to one of Ash's poems, quoted at the head of the first chapter and then again, in its entirety, in Ch. XXVI of the novel (*The Garden of Proserpina*), allowing us to see just why Maud is invited into the garden: carnality and textuality are merged in a riot of creativity, of the kind that overwhelmed the pair of Victorian poets.[83] This literary and carnal union is elegantly prefigured in

82 See the shrewd characterisation of Blackadder in Ch. III, where he is said to have been sent up to Cambridge by his Scottish father (27).

83 On the significance of the garden as an image of creativity, Byatt gave some important indications in the interview with Nicholas Tredell cited above: 'It's exactly the

a fleeting moment of involuntary intimacy, when the pair of scholars fall asleep next to each other:

> He slept curled against her back, a dark comma against her pale elegant phrase. (424)

It has already been pointed out that Maud is a direct descendant of Christabel La Motte, which explains her having a number of physical features in common with the poetess, as is repeatedly emphasised: she has a pale complexion and very blonde hair – which she is reluctant to flaunt, paradoxically inhibited by the probable reaction of her feminist colleagues; her eyes are green, which is also the dominant colour of the clothes and jewellery worn by both women. One particularly important item is a Victorian green and jet brooch with the figure of a mermaid on a rock, an heirloom of Maud: the allusion to the fairy Melusina is clear and immediately recognised by Maud (Ch. XIII, 260). While Christabel spent the last years of her life writing poetry in the gothic tower of Seal Court, like a latter day *Lady of Shalott*, Maud now carries out her researches in a room on the top floor of Lincoln University's Tennyson Tower, while her flat is on the ground floor of a red-brick Georgian house near the city. This abundance of detail, which critics have sometimes found excessive, is a recurrent trait in A.S. Byatt's work. Its real function is to enhance the symbolic value of certain details, which act in an intricately connective web. Djordjevic has perfectly captured the significance of these itemised descriptions:

> [...] this kind of 'metonymic detail' lends itself to *contamination by symbolism*. Absorbed in the visualisation of the objects described, we do not notice – not consciously that is – that a hefty dose of symbolism is being let in by the back door. (Djordjevic 1997: 79)

---

same image as in *The Virgin in the Garden*: language is flowers [...]. The reason I love North Yorkshire so is that for me language and the earth are really intertwined there' (65). On other occasions the novelist has dwelt on the image of open space beyond a fence, like the one which appeared to her beyond the playground of the school she attended in childhood, a prospect which seemed then to promise a special kind of happiness. See also her recollection of childhood memories in the essay 'Identity and the Writer' (1987) where, in her attempt to define the poetic self, she recalls her perception of external space as defined by the edges of the pram in which she was lying: 'And I remember – and this is to betray the memory in a way – I remember constituting the person (Lacan is wrong: the sense of identity begins long before language). And there was this sense of waking from sleep and realising that I was there, in that place, not in another place, seeing these things. And this was intensely pleasurable. [...] *this memory, this sense, is behind most of the moments when I'm quite sure I know what I'm doing in my work. It is to do with the working self*' (24, my emphasis). We will return to the symbolism of *The Garden of Proserpina* in the next section.

I find this observation accurate, inasmuch as a critical reading of the novel cannot possibly neglect to consider the metonymic function of the details, which becomes a narrative procedure in its own right. Even the characters of the two female figures have a similar set of particularities in common. Christabel's proud independence is reflected in Maud's presumed haughtiness, which in fact hides the timidity of a beautiful woman who feels a victim of other people's gaze: 'You can become a property or an idol. I don't want that. It kept happening' (506).

Behind her wall of self-imposed abstinence, defended by typically English reserve, Maud seizes on the metaphor of the self-sufficient unit, making into her own the image of an egg contained in an enigmatic story by Christabel La Motte, addressed to Mr. Ash:

> an Egg, a perfect O, *a living Stone*, doorless and windowless […].
> An Egg is my answer. What is the Riddle?
> I am my own riddle. […] my solitude. It is a thing we women are taught to dread – oh the terrible tower […] The Donjon may frown and threaten – but it keeps us very safe – within its confines we are free in a way you, who have the freedom to range the world, do not need to imagine […] my Solitude is my Treasure […]. (137, *emphasis* added)

But Maud, too, like Roland, undergoes a transformation, recognising that the egg described symbolises an ego shut up in itself, destined to chill and harden since it lacks the spark of life. Once she regards Roland's presence as worthy of her special attention, Freud's remarks on falling in love make it obvious to her that Christabel's egg is a metaphor:

> It is only when a person is completely in love that the main quota of libido is transferred on to the object and the object to some extent takes the place of the ego. (430)

Only in the concluding chapter is Maud's personality, now open to the change introduced by her relationship with Roland, fully revealed. She herself tells Roland of her empathetic rapport with the poet she has studied for so long:

> I feel as she did. I keep my defences up because I must go on *doing my work*. I know how she felt about her unbroken egg. Her self-possession, her autonomy. (506)

Leonora Stern is an opposing figure, intimidating and threatening Maud's English reserve with her own American brand of intrusive, brash exuberance. The description of Stern is a particularly telling, irresistible caricature. Her formidable sexual appetite, unbounded by the confines of gender, is a salient feature of the portrait:

> Leonora was a kind of verbal Cleopatra, creating appetite where most she satisfied, making an endless pillow-book out of the new oratory of the couch. (315)

Byatt uses her satire of Stern to launch an attack on the kind of feminist and psychoanalytical critical theories which, in her view, misrepresent the meaning of literary texts.[84] Furthermore, even Maud's splendid, regal autonomy is indirectly satirised through the parody of her American colleague:

> I got to be quite in love with myself, and then I thought I was unhealthily attached to me, and should give myself up. So I found Mary-Lou. (316)

The egg metaphor which Maud had appropriated for herself appears quite inadequate for Leonora, who has no fear of openings or contact with others, seeming to devour existence.[85] She also has an important part to play in the plot, given that she supplies the clue which leads all the academic characters in the book to Brittany, in search of records of Christabel's presence there. Her correspondence with a French academic from the University of Nantes, an expert in women's writing, reveals the existence of a letter from Sabine de Kercoz, Christabel's cousin, confirming that the latter was in Brittany for a period, shortly after the trip to Yorkshire. Like Arianna in the Greek myth, the French scholar – whose name is indeed Ariane Le Minier – lays down another thread to follow by revealing that the papers were left by one of Sabine's descendants. Typically, Stern's initial reason for contacting Le Minier is to further her studies on the 'sexualisation of the landscape elements in the *Fairie Melusina*' (313).

---

84 On this point see the views expressed by Byatt in the interview with Nicolas Tredell cited above, where she builds on her description of Stephanie in labour in *Still Life* to refute the validity of certain research methods: 'I read a very good article about descriptions of childbirth by women which assumes that my accounts of childbirth in the 1950s and '60s are informed by feminist perspectives, whereas in fact they are simply accurate memories of, for instance, the rage I felt at not being allowed to walk up and down when I was in labour. It's nothing to do with feminist theory having told me that, I observed it. *I think in metaphors, not in propaganda*. […] I think I'm fighting a different theoretical battle, for the work of art not to be propaganda' (61, my *emphasis*). In turn, Byatt's approach to questions of gender and post-structuralist theory has been discussed by Franken (2001) who, in her nuanced analysis of the novel, attributes the author's ambivalence on these issues to her split role as both writer and critic. See also Pereira (2004: 149–164).

85 Certain details of Leonora's biography appear significant: her first husband was a Princeton scholar, a representative of the now outmoded New Criticism and incapable of surviving the 'cut-throat ideological battles of structuralism, post-structuralism, Marxism, deconstruction and feminism'; her second marriage was to an athletic and violent man, since which she has had exclusively female partners. Despite referring to her first husband as that 'poor sap', she has retained his surname and its aura of prestige (Ch. XVIII, 310–311).

This amusing portrait of the international academic scene reaches its climax with the advent of the American Mortimer Cropper, the object of Byatt's sharpest satire. Elegant, self-confident, rich and famous, Cropper moves with efficiency and dynamism in a field in which his British rivals dither endlessly, bogged down in their inconclusive research methods, like Beatrice Nest. As well as being the author of a major biography of the poet Ash, which is revealed to be full of inaccuracies, Cropper boasts of being the keeper of the richest collection of manuscripts and artefacts which once belonged to Randolph Henry Ash, preserved at Robert Dale Owen University in Harmony City, New Mexico. Cropper is a conceited materialist who flashes his business card and a fat cheque book whenever he comes across an item which might be added to the prestigious Stant Collection of his home institution. He cruises the British Isles in a luxurious black Mercedes with the number plate ANK 666. When his rival James Blackadder, having become an ally of Leonora Stern in the fight against Cropper, meets up with him again in Brittany, travelling in the infamous limousine now damaged in a collision with Leonora's own car, he exclaims: 'Cropper is the Ankou' (429).

Once again this is a detail which hides interesting symbolic meanings: the Ankou is a common figure in Breton mythology, an implacable harbinger of death who travels in a creaking wagon loaded with human bones. Often the Ankou is depicted as a skeleton covered with a sheet and holding a lance or scythe: an image which is recreated when, in Ch. XXVIII, Cropper wields a spade to dig up the remains of Ash. The registration number 666 (319) seems, on the other hand, to be connected to the 'Number of the Beast' in the Book of Revelation in the New Testament, where it may be a symbol of the Anti-Christ.[86] Hence the colours of Cropper's dressing gown when he makes his first appearance in the novel are black and red, the colours of Satan (Ch. VI, 93).

Cropper's name may suggest the harvest of the grim reaper, as well as his habit of accumulating a 'crop' of texts and memorabilia, just as his first name Mortimer contains an echo of mortality. In reality he wishes to emulate Ash, not to understand him. Lacking in awareness of his true self, he tries to fill the inner emptiness by collecting other people's objects, an aspect which is cleverly parodied by the placing of one of Ash's poems, 'The Great Collector', in the chapter centred on Cropper (Ch. VI, 92). Driven by an inflated sense of his own importance, Cropper

86 I owe many of these observations on the figure of Mortimer Cropper to the essay by Ivana Djordjevic (Djordjevic 82). For the symbolism of the 'Number of the Beast', see Drabble (1985: 74).

even writes his own autobiography, *The Early Life* (99), in which he examines the history of his family and his grandmother Priscilla Penn Cropper, the daughter of convinced abolitionists and an energetic apologist for female emancipation.[87] An important detail revealed in the description of Cropper's family tree is that Priscilla entered into a correspondence with Randolph H. Ash on paranormal phenomena and Spiritualism. Byatt uses Cropper's autobiographical writings to offer a sketch of cultural history in the United States, thereby completing the symmetry of the novel's setting, structured and regulated as always by the play of mirrors between different worlds and epochs. The history Byatt gives of the utopian socialist experiments conducted by Robert Owen and Charles Fourier in the southern United States, which led to the setting up of various communities at New Harmony, is a clear example of how she extends her narration to include roots in the New World, allowing even Mortimer Cropper some ancestors of whom he can be proud (Ch. VI, 101–102).

The characterisation of the wealthy American academic culminates in the following description of his megalomania:

> He was an important man. He wielded power: power of appointment, power of disappointment, power of the cheque book, power of Thoth and the Mercurial access to the Arcana of the Stant Collection. He tended his body, the outward man, with a fastidiousness that he would have bestowed on the inner man too, if he had known who he was [...]. (99)

The picture would not be complete, however, without a description of his luxurious Mercedes:

> His car was a long black Mercedes, of the kind more normally seen driving dignitaries in countries behind the Iron Curtain, a swift funereal car. He knew that in England it was overstated, unlike his tweed jacket. He did not care. It was beautiful and powerful, and he had a flamboyant side to his nature. (98)

George Bailey's sensibility balks at the thrusting materialism of Cropper, who intends to use the lure of his dollars to secure the precious letters he suspects are in the Englishman's hands:

> English things should stay in England in my view. (321)

is his aristocratic defence. Cropper's response is typically arrogant and dismissive:

87 This is also the first element to introduce the theme of the female condition, subsequently explored in greater depth through the vicissitudes of Christabel La Motte, Blanche Glover and Ellen Ash.

> Understandable. An admirable sentiment. But in these days of microfilm and photocopying – how relevant is sentiment? (321)

Cropper is a living embodiment of the view that communication is the most vital tool in today's world: always abreast of the new technologies, his manipulation of the media and people of influence – including the United States Ambassador – is accomplished. His multimedia conference on the 'Art of a Biographer' is an attempt to outmanoeuvre his British colleagues, also engaged in the search for the truth about Ash and La Motte (Ch. XX).

British academia, on the other hand, is depicted as a grouping of slow and sometimes ineffectual scholars of the calibre of James Blackadder, who spends his life writing and then deleting notes to his critical edition of the works of Ash:

> He used a pen; he had never learned newer methods. (299)

He is an archetypal inheritor of the British tradition forged by F.R. Leavis and in consequence has stifled his own, more genuine creativity in an excess of self-punishing rigour:

> The young Blackadder wrote poems, imagined Dr. Leavis's comments on them, and burned them. (27)[88]

Nonetheless, forced into action by the American invasion, even Professor Blackadder emerges from the dark corridors of the British Library, mobilising powerful institutions, ministries and the National Heritage Trust in the fight to prevent the precious papers from being taken abroad. He even summons up the courage for a television appearance to defend the cause of Randolph Henry Ash and the preservation of his unpublished letters, alongside his new-found ally Leonora Stern. The television episode is a hilarious parody of the fate of English literature teaching, overwhelmed by the latest media-driven trends and a wave of cultural transformations. The television journalist who occasionally finds five minutes of screen time for culture on her magazine programme 'Events in Depth' (399) is a beautiful Indian woman with a smattering of contemporary American and postcolonial English literary knowledge. She has never heard of Ash or his work. With the assistance of Leonora – made up to kill for the cameras and 'red in tooth and claw' in Tennyson's famous phrase (403) – the grey and boring Blackadder, polished up as best can be by the make-up department, manages to produce a concise but passionate overview of the Victorian writer's love poetry.

88 A.S. Byatt has often been ambivalent in her attitude towards Leavis and his teachings.

An important part is also played in the assessment of the Ash-La Motte correspondence by Beatrice Nest, Blackadder's English colleague who, as a woman, is relegated to a subject judged to be of secondary importance by the academic old guard: the diary of Ellen Ash. As we have seen, Beatrice Nest is a kind of projection of the long-dead Mrs. Ash, like her a prisoner in a confined space, the 'Ash Factory' headed by Blackadder. The metaphor of the spider, which for Christabel was a symbol of creativity, takes on a different meaning for Beatrice, who appears to Blackadder as

> one of those puffed white spiders, bleached by the dark, feeling along the threads of her trap from her central lair. (112)

Beatrice is thus an emblem of repressed creativity, reading with subtle and penetrating perspicacity the diary of Ellen Ash, a woman herself repressed by the dominant personality and creativity of her husband. It is Beatrice who intuits, for instance, that the diary of Ash's wife was anything but confessional, that perhaps she wrote to disorientate, not to reveal, and that Ash's love poems suggest a female presence far more real than that of a remote muse or an abstract idealisation of woman (113), as erroneously hypothesised by Mortimer Cropper (110).

The present-day setting is completed – and the plot complicated further – by a series of minor characters, such as the smug deconstructionist critic Fergus Wolff, who has his eyes on the icy Maud;[89] Roland's young girlfriend, Val, who finds greater satisfaction and a new life in the arms of a wealthy, but honest solicitor by the name of Euan MacIntyre, who also takes charge of the complex legal issues surrounding the copyright and ownership of the precious letters; the trio of down-at-heel gentry, Sir George and Lady Joan Bailey and Lord Hildebrand Ash, surviving descendents of the Victorian poets. The actions of all these characters ground the main events firmly in a social context that bears all the signs of the era of Thatcherite conservatism and its accompanying yuppie fashions.

89 Wolff is clearly a caricature of certain fashionable tendencies in literary criticism: 'He was older than Roland, a child of the Sixties who had temporarily dropped out, opted for freedom and Parisian revolutions, sitting at the feet of Barthes and Foucault, before coming back to dazzle Prince Albert College' (32). We also learn that, although a researcher in the English department, Wolff is working on a deconstructionist analysis of the novels of Balzac, a fact which once raised several doubts in Roland's mind: Byatt satirises the national fears over French cultural contamination with obvious relish.

5.6 The Timeless Dimension: Fairy Tale and Myth

In addition to the two period settings which we have so far discussed, *Possession* also has a further narrative ambit, of fairy tale and myth, which by tradition cannot be located in any precise era. Indeed. this particular narrative ambit has a connective function, defining the relations between persons and events in the two distinct temporal dimensions. This wealth of material from fairy tales and mythology is frequently inlaid in the parallel plots. As already detailed above, it includes poems inspired by classical and Norse myths and a series of fairy tales and poems based on Breton legends ('The Fairie Melusine', 'The City of Is', 'Gode's Story') and on traditional fairy tales ('The Glass Coffin' and 'The Threshold'). With the exception of the wonder-tale 'Gode's Story', the author of all these pieces is Christabel La Motte, who collected her fairy tales in the volumes entitled *Tales Told in November* and *Tales for Innocents* (36), with illustrations by Blanche Glover (52). Christabel, of mixed English and Breton parentage, is the main character on whom the material from fairy tale and myth is polarised, partly because of her particular relationship with her father, Isidore La Motte, who had been influenced by the German movement to recover folk tales (see p. 36) and had become famous in his own right as a collector and scholar of fairy tales. Thanks to this explicit reference to the German origins of Christabel's father's researches, we have a key to interpret some of the tales which feature in *Possession*, since several are inspired by those of the brothers Grimm and Ludwig Tieck (see p. 52). One such is 'The Glass Coffin', the first of the tales in the novel (Ch. IV) that Roland reads at Maud's suggestion; another is 'The Threshold', which takes up the whole of the ninth chapter and is signed by Christabel La Motte. The two tales have common themes in a choice that must be made and a journey undertaken towards a goal or an object – a quest – and are connected with Freud's famous essay on Shakespeare's *King Lear* and *The Merchant of Venice*, 'The Theme of the Three Caskets' (1913), which Byatt drew on directly for her work (cf. Sanchez 1995: 40).

The title of the first of the tales, 'The Glass Coffin' is taken from one of the Grimms' fairy tales, *Der gläserne Sarg*. The protagonist is a little tailor that, thanks to the gift of a glass key, manages to free a lady who, together with all the other inhabitants of the castle where she lives, has had a spell cast on her by a magician; shrunken and placed in glass caskets, they are sunk in a deep sleep. Her brother has also been changed into a hound, which must then fight with a bull. Byatt takes the same plot, but introducing a number of variations: the key has to be chosen from various objects and there are more animals (a large grey dog called Otto, a black-and-white goat, a calico cat and a dun cow), treated with special kindness by the little tailor. Unlike the Grimm brothers' version, in *Possession* the little tailor, whose craft skills are constantly praised, continues to ply his former trade after freeing the lady and killing the evil magician with a shard of glass from the coffin. Moreover, he does not claim the right to live with her ever after simply because he freed her from the coffin, which here takes the shape of 'a green ice egg' (63), in what is patently a prefiguration of Christabel and Maud's egg enigma. He even accepts the presence of the lady's brother, now returned to his own shape and form.

The remote and timeless dimension of the fairy tale pre-echoes several of the elements in the story of Roland and Maud. Like the little tailor, Roland is kind to animals, in his case the numerous cats at his Putney home, which he looks after despite all the nuisance they create for him (Ch. II and Ch. XXVI). Their purring and the myriad colours of their eyes accompany the welling up of the poetic vocation in Roland, who will at last gain admittance to the garden that Mrs. Irving had forbidden him to enter (473–474). Roland, too, is a craftsman, a wordsmith who can assay and judge the quality of the letters of Ash and La Motte, rather in the way that the little tailor recognises the fine workmanship that made the preciously carved glass key. As the tailor frees the princess from a spell that isolates her in a long sleep, Roland brings Maud back to the life outside her cocoon.

The second fairy tale, 'The Threshold', is entirely dedicated to the theme of the choice and is more descriptive in content, with little action, although there is once again a journey, undertaken by the young hero in search of a 'herb of rest' (54) that can relieve his father's sufferings. After receiving various suggestions as to the route he should follow from a cantankerous old woman, the young Childe travels across wild heaths and dangerous pathways until he meets three splendid ladies, each with a precious casket (gold, silver and lead) containing a promise. The type of each casket reflects the appearance of its owner, but the young man chooses the leaden one because it is the only one to promise the 'herb of rest'. After making his choice, he is admitted beyond 'the threshold', along a path that winds downward through flowery meadows, seeming to presage a happy adventure – perhaps also the one in which Roland will be involved.

Both tales have in common an interruption in the traditional narrative, made by Byatt in order to underline the freedom of choice of the protagonists. In particular in 'The Glass Coffin' the maiden is free to choose her own companion, notwithstanding she has been awakened by the little tailor who, in a conventional fairy tale, would thereby be entitled to marry her. The novelist also interrupts the narrative to address the external reader, thereby introducing an element of modernity in the traditional pattern of the fairy tale:

> And you, my sagacious readers, will have perceived and understood that Otto was the very same hound into which the young brother of the lady of the coffin had been transformed. (67)

Similarly, in 'The Threshold', the narrative voice introduces a digression emphasising the wisdom contained in fairy tales, whereby the choice always falls on the least glittering casket/lady that contains 'the true choice'. At the same time the possibility of varying the conventional scheme is mooted:

> And one day we will write it otherwise, that he would not come, that he stayed, or chose the sparkling ones, or went out again onto the moors to live free of fate, if such can be. But you must know now, that it turned out as it must turn out, must you not? *Such is the power of necessity in tales.* (155, *emphasis* added)

In this way the fairy tale, normally characterised by a series of formal elements which have been accurately singled out by Victoria Sanchez (41), following the schema drawn up by Max Lüthi (1970), undergoes a process of self-analysis. It is one we find again in the third fairy tale inspired by Breton myths, 'Gode's Story', which thereby takes on a kind of meta-language characteristic of the novel as a whole. Sanchez groups the typical elements of fairy tales into three principal characteristics: linear, spatial and temporal narration, whereby there is no separation between the spiritual or supernatural and the ordinary world; absence of depth of characterisation, with no revealing of the thoughts or state of mind of the characters (who are often also isolated from their family context), lastly, abstraction of the story, which thus can also perform a useful psychological function for the reader. Sanchez makes a number of interesting observations concerning the use of fairy tale and narration in *Possession*, noting that the above characteristics are also applied in part to the present-day characters in the novel, enabling the Romance to re-emerge in the contemporary context, personified in the experiences of Roland and Maud.[90]

Lastly, both tales feature metaphors and adjectives which are found elsewhere in the novel, whenever analogies are intended between characters and events. These elements form a connective web in Byatt's writing, one which extends to other fiction in which she has used similar symbolism. Elements such as glass, water, ice, snow and mirrors constantly recur in her metaphors, forming a kind of

90 For an exhaustive analysis of the two fairy tales, the reader may refer once again to the essay by Sanchez, in which she examines in detail 'The Glass Coffin' and 'The Threshold', relating all the elements in their make-up to the classification of folk material made by Stith Thompson in *Motif-Index of Folk Literature*, rev. edn., 6 vols (Indiana: Indiana UP, 1955–1959). See also Ashworth (1994: 93–94) and Todd (1997: 39–47).

coded language in which a number of symbolic values are encrypted. Although they derive from a common folk heritage, these elements are transformed by Byatt into a personal figurative language by grafting them onto different literary genres. As the novelist herself has explained:

> One of the surprising things about glass, to northerners, must have been its resemblance to ice, and its difference from ice. Glass is made from sand, heated and melted; ice is a form of water, which shifts from solid to liquid with the seasons. The fairy stories which I now see provided much of my secret imagery as a child are northern tales about ice, glass and mirrors.[91]

In the essay Byatt cites several tales which are particularly dear to her and which contain this particular symbolism: in *The Snow Queen* by Hans Christian Andersen, for instance, the episode of the shattered mirror seems to prefigure another episode, added by the novelist to the tale of 'The Glass Coffin' in her own adapted version, in which the magician is killed by a shard of glass. *Snow White*, on the other hand, seems to be the origin of the powerful image of the snow falling and freezing human life, consigning it to a kind of permanent sleep between life and death. It is worth noting that this symbolism reappears in the twentieth-century plot of *Possession*, where a snowfall blankets the landscape around Seal Court, once the last refuge of Christabel La Motte and now the home of her descendants, George and Joan Bailey. Chapter VIII of the novel features a detailed description of Maud making her way around the snow-bound Seal Court grounds, as if to underline the separation of Maud, and later also of Roland, from a more concrete and earthly dimension of existence. Both of them are about to cross a threshold and be admitted to the sole, timeless dimension of the fairy tale and the realm of Melusina.

A.S. Byatt's essay also focuses on the juxtaposition of particular nouns and adjectives, such as 'white and red, ice and fire, snow and blood, life and death', taken from the set of Snow White stories, in the Grimm and Andersen versions, as well as from *The Sleeping Beauty* and *The Glass Coffin*. These references have since been interwoven with elements from English literature, above all the now familiar *Lady of Shalott*, emblematic of a state of seclusion from life, interrupted by the passing of a knight with shining, dazzling helmet, who causes the Lady to fall from her tower, together with her mirror which shatters. The figure of Queen Elizabeth I, which appears constantly in *The Virgin in the Garden*, is associated

91 A.S. Byatt, 'Ice, Snow, Glass'. *Mirror, Mirror on the Wall*. Ed. Kate Bernheimer (New York: Anchor, 1998) 60–79 (here 60). My thanks are due to A.S. Byatt for providing me with a copy of her typescript before publication.

with the colours of Snow White, red and white, which for Byatt are emblems of the queen's ability to master her passions and hold onto power.[92] Water, snow and ice also recur in Coleridge (*Kubla Khan* and *The Rime of the Ancient Mariner*), while Queen Hermione in *The Winter's Tale* has the appearance of a statue which comes back to life after a long period in which all believe her to be dead. Clearly snow and ice have crystallised in the novelist's imagination as elements linked to the cyclical passing of the seasons, capable of enclosing and preserving life beneath their transparent, freezing surface.

Another water creature inspires the long poem by Christabel La Motte which so fascinates Maud Bailey and other women's studies specialists. Passages from 'The Fairie Melusine' take up part of Ch. VII and all of Ch. XVI, where it is cited in a page of Ellen Ash's diary being read by Roland. Other comments on the fairy Melusina appear in the Ash-La Motte correspondence, allowing the novel's modern scholars to date the poem, which however never appears in full. The story of Melusina is woven into *Possession* in various ways, as are the various explanations which have been put forward for the myth. Randolph Ash, for instance, cites in a letter the version of the myth attributed to Paracelsus (171), who apparently considered the creature to be a lesser spirit fated to wander the earth for ever more. It is Fergus Wolff, however, who offers the first information about the fairy:

> Do you know about Melusina? She was a fairy who married a mortal to gain a soul, and made a pact that he would never spy on her on Saturdays, and for years he never did, and they had six sons, all with strange defects [...]. (33)

Melusina is thus a fairy who enters the world of mortals, where she meets and enters into a pact with a hero, only to be betrayed by him. One of the best-known versions of this story is the one written in 1392 by Jean d'Arras for Jean Berry and his sister Maria, Duchess of Bar, who belonged to the noble family of the Counts of Lusignan. After the punishment inflicted on her by her mother Pressina, a part of Melusina's body is transformed once a week into a serpent, and she must not be seen by anyone during her metamorphosis. Her husband Raymond, whom she meets one day by a magic well of thirst, is the first to break this prohibition,

92 'A poem written about her: *Under a tree I saw a Virgin sit/The red and white rose quartered in her face...* was ostensibly about her combination of York and Lancaster in the Tudor Rose, but I read it as a combination of Snow White and Rose Red in one self-sufficient person' (Byatt, 'Ice, Snow, Glass', 66). Once again these reflections reveal Byatt's characteristic narrative procedure, underpinned by a tangle of continuously intersecting metaphors.

spying on her through a keyhole. He then accuses Melusina of being a monster and in her anger the fairy disappears, transformed into a winged creature or dragon.[93]

In Breton mythology Melusina is always associated with the mysteries of water, fountains and wells, and her appearance reflects the natural woodland settings of such places, made more disquieting by the moonlight. Christabel's poem gives a similar picture of the fairy, surprised at the well of thirst as she tresses her blonde hair, singing a song that charms Raymond:

> As milky roses at the end of day
> In some deserted bower seem still alight
> With their own luminous pallor, so she cast
> A softened brightness and a pearly light
> On that wild place, in which she sate and sang.
> She wore a shift of whitest silk, that stirred
> With her song's breathing, and a girdle green
> As emerald or wettest meadow-grass. (296)

As Harf-Lancner points out, the legend of Melusina arises from the collision of two cultures, one a pagan, oral tradition that typically prefers the sensual and supernatural identity of the lady of the forest, the other a cultured, Christian view which modifies and rationalises that picture,[94] while A.S. Byatt's own version presents still another variation. In *Possession*, Melusina is both mother and artist, a characterisation which once again breaks up the conventional scheme of the tale. Byatt herself has stated that she took the idea of reworking the Melusina legend from a lecture by the French scholar Luce Irigaray on 'Melusina and the Swan Knight' and from her essay on the dangerousness of female divinities entitled 'Femmes Divines', with the intention of bringing them into Christabel's poem as 'a parody of both Irigaray and the feminist epic that was never written in the nineteenth century'.[95]

---

93 See Laurence Harf-Lancner (1989: 186–208).

94 To be more precise, Melusina belongs to the fairy figures which in part derived from the ancient Parcae and thus have the power to predict the destiny of men, and which later, from the twelfth century, were associated with the Celtic mother divinities, connected with cults of fertility and abundance, that populated the Breton forests. The learned, Christian culture of the Middle Ages assimilated these pagan divinities in 'an orthodox system of thought' that was expressed in their dual nature, half-human and half-demon. See Harf-Lancner 1–41.

95 Qtd. in Tredell, 61. Cf. Irigaray (1993: 55–72).

The ambivalent nature of Melusina, reincarnated in Christabel, is also conveyed through the dual nationality of the poet, who as we have seen is of French origin on her father's side. This aspect of her background is amplified by the journey she makes to Brittany, seeking a refuge for the last stages of her pregnancy. Once there, her own story is interwoven with the multiple suggestions of the Breton stories handed down from generation to generation in the family ambit of her uncle Raoul La Motte and her cousin Sabine de Kercoz. Christabel's stay in Brittany is also connected with another poem extensively quoted from in the novel: 'The City of Is' (Ch. XIX, 330–331 and Ch. VIII, 134–135). It is based on the ancient legend of the city of Is, once governed by the fairy queen Dahud, daughter of King Gradlon. For having refused to abandon the druidical religion and submit to Christianity, Dahud is punished by being turned into a mermaid, while her realm is flooded by the sea.[96] Chapter XIX of the novel includes a passage from Christabel's poem describing the terrifying moments experienced by Dahud and her lover just before they are overwhelmed by the ocean. The description is closely followed by the Channel crossing made by Roland and Maud aboard the ferry Prince of Brittany, another allusion to the idea that the two young scholars have themselves crossed the legendary threshold. In choosing the upper berth in their cabin, Maud recalls Lilith, another prefiguration of the legend of Melusina, who refused to submit to Adam and so was driven out by him (332).

A second extract from the City of Is poem is given in the eighth chapter, together with the critical commentary of Leonora Stern, in the edition published by the Sapphic Press in Boston. This part of Christabel's work is interesting because it highlights the same symbolism that occurs in the novel and its fairy tales. The women of Is have transparent 'spun-glass skin' (134), so the blood can be seen coursing in their veins 'like spider-thread […] woven with red' (134). Their world is reflected by the transparent surface of forms, 'As though the world […]/Were stored inside a glassy box' (135). The same chapter also includes another, shorter poem by Christabel which evokes an image of snow and a pale feathered creature (128). Clearly this meticulous adjectival imagery has the function of transmitting the symbolism which underlies the narration in all its dimensions. Once again the layer of snow stands for a separation from

96 Dahud was probably a druid, turned into a witch by Christian writers. Cf. Peter Berresford Ellis, *Il segreto dei Druidi* (Casale Monferrato: Edizioni Piemme, 1997) 129. Trans. of *The Druids* (London: Constable & Co, 1994).

reality, a kind of death in life; red stands for passion and white for its opposite. Glass is the filter through which the artist/spider observes the world outside.

The Breton trip is also enriched by the accounts of Sabine Kercoz in her diary, detailing the presence of Christabel there and the outcome of her pregnancy. Sabine herself is later to write a series of novels inspired by Breton mythology, with one in particular centred on the figure of the fairy queen Dahud (see the letter from Le Minier, 380). By introducing the character of Sabine, Byatt gives a voice to numerous ideas on fairy tales and the role of the narrator, again expanding the meta-literary content of *Possession*. In her diary, Sabine notes down all the conversations between herself, Isidore and Christabel, a highly cultivated family group in the heart of Brittany.

In their discussions, a special place is given to the folk tales which are told every year in the period following All Hallows, from 1st November to Christmas. This is the time when in Brittany the realms of the living and the dead merge together, during the two so-called 'black months' (352). Sabine is particularly aware that there is a substantial difference between oral and written narration, observing in her diary that the ancient druids believed the spoken word performed a vital function, identified with breathing, and the written word a mortiferous one (355). These reflections are exemplified in the story of Gode, housekeeper to Raoul and Sabine, who has the reputation of being a witch and represents the most direct link with Breton oral tradition. By placing this simple and intuitive woman, an emblem of folk wisdom, alongside Sabine's father and Christabel's cousin, Raoul La Motte, Byatt joins the folk voice with the more cultured, but controlled voice of written tradition.

Gode's Story adds another variant to the types of narration used in *Possession*. It is more a wonder-tale than a fairy tale and, mysterious as it is, escapes any precise interpretation, a fact of which Sabine is well aware. She understands that the story and Gode's oral narrative style form an indissoluble whole:

> And Gode's telling is a play with all these things, with the firelight and the gesturing shadows and the streamers of light and dark – she brings all their movements together as I imagine the leader of an orchestra may. (356)

In the story, a sailor wishes to give a silken ribbon to a miller's daughter, who, however, insists on paying for it. Offended, the young man sails away across the ocean, forcing the maiden to suffer long waits and sleepless nights. During one such night the miller hears a strange noise in the hayloft and afterwards finds traces of blood there. He wakes up her daughter, but although her face has turned pale she can offer no explanation as to what happened. In the end the sailor marries Jeanne, the blacksmith's daughter, and on their wedding night the miller's daughter follows the spectre of a dancing creature that leads her to her death on the cliffs. Thereafter the sailor is wracked by guilt and in turn suffers a vision of a dancing creature that leads him to the Baie des Trépassés, a meeting place for the living and the dead (355). After spending much time tormented by the obsessive recollection of the vision of the dancing creature, the sailor also dies, while Jeanne marries another man.

The tale is characterised by a cyclical narration which lingers insistently on descriptions of episodes that recur several times. Despite its covering veil of mystery, the miller's daughter may perhaps be identified with Christabel and the sailor with Ash, who likewise had to suffer a long wait before hearing news of Christabel and her presumed pregnancy (the spot of blood). The Baie des Trépassés is thus a place beyond the confines of space and time where the living meet with persons now dead.[97]

The timeless dimension *par excellence*, however, is contained in the concluding postscript to the novel, in which the omniscient narrator describes a hypothetical encounter between a poet and a girl to whom he entrusts a message:

> Tell your aunt [...] that you met a poet, who was looking for the Belle Dame Sans Merci, and who met you instead, and who sends her his compliments, and will not disturb her, and is on his way to fresh woods and pastures new. (510)

The girl's name is Maia and she is of course the daughter of Ash and La Motte, at last allowed to enter the scene and the mythical time of the novel. Her name is mythical, too, since Maia in Roman mythology was the goddess of Nature, after whom the month of May is named. Indeed, poet and girl meet 'on a hot May day' (508), in a beautiful flowery meadow which underlines the awakening of life and the cycle of the seasons. In exchange for a lock of her hair, the poet weaves a garland of flowers with which he crowns the girl's head, comparing her to Proserpine while asking 'Do you know

> "that fair field
> Of Enna, where Proserpine gathering flowers,
> Herself a fairer flower, by gloomy Dis
> Was gathered, which cost Ceres all that pain
> To seek her through the world"?' (510)

The lines are from Milton (*Paradise Lost* IV, 268–271) and they frame this fleeting moment between the poet and the child, through the versified evocation of the legend whereby the rape of Proserpine took place in Sicily. The

97 This is the interpretation given by Richard Todd (Todd 1997: 47).

figure of Proserpine, forced by Pluto to spend half of the year underground in Hades, is naturally connected to the germination of seeds that heralds each new life cycle. In the light of these reflections, it becomes obvious why one of the poems of Randolph Henry Ash, which heads the first chapter and the chapter in which Roland Michell becomes aware of his own poetic gift, should be called *The Garden of Proserpina* (1 and 463–465).[98] Poetry and life are continuously intertwined, because they both spring from a single source. This also explains why the primordial imagery of the genesis of the universe found in Ash's epic poem *Ragnarök*[99] should return with particular force in this final poem.

5.7 Unlocking the Text: Romance and *pastiche*

It is possible to read *Possession* without being fully aware of the range of intertextual references that characterize its cultural scope. The novel undoubtedly offers the straightforward pleasure of reading for entertainment, which in part explains its huge success with a general readership, from the moment of its publication. Indeed, some readers skip the poems which appear in each chapter, or even neglect the substantial inserts of fairy tales and letters, although they play such an important part in the structure of the work. It should be added that not only the less cultivated readers have preferred this selective approach: even the editor at Random House in charge of preparing the U.S. edition exerted considerable pressure on A.S. Byatt to cut much of the material of that kind from her novel. The whole controversy over the American edition is described in detail in a correspondence with Helge Nowak, who has compared the British and U.S. editions.[100] In this regard, it will be worth citing briefly some of the observations made by the novelist in a letter quoted by H. Nowak, since they reveal facts which many European readers are unaware of, as well as providing a reminder that there are two quite different editions of *Possession* in circulation in the various continents:

---

98 It is no coincidence, either, that Ash's poem is itself an allusion to Victorian literature: 'The Garden of Proserpine' is the title of a poem by Algernon Charles Swinburne (1837–1909). Both Ash and Swinburne use the mythical representation of the garden as a tryst-place, and the idea of Proserpine as a point of intersection between life and death.

99 See the previous section for a commentary on Ash's epic.

100 A.S. Byatt, letter to Helge Nowak (4 October 1996), qtd. in Nowak (1997) <http://webdoc.sub.gwdg.de/edoc/ia/eese/rahmen22.html> [accessed 21 July 2015]

> When the [American (HN)] editor first proposed to buy *Possession* she told me that the book would have to be very heavily cut for the American market – "You have spoiled a fine intrigue with extraneous matter" "most of the correspondence, journals etc will have to go" "there must be few poems and those there are short". I said this was unacceptable […] She had decided that Roland was not "sexy" or sympathetic enough to appeal to "our American audience" and that I was to amend the descriptions of him. The whole project made me quite ill […] She proposed sex between Maud and Roland where I had avoided it, and kept writing in the margin "You have missed a great opportunity for a climax!!! […] I am sure the quotes are more or less exact – they are burned on my memory". (Nowak ibid.: n. pag.)

As things turned out, the American editor fell into line with the fate of the book, which in the meantime had achieved enormous public success in Britain and won the Booker Prize. Nonetheless a compromise was reached concerning the characterisation of Roland who, in the American edition, conveys a 'much more visual' and 'heightened' impression to the reader (Nowak ibid.).[101]

This aspect of *Possession*'s publishing history is interesting because it points up its stylistic specificity and the differing reactions which this can provoke among its readers. Another reason why the U.S. editor did not succeed in introducing further revisions into the text was that so many readers proved to enjoy the initiation into Victorian studies that the work enjoined, so much so that pilgrimages have been made by literary tourists to the places frequented by Christabel and Randolph on the Yorkshire coast. Not a few readers have visited libraries, asking for more books by or on Byatt's imaginary authors. In short, the history of the novel itself and its reception in various countries since its first appearance has become a kind of 'editorial fairy-story' (Byatt qtd. in Nowak ibid.).

Certainly the novel has an undeniable cultural weight due to the interweaving of genres, erudition and imaginative narrative, and goes beyond the dimension of pure entertainment, which in turn is guaranteed by the clever, detective story plot constructed on the basis of its own finale. Using all the critical tools at her disposal in the service of literary invention, Byatt conceals her own ventriloquism behind Ash's (Hulbert 1993; Broich 1996: 623), which, allied to the technique of *pastiche* in a postmodern context already approaching *cliché*, allows the

101 Despite this compromise, a variety of changes concerning the bibliographic and linguistic code in the British and American editions remain. Nowak also points out that the American edition has corrected chronological errors in the fictional time-scheme which were in the original British hardcover edition, though later paperback reprints in Britain have reproduced those changes (Nowak ibid.: n. pag.).

novel's many voices to give shape to a multiplicity of genres. Indeed, the author's knowledge of the literary past seems to generate an almost incantatory effect:

> [...] as a girl I read a great deal of Wordsworth's poetry, Coleridge, Browning, Tennyson. I learn things by heart very easily, and my mind is possessed by very long quotations, which sing about when I'm sitting in taxis. (qtd. in Wachtel 1994: 81)

We have already seen that several genres co-exist within *Possession*: campus novel, epistolary and Gothic novel, detective story, Romance. The attention paid by the author to the proliferation of texts and their reception, together with the description of their multimedial circulation through parodies of lectures and television programmes, is a sign of a typically postmodern orientation in line with contemporary trends in the novel at the turn of the millennium. At the same time, the manifold narratives and genre patterns can also be seen as expressions of cultural memory, itself 'generated and transmitted by "memory genres"' (Erll and Nünning 2006: 18) through 'continual repetition and actualization' (ibid.: 17).

In her reading of the novel, Steveker reiterates this point further, stating that 'genres encode and communicate cultural knowledge'. Drawing on a number of theoretical sources, she shows how '[a]uthors use generic repertoires in order to solve the aesthetical problem of matching matter to form, whilst readers rely on them for orientation during the reading process' (Steveker: 127). In turn, Sarah Heinz qualifies the use of Romance in the novel as a '*Rahmen-Genre*' (lit. a frame-genre), suitable to encode the multiplicity of voices and forms characterizing *Possession* (Heinz 2007: 318).

The term Romance appears not only on the cover of the novel as its subtitle, but also in the text, where a quotation from the preface to *The House of the Seven Gables* by Nathaniel Hawthorne serves as an introduction:

> When a writer calls his work a Romance, it need hardly be observed that he wishes to claim a certain latitude, both as to its fashion and material, which he would not have felt himself entitled to assume, had he professed to be writing a Novel. The latter form of composition is presumed to aim at a very minute fidelity, not merely to the possible, but to the probable and ordinary course of man's experience. The former – while as a work of art, it must rigidly subject itself to laws, and while it sins unpardonably so far as it may swerve aside from the truth of the human heart – has fairly a right to present that truth under circumstances, to a great extent, of the writer's own choosing or creation... The point of view in which this tale comes under the Romantic definition, lies in *the attempt to connect a bygone time with the very present* that is flitting away from us.[102]

102 Nathaniel Hawthorne, preface to *The House of the Seven Gables*, qtd. by Byatt in the introduction to *Possession*. My *emphasis*.

Like Hawthorne, Byatt uses the mythical time of the novel to weave together two different epochs that form the backdrop to the novel itself and furthermore to gain access to a veiled, but still present truth that evades the immediate representation of reality, of the 'probable and ordinary course of man's experience' as Hawthorne puts it. Both writers appeal to the poetic freedom which allows them to identify 'the truth of the human heart', destined to be embodied cyclically in the affairs of men and women, like eternal prototypes. Since the Romance typically involves the suspension of the circumstances of ordinary life, thanks to the intervention of fantastic or magical elements which demonstrate a moral principle, A.S. Byatt uses the form to highlight patterns of human experience. Indeed, both Northrop Frye, like Gillian Beer already underlined the function of the archetypes contained in the Romance, which make it, in this sense, analogous to the fairy-tale and the myth:

> The romancer does not attempt to create 'real people' so much as stylised figures which expand into psychological archetypes. It is in the romance that we find Jung's libido, anima and shadow reflected in the hero, heroine and villain respectively. That is why the romance so often radiates a glow of subjective intensity that the novel lacks, and why a suggestion of allegory is constantly creeping in around its fringes.[103]

In the preceding pages, we noted how the fairy tales included in *Possession* contain elements which function as a link between the two temporal dimensions of the novel, and how the present-day time is subtly made to drift towards the fairy-tale, allowing Roland and Maud to enter that dimension fully. It is only when their journey/discovery is fulfilled that we begin to perceive their individuality, since at that point the novel/romance begins to cast on them that 'glow of subjective intensity' which Frye speaks of. The spotlight moves from the nineteenth century to the archetypal dimension of the fairy-tale, with its transfiguration of the fairy Melusina into contemporary time, where the characters of Roland and Maud acquire a fresh identity thanks to their unusual journey of initiation.

Through this grafting of styles A.S. Byatt effectively subjects her own particular brand of realism to a sophisticated warping operation that increases its complexity. The quest and the love intrigue that characterise the romance become polarised around Roland and Maud, at which point the atemporal dimension is superimposed on the present. It has been observed that the nineteenth century plot involving Christabel and Randolph is not itself contaminated with the romance form, its representation remaining within the schema of the realistic novel, except for the variant constituted by its fragmentation and the insertion

103 Frye (1965: 304). See also Beer (1970: 19).

into various points of the overall structure in the shape of letters and diary extracts. When the novel reaches its conclusion and the final order of the couples is established, along with a new social pattern, the romance is also left off, to be replaced by conventional realism. Following the typical lines of the finale to a comic drama, in Ch. XXVII we find all the academic characters, except for the villain of the piece, Mortimer Cropper, brought together in one scene set in Beatrice Nest's flat, where the whole story of Randolph and Christabel's clandestine affair and the rediscovery of their papers is summarised and commented on in a climate of general merriment and reconciliation.[104]

5.8 Self-Reflexivity in *Possession*

Possession is a story about reading, but it is also presented as a kind of exposition of texts which question each other. The novel is littered with a myriad of reflections on the function of writing and the genres into which it can be categorised. Often it is the novel's own characters who express these reflections, which taken together allow a glimpse of a fourth, meta-literary dimension in the book.

In a letter to Christabel La Motte, Randolph Henry Ash himself observed with patent irony and postmodern self-awareness: 'We are rational nineteenth-century beings, we might leave the *coup de foudre* to the weavers of Romances' (193). Reading their correspondence in the following century, Roland notes as follows:

> Letters [...] are a form of narrative that envisages no outcome, no closure. His time was a time of the dominance of narrative theories. Letters tell no story, because they do not know, from line to line, where they are going. (130–131)

Later, Roland shows the typical awareness of a scholar brought up on deconstructionist and post-structuralist theories when he notes that letters prevent the reader from becoming a sort of co-author of the letters themselves; in reality, every letter is addressed to a single, privileged reader, not a public readership. Behind his observation we can detect the novelist's own voice, polemical with those academics who, like Mortimer Cropper, consider it possible to arrive at a

104 I am indebted for these observations to Alexa Alfer who, in an unpublished essay, illustrates these aspects of the novel in the light of Paul Ricoeur's studies on metaphor, pointing out that the two Victorian poets' engagement with myth remains confined to their creative work only: Alexa Alfer, 'Realism and Romance – A.S. Byatt's *Possession*' (March 1996).

conclusive truth which they may then appropriate. The postscript to the novel makes her views on the subject explicit.

Fairy tales, too, are usually regulated by that 'power of necessity' discussed in Section 5.6 and question their own form by addressing the external reader and interrupting the narration. In all the types of literary genre present in *Possession*, there is thus an attempt to slide forms towards a point of aperture, which however is suddenly contradicted by the surprise finale contained in the postscript and by the novel's happy ending, which orientates the narrative towards a definitive and rapid closure.

In Sabine de Kercoz's diary, which records most of the events that befall Christabel (Ch. XIX), writing itself again takes centre stage. Christabel's cousin also aspires to become an author, noting down all her reflections on her attempts at writing and the advice offered by her poetess relative. She even goes so far as to detail the procedures which precede the ordering of material on the written page, arriving at an awareness of the function of the narrator which seems postmodern in tone: 'I have something to tell which is not to do with Gode's tale, thought it was then that. Start again. Write it like a story, write to *write* it'. (356)

Sabine also includes in her diary a conversation with Christabel in which the poet spoke of her opinion of the Romance genre. It becomes clear at this point that her pregnancy coincided with the genesis of the *Fairie Melusine*:

> She talked of *Melusina* and the nature of epic. She wants to write a Fairy Epic, she says, not grounded in historical truth, but in poetic and imaginative truth – like Spenser's *Fairie Queene*, or Ariosto, where the soul is free of the restraints of history and fact. She says Romance is a proper form for women. She says Romance is a land where women can be free to express their true natures, as in the Ile de Sein or Sid, though not in this world./She said, in Romance, women's two natures can be reconciled. I asked, which two natures, and she said, men saw women as double beings, enchantresses and demons or innocent angels. (373)

The mythological time, allied with the representation of the female as free and independent, is joined to the Romance and becomes in turn an object of self-analysis, in similar fashion to all the other narrative genres.

Self-reflexivity in the writing of *Possession* highlights the tension derived from the constant comparison between forms consolidated by literary tradition and the attempt to unhinge them, between realism and postmodern. Through Roland and Maud's reflections on postmodern deconstruction of the subject, the concept of subjectivity and the relationship between author and work, the writing conducts an interrogation and a dialogue with itself. The proliferation of texts and narrative genres is suddenly halted in the novel, when the fragmentary narration is replaced by unexpected unity and by the Romance that gives it a happy ending.

Here, the studies of Linda Hutcheon have a special relevance insofar as they lay stress on the self-awareness inherent in the irony and parody that are so typical of A.S. Byatt: 'Parody is one of the major forms of modern self-reflexivity; it is a form of inter-art discourse' (Hutcheon 1985: 2).

Hutcheon reiterates the substantial distinction, borrowed from Genette, between parody and pastiche. According to this, in parody the text differentiates from the literary model by transforming it, whereas pastiche is determined by the imitation of a pre-existing text. It remains true, however, that parody can make use of pastiche, and that *Possession* offers highly unusual instances of both forms. As has been seen, Byatt's novel contains a complex web of textual quotations and references. However, whereas pastiche is used in its nineteenth-century dimension and concerns mainly texts invented by the author, interpolated with fictional documentation of the Ash-La Motte affair, thus retaining the literary taste of the epoch imitated, parody is used only in its contemporary dimension. As has been noted above, this part of the novel shows the marks of knowledge as a 'badge of learning' in the terms in which Hutcheon describes the properties of parody (Hutchoen ibid.: 99). While the numerous intertextual references present in the nineteenth-century narrative are harmoniously integrated in the output of Ash and La Motte or in the portrayal of their ambience (with the sole exception of the texts cited in the introduction and the poems interspersed in the narrative as epigraphs), the contemporary story shows quite clearly the seams between citation and invention.

In her novel, A.S. Byatt has in practice saved the narrative from the effects of linguistic fragmentation which might have upset the novel form completely. After keeping the reader occupied for many a page with an almost endless series of stories contained one within the other, the author inserts the postscript which, as has been observed, is the last of many *coups de théâtre*. In so doing, Byatt adopted a twofold decision, demonstrating on the one hand her conviction, already expressed in the story *Sugar*, of the impossibility of arriving at a single and definitive truth, which instead may only ever be partially known; on the other, her determination not to give up the principles of unity and coherence that give meaning to the perception of the real reflected in the novel: the Romance answers that particular requirement.

In summing up, the preceding pages have sought to highlight the structural complexity of the novel while uncovering the polyphony of intertextual voices disseminated along its different temporal planes. I began with a preliminary survey of the ideas underlying the genesis of the novel and went on to uncover the amalgam of heterogeneous materials underpinning its temporal axis, orienting the reader in the ongoing shifts between the different worlds portrayed. I have endeavoured to display the full range of textual and contextual references woven into the narrative, measuring its cultural scope and demonstrating its mnemonic function as a textual locus. In the process, I have paid special attention to the craft with which the author has orchestrated the many voices, language forms and genre patterns in *Possession*, producing its own incantatory effect as if under the spell of a self-generating tangle of narrative clues. Finally, I have sought to illuminate aspects of its publishing history while surveying the critical terms current in the various stages of its reception.[105]

105 As I revise these pages for publication, I become aware that a new study celebrating the author 'before and after *Possession*', edited by Armelle Parey and Isabelle Roblin, has just appeared. I thank Barbara Franchi, whose contribution to the volume I could read in manuscript, for kindly providing this information (Franchi 2018).

Conclusion

This study attempts a comprehensive reading of Byatt's major novels. It maps a way into the intricate complexities of her writing, highlighting the author's main concerns and textual strategies. Byatt's fiction is notoriously challenging for many readers. To write of memory, Renaissance forms of theatrical reinvention in post-war culture, ekphrasis, visuality and the cognitive processes of the mind, gender and science, the creative potential of language and its verbal texture, is to touch upon a formidable network of theoretical questions. Furthermore, the author's characteristic handling of narrative patterns, encompassing different forms of knowledge and imaginative subject matter, adds to the challenge of interpreting her texts.

The all-inclusive, encyclopaedic nature of her writing is ideally suited to a critical approach informed by theories of cultural memory, which I have illustrated in the introductory chapter and applied in my analysis of the novels. Nonetheless, the aim of the present study has not been to superimpose a rigid theoretical structure onto Byatt's fiction, but to illuminate the author's fictional world from within, paying close attention to the narrative patterns and elaborate system of mnemonics underpinning it. Building on the existing analyses of Byatt's novels, I connect previous approaches to produce a more encompassing account of her work. Special attention has been devoted to the craft with which the author intertwines various forms of knowledge, translating complex issues into imaginative fiction.

The preceding chapters have argued that in Byatt's series of novels that began to appear in 1978 and ended in 2002, a subtle process of transmutation from literary culture to visuality has taken place. They highlight a gradual shift from the art of memory as conceived by the classics and re-enacted in Renaissance forms of theatricality, to a more visual culture, encompassing both a museological practice and popular forms of entertainment. Although these thematic concerns have long preoccupied cultural theorists, rarely have they engaged the attention of a creative writer to such a degree and in so many different forms.

Chapter 1 explored the author's densely layered narrative and elaborate system of mnemonics underpinning *The Virgin in the Garden*, which I read as a memory theatre of a literary kind. Drawing on classical and Elizabethan conceptions of the art of memory, I demonstrate how the novelist turns an ancient and long forgotten art into a conceptual framework accommodating different forms of memory within her personal reinvention of the 1950s. The topographical setting of the novel is shown to be strictly linked with the arrangement of its subject matter, thus re-enacting a visual strategy connected with the ancient *ars memoriae*. This was in origin a process of memorization functioning as an inner pictorial technique and I argue that, prompted by her reading of Frances Yates, A.S. Byatt translates this technique into a literary strategy. Weaving together place and the various inscriptions constructed in her narrative, I show how the novelist acts as a mnemonist engaged in mapping the orderly arrangement of memory traces along the path of an archaeological site. These memory traces may contain intertextual allusions to previous texts belonging to the literary canon or relate to images connected with Renaissance iconography. Frequently, they function as 'conceptual images' (*imagines agentes*) aiding the author's process of recollection. Thus, D.H. Lawrence or Elizabeth I may equally fulfill this function, since they haunt the imagination of the characters in the novel.

Chapter 2 illustrates the intellectual concerns underpinning *Still Life*, a novel preoccupied with the question of pure representation and the functions of language as a vehicle for direct description. Here, Byatt's approach to memory centres on its iconic and spatial aspects, and the novel unfolds gradually as a *mise en scène* relying both on memories of artwork and knowledge. I argue that visuality fulfills multiple functions in *Still Life*, both as a means to test the power of visual and verbal language to describe reality and as an overarching cultural practice which becomes historicized through the institutional context in which it is enacted – the museum. Hence, I illustrate how the ekphrastic description of Post-Impressionist paintings is woven into the narrative, and how this is intertwined with countless allusions to Romantic poetry relating not only to the evocation of childhood, but also to questions of sense perception and mental processes. It is here that the art of Van Gogh becomes associated with phenomena relating to visual perception and the poetry of S.T. Coleridge. Although the influence of Romantic poetry on Byatt's narrative has been perceptively highlighted by Judith Plotz (2001), this contribution centres on the Wordsworthian evocation of childhood in *The Virgin in the Garden*. My analysis of *Still Life* illuminates a new facet of Byatt's handling of a Romantic theme by focusing on aspects relating to sensory perception and the visual faculty. I demonstrate how these are embedded in the subliminal world of Coleridge's *The Rime of the Ancient Mariner*, which influences Byatt's iconic and intertextual mnemonics in her writing process. Indeed, my analysis shows that in this novel memory is conceptualized as an overarching category interrelating different modes of thought and ways of apprehending the world.

One of the most fascinating aspects of Byatt's fiction is the way in which the author interrelates her recollections of a specific time and place with intellectual concerns. Such intellectual concerns figure in her writing not just as decorative. They are as much part of the lived, felt substance of her work as are the motives driving her characters. The ideas demand to be heard for their conceptual energy, for what they have to say about human beings in the world. Thus, questions of mimetic representation probing the limits of language, visuality and cognitive science, are juxtaposed with the reconstruction of women's lives in post-war English society and, in particular, with their evolving position in the domestic and public sphere. Entering Byatt's fictional world portraying life in England in the post-war period involves surveying a period of social history as much as the history of ideas and changing mental patterns, all rendered in imaginative ways. Significant examples of this double perspective on narrative, which I have highlighted in my reading of the novels, are excerpts from *Still Life* describing a baby's first response to light at birth, which I discuss in Chapter 2, or a television studio pictured as a visual and textual frame reproducing the mesmerising effects of television on people's consciousness, which I examine in Chapter 4. In this chapter, I highlight how Byatt associates these effects with the transformative, shape-shifting games of *Alice in Wonderland* in an imaginative manner. In both cases, fictional events are interwoven with observations regarding the physiology of mind and brain, questions of visual perception reaching into the areas of art history and the changing technology of television during the two decades that form the backdrop to Byatt's *roman fleuve*. In parallel, new trends in culture and society are also foregrounded, magnifying the scope of Byatt's exploration of the past. Hence, new attitudes to questions of gender and sexuality, a growing awareness of feminist issues, the counterculture of the sixties and the turmoil following 1968, all find their place in Byatt's chronicle of the period.

The novels analysed in Chapters 3 and 5 (*Possession* and *Babel Tower*) bring into focus the author's use of intertextuality. Although these novels are entirely separate from one another and belong to different projects, they are characterized by an almost flamboyant use of intertextual sources and reveal the author's systematic attempt to relocate a wealth of language forms within the space of her novels, transformed into actual textual loci with a mnemonic function. As I noted in Chapter 3 focusing on *Babel Tower*, this novel is preceded chronologically by the publication of *Possession*, marking a gap in the ongoing project of the tetralogy. The gap is significant in that it reveals Byatt's increasing exploration of more experimental forms of narrative and a variety of genres. We have seen how the polyphony of the many voices woven into *Possession* are harmoniously integrated within the nineteenth-century core narrative. In contrast, the contemporary narratives in both *Possession* and *Babel Tower* show quite clearly the effects of linguistic fragmentation, which only in *Possession* are offset by the final postscript.

My study has displayed how the cognitive processes of memory and the persistent reference to cultural memory in its ongoing dialogue with the literary canon and intertextuality inform Byatt's fictional world. Connections between narrative, cognitive science and intertextuality highlight the author's handling of mnemonic processes in their interrelation with a tightly-knit framework of cultural references giving shape to her personal reinvention of life in England during two decades. The final volume in the tetralogy foregrounds especially the interplay of gender and cognitive science, producing a series of recurring metaphors which I re-trace as a subtle framework underlying Byatt's narrative.

The elaborate process of fictional reinvention that led to Byatt's personal system of mnemonics is described in 'Memory and the Making of Fiction' (Byatt 1998), which is crucial for an understanding of her approach to memory. Hence, I have emphasized in my investigation the fundamental interplay of vivid imagery characterizing the ancient art of memory, with pictorial representation and contemporary visual culture, as well as shifting modes of perception and processes of cognition.

The two types of mental pictures which Byatt associates with creativity and the writing process as it unfolds, are significant for an appreciation of her work. These are the two images of a feather 'being preened' (Byatt 1998: 65) and of a fishing net 'with links of various sizes' (ibid.). As I repeatedly pointed out throughout my study,[106] these striking analogies convey something essential about the nature of cognitive processes regulating mnemonic activity and cultural construction through a network of associations. Literary studies have meanwhile transformed the interplay between embodied cognition and fiction into a widespread theme, but the 'art and craft' with which the novelist transmutes these mental pictures into a long narrative conveying the flow of mental processes as well as cultural construction deserves special attention.

This leads me to a final question that has remained open throughout my investigation. Given the author's characteristic way of incorporating cultural knowledge into her novels, the question we may ask is how precisely knowledge interlocks with the imaginative quality of her storytelling. In the introduction to the present study, I have suggested that one way to answer this question is to reflect on the ancient practices of memorization and Renaissance forms of systematizing thought derived from antiquity in the light of recent cognitive

106 See Introduction (ii), Chapter 1 and Chapter 4.

theories developed by Mark Turner and Gilles Fauconnier. As I have already emphasized, Byatt has drawn inspiration from this early approach to memory. Indeed, the link between spatiality and visuality is an essential component in both the ancient memory system and in Byatt's narrative, where a kaleidoscope of images and iconic signs frequently proliferate as a series of 'inset structures' and narrative frames (Harries 2008: 87). Significant examples of this elaborate system of mnemonics are the many real and symbolic gardens patterning the structure of various episodes in *The Virgin in the Garden* or the prologues to both *Virgin* and *Still Life*, where the National Portrait Gallery and the Royal Academy of Arts function as conceptual frames for different inset structures corresponding to the characters' individual stories.

Section v of the introduction provided a concise description of how Turner and Fauconnier conceptualize their investigation into the very sources of knowledge and creativity. The theory known as *conceptual blending* or *conceptual integration* developed by the two cognitive scientists aims at illuminating the human capacity for thought and language and the consequent construction of meaning and memorization. It provides a fitting description for Byatt's characteristic narrative patterns through visualisation, narrative frames and embedded stories.

I suggest that this is the area that might offer a new critical perspective on Byatt's work. With the exception of Celia Wallhead, who has engaged with the conceptual metaphors structuring Byatt's narrative, and Elizabeth W. Harries's analysis of narrative framing in Byatt's fairy tales, no other attempt has been made to map out the author's characteristic handling of narrative patterns intertwined with complex imagery. What I illustrate below is a mere tentative sketch for possible investigation in future research.

Blending theory proposes that cognition is a process generating an ongoing sequence of mental spaces interrelated through a new *blended* or *generic space*, consisting in a compression of input spaces, which then becomes the *emergent structure*. Both creativity in individuals and processes of cultural construction in society are characterized by such a capacity 'for setting up a blend' (Fauconnier and Turner 2002: 72). In the introduction I mentioned that Fauconnier and Turner see the ancient art of memory as a characteristic example of this blending process, by which cultures ensure the transmission of knowledge.

As I pointed out at the end of Chapter 4, suggestively similar reflections are embedded in Byatt's narrative. We may remember, for example, that one of the expert characters participating in the fictional academic conference occurring at the end of *A Whistling Woman* remarks that human beings cannot think without metaphors. Similarly, the protagonist of *Still Life* thinks that 'we cannot resist the connecting and comparing habit of the mind' (*Still Life* 1986: 236). Therefore, my claim is that Byatt's characteristic narrative pattern, grafted by a process of accumulation of symbolic and semantic structures, resembles the method conceptualized by cognitive scientists.[107]

Byatt's novels – whether depicting life in post-war English society or Victorian culture in its dialogue with the present through the interpolation of myth and fairy tales – encompass a large display of blended spaces mapping a huge palace of memory. As I remarked in the introductory chapter, the connection between creative and scholarly modes characterizing her work can be seen to serve a kind of museological practice. In their introduction to *The Exhibit in the Text. The Museological Practices of Literature* (2009) Caroline Patey and Laura Scuriatti aptly suggest that 'museums and galleries are at the core of contemporary culture, manifesting its potentialities and at the same time exposing its frailties, its wounds and the disappearance of its treasures' (Patey and Scuriatti 2009: 5). Significantly, they highlight a common terminology in use in cultural theory and museum culture, favouring words like 'fragments, *débris*, displacement and discontinuities' (ibid.: 5), which in turn have been enhanced by the culture of modernity and postmodernity.

All these broad observations continue to illuminate Byatt's narrative. Blending theory can be seen to operate in two ways in her work, i.e. as a device structuring single episodes or aspects concerning characterization in the novels, or else as a strategy affecting larger conceptual paradigms. If we return, for example, to the central image of a spiralling shell governing the intricate symbolic network at the core of *Babel Tower*, we note a number of interrelated images, i.e. the double helix of DNA, neurons in the brain, the Tower of Babel, the endless intertextual proliferation of language forms, and the narrative pattern structuring the fictional novel within the novel, entitled 'Babbletower'. As well as producing a well-known *mise-en-abyme* effect,[108] these interrelated verbal images suggest a series of blended spaces, i.e. 'a complex online set of mappings from source to target' domains (Popova 2014: 247). In the novel, the overarching structuring

107 It is useful to remember that cognitive science is 'the umbrella discipline that turns on the study of the mind/brain, embracing philosophy of mind, psychology, neuroscience, artificial intelligence (AI), linguistics, and anthropology' (Caracciolo 2014: 16). In his insightful study, Caracciolo outlines the distinction between first-generation and second-generation cognitive science, showing a genealogy of interrelated disciplinary inputs and their future direction.

108 For a detailed description of the concept see Chapter 1.

metaphor, however, is that of language as a system, compared to a spiralling organism producing a polyphony of voices.[109]

The second example where blending can be seen to operate in Byatt's work is at the point of convergence between different conceptual paradigms or epistemological domains subsumed within her narrative. I am thinking in particular of the episode describing Stephanie giving birth in *Still Life*. As I expounded in Chapter 2, birth is here described as a journey of the human body through light, an idea which closely resembles platonic and neoplatonic conceptions of the soul. For Plato 'the soul is like the eye […] radiant with intelligence' (*Republic* VI: 508). It is important to remember that Byatt's first novel derived from her unfinished dissertation 'on the nature of religious metaphor – the relations between the world of sense and the world of spirit – in the English Renaissance' (Byatt 1993: 17). Echoes of this early scholarly work reverberate throughout *The Virgin in the Garden* and *Still Life*, evoking a well-known topos informing, for example, Dante's spiritual journey towards pure light in 'Paradise' in the *Divine Comedy*, as I showed in Chapter 2.

Chapter 2 details how the novelist replaces a medieval conception of the universe with a secular one, informed by the art of Van Gogh and the cognitive sciences rather than a theological order. Accordingly, *Still Life* displays an ongoing secular debate between words and things, between image and the language used to described it. Thus, we can observe how different forms of knowledge are at play in this novel, blending distinct epistemological domains. The same principle of connectivity and blending can be observed throughout Byatt's major novels. We have seen, for example, how the idea of a memory theatre, modelled on the old conceptual framework designed by Giulio Camillo and related to the Elizabethan memory of Robert Fludd (Yates 1966: 320 ff.), provides a first instance of a blended space in which different forms of knowledge are connected with the embedded symbolic images of *The Virgin in the Garden*,

109 Thus, language as a system could be seen to occupy the area of the metaphoric target. The property evoked is that of a spiralling movement or internal dynamism, which corresponds to the generic space in blending theory, while the metaphoric source is the shell. The actual blend is a fourth space, or emergent structure, which contains new features emerging from the generic space. We could venture to say that this fourth space takes the shape of the novel itself. It is a new narrative dimension emerging from the textual domain of language merging with the shape of a spiralling shell, bearing the genetic code of the species as a visible inscription. By analogy, *Babel Tower* bears witness to the literary past through its many intertextual echoes proliferating in spiralling motion.

which in turn are intertwined with the iconography of Elizabeth I. Similarly, *A Whistling Woman* conflates the transformed image of Frederica, the novel's protagonist making her first entrance into the world of simulacra, with the shape-shifting games of *Alice in Wonderland*. Like Alice and the surrounding space in which she moves, Frederica multiplies her human identity in the virtual domain of a television studio. Both can be compared to the metaphorical structure of a fractal, i.e. an irregular shape capable of infinite repetitions and variations. Fractals remain substantially identical because of the underlying principle of 'self-similarity' characterizing their core structure (Hemenway 2008: 125). As Susana Onega comments with regard to *Babel Tower*, fractals provide 'an infinitely flexible formula for the ordering of chaos' (Onega 2007: 61), allowing Byatt to create new narrative patterns within her novels.

Though I have tried to offer a comprehensive reading of some of Byatt's major novels, her work opens more fields of enquiry than it has been possible to explore in the present volume. A.S. Byatt has continued to produce fiction, yielding new possibilities of investigation and challenging authors of new critical studies attempting to offer a systematic analysis of her work. I have chosen to end my study on a minimal 'narratological' note because this is the area which seems to offer potentially fruitful possibilities of scholarship. As the narrative voice suggests at the end of *The Virgin in the Garden*, '[t]hat was not an end, but since it went on for a considerable time, is as good a place to stop as any' (Byatt 1994: 566).

Bibliography

I. Primary sources
II. Other literary works cited
III. Secondary sources

I. Primary sources

Byatt, A.S. (1970) *Wordsworth and Coleridge in Their Time*. London: Nelson. Rpt 1989 as *Unruly Times: Wordsworth and Coleridge in Their Time*. London: Hogarth.

Byatt, A.S. (1986) *Still Life [1985]*. Harmondsworth: Penguin.

Byatt, A.S. (1987) 'Identity and the Writer'. *The Real Me. Postmodernism and the Question of Identity*. Ed. Lisa Appignanesi. ICA Documents 6. London: ICA. 23–26.

Byatt, A.S. (1991a) *Possession* [1990]. London: Vintage.

Byatt, A.S. (1991b) *The Shadow of the Sun* [*Shadow of a Sun*, 1964]. London: Vintage.

Byatt, A.S. (1993) *Passions of the Mind* [1991]. London: Vintage.

Byatt, A.S. (1994) *The Virgin in the Garden* [1978]. London: Vintage.

Byatt, A.S. (1995) *Sugar and Other Stories* [1987]. London: Vintage.

Byatt, A.S. (1997a) *Babel Tower* [1996]. London: Vintage.

Byatt, A.S. (1997b) Personal interview. 4 November 1997.

Byatt, A.S. (1998a) 'Memory and the Making of Fiction'. *Memory*. Eds. Patricia Fara and Karalyn Patterson. Cambridge: Cambridge University Press. 47–72.

Byatt, A.S. (1998b) 'Ice, Snow, Glass'. *Mirror, Mirror on the Wall*. Ed. Kate Bernheimer. New York: Anchor. 60–79.

Byatt, A.S. (2000a) *The Biographer's Tale*. London: Chatto & Windus.

Byatt, A.S. (2000b) *On Histories and Stories. Selected Essays*. Cambridge: Harvard University Press. Contains: 'Ice, Snow, Glass'. First published in Kate Bernheimer, ed. (1998).

Byatt, A.S. (2002a) *A Whistling Woman*. London: Chatto & Windus.

Byatt, A.S. (2002b) *Portraits in Fiction* [2001]. London: Vintage.

Byatt, A.S. (2004) 'Soul Searching'. *The Guardian* 14 February, *Review*: 4–6. Available at: http://www.theguardian.com/books/2004/feb/14/fiction.philosophy. Accessed 24 February 2004

Byatt, A.S. (2005) 'Fiction Informed by Science'. *Nature* 434 17 March: 2–5.

Byatt, A.S. and H. Harvey Wood Eds. (2008) *Memory. An Anthology*. London: Chatto & Windus.

Byatt, A.S. (2008) 'Introduction'. *Memory. An Anthology*. Byatt and Harvey Wood. xii–xx.

Byatt, A.S. (2009) *The Children's Book*. London: Chatto & Windus.

Byatt, A.S. (2016) *Peacock and Vine: Fortuny and Morris in Life and at Work*. London: Chatto & Windus.

II. Other literary works cited

Bruno, Giordano (1955a) *La cena de le ceneri* [1584]. Ed. Giovanni Aquilecchia. Torino: Einaudi.

Bruno, Giordano (1995b) *The Ash Wednesday Supper*. Ed. and tr. Edward A. Gosselin and Lawrence S. Lerner. Toronto: University of Toronto Press.

Camillo, Giulio (1991) *L'idea del theatro* [1550]. Palermo: Sellerio.

Dante (2007) *Paradiso*, trans. Robert Hollander and Jean Hollander. New York: Anchor.

Eliot, George (1985) *Middlemarch* [1871–2]. Ed. W.J. Harvey. Penguin Classics. Harmondsworth: Penguin.

Eliot, Thomas Stearns (1973) 'Tradition and the Individual Talent' [1919]. *The Oxford Anthology of English Literature*, Vol. 2. Eds. Frank Kermode and John Hollander. Oxford: Oxford University Press. 2013–2019.

Eliot, Thomas Stearns (1979) *Four Quartets* [1944]. London: Faber and Faber.

Lawrence, David Herbert. (1979) *Women in Love* [1921]. Harmondsworth: Penguin.

Marvell, Andrew (1985) 'A Dialogue between the Soul and the Body'. *The Metaphysical Poets*. Ed. Helen Gardner. Harmondsworth: Penguin. 245–247.

Milton, John (2005a) 'Areopagitica' [1644]. *Paradise Lost*. Ed. Gordon Teskey. New York: Norton. 339–374.

Milton, John (2005b) *Paradise Lost* [1667]. Ed. Gordon Teskey. New York: Norton.

Rossetti, Christina (1970) 'Goblin Market'. *A Choice of Christina Rossetti's Verse*. Ed. Elizabeth Jennings. London: Faber and Faber.

Woolf, Virginia (1990) *Orlando* [1928]. London: Grafton.

III. Secondary sources

Alfer, Alexa (1996) 'Realism and Romance: A.S. Byatt's *Possession*'. Unpublished essay.

Alfer, Alexa (1999) '"A Second that Grows First, a Black Unreal/In Which a Real Lies Hidden and Alive": The Fiction of A.S. Byatt'. *Anglistik* 10.2: 27–48.

Alfer, Alexa and Amy J. Edwards De Campos (2010) *A.S. Byatt: Critical Storytelling*. Manchester and New York: Manchester University Press.

Alfer, Alexa and Michael J. Noble Eds. (2001) *Essays on the Fiction of A.S. Byatt: Imagining the Real*. Westport: Greenwood.

Allen, Graham (2000) *Intertextuality*. London: Routledge.

Aquilecchia, Giovanni (2001) *Giordano Bruno*. Torino: Einaudi.

Aragay, Mireia (1994) 'The Long Shadow of the Nineteenth Century: An Interview with A.S. Byatt'. BELLS: *Barcelona English Language and Literature Studies* 5: 151–164.

Ashworth, Ann (1994) 'Fairy Tales in A.S. Byatt's *Possession*'. *Journal of Evolutionary Psychology* 15.1–2: 93–94.

Assmann, Aleida (1999) *Erinnerungsräume*. München: Beck.

Assmann, Jan (1997) *Das kulturelle Gedächtnis*. München: Beck.

Bakhtin, Michail M. (1981) 'Discourse in the Novel'. *The Dialogic Imagination*. Ed. M. Holquist. Austin: University of Texas Press. 269–422.

Barthes, Roland (1968) *Writing Degree Zero* [*Le Degré zéro de l'écriture*, 1953]. New York: Hill and Wang.

Barthes, Roland (1977) *Image, Music, Text*, trans. Stephen Heath. New York: Hill and Wang.

Barthes, Roland (1989) *The Rustle of Language* [*Le bruissement de la langue*, 1984], trans. Richard Howard. Berkeley and Los Angeles: University of California Press.

Barthes, Roland (1995) 'The Reality Effect' [L'effet de reel, 1968]. *The Realist Novel*. Ed. Dennis Walder. London: Routledge in association with the Open University. 258–261.

Becker-Leckrone (2005) *Julia Kristeva and Literary Theory*. Basingstoke: Palgrave MacMillan.

Beer, Gillian (1970) *The Romance*. London: Methuen.

Beer, Gillian (1983) *Darwin's Plots*. Cambridge: Cambridge University Press.

Bernini, Marco and Marco Caracciolo (2013) *Letteratura e scienze cognitive*. Roma: Carocci.

Bigliazzi, Silvia (1999) '"Art Work": A.S. Byatt vs Henri Matisse or The Metamorphosis of Writing'. *Textus* 12.1: 185–199.

Billi, Mirella and Nicholas Brownlees Eds. (2003) *In and Around the Sixties.* Viterbo: Sette città.

Boccardi, Mariadele (2009) The Contemporary British Historical Novel. Basingstoke: Palgrave Macmillan.

Boccardi, Mariadele (2013) *A.S. Byatt.* Basingstoke: Palgrave MacMillan.

Bolter, Jay David and Richard Grusin (2000) *Remediation.* Cambridge: MIT Press.

Bolzoni, Lina (1991a) 'Lo spettacolo della memoria'. Foreword. *L'idea del theatro.* By Giulio Camillo. Palermo: Sellerio. 9–34.

Bolzoni, Lina (1991b) 'The Play of Images. The Art of Memory from Its Origins to the Seventeenth Century'. *The Enchanted Loom. Chapters in the History of Neuroscience.* Ed. Pietro Corsi. Oxford: Oxford University Press. 16–26.

Bolzoni, Lina (2001) *The Gallery of Memory* [*La stanza della memoria* 1995], trans. Jeremy Parzen. Toronto: University of Toronto Press.

Brewer, William F. (1996) 'What is Recollective Memory?' *Remembering Our Past: Studies in Autobiographical Memory.* Ed. David C. Rubin. Cambridge: Cambridge University Press. 19–66.

Bridgeman, Teresa (2007) 'Time and Space'. *The Cambridge Companion to Narrative.* Ed. David Herman. Cambridge: Cambridge University Press. 52–65.

Broich, Ulrich (1985) 'Formen der Markierung von Intertextualität'. *Intertextualität. Formen, Funktionen, anglistische Fallstudien.* Eds. Ulrich Broich and Manfred Pfister. Tübingen: Niemeyer. 31–47.

Broich, Ulrich (1996) 'A.S. Byatt's Possession – Ein Pastiche postmoderner Fiktion?' *Expedition nach der Wahrheit.* Eds. Stefan Horlacher and M. Islinger. Heidelberg: Winter. 617–633.

Brosch, Renate (1999) 'Inszenierung, Visualisierung und Fiktionalisierung als Strategien der Herstellung von individueller und kultureller Identität: Vom historischen zum historiographischen Text in A.S. Byatts Romantetralogie'. *Anglistik* 10.2: 49–65.

Brosch, Renate (2008) 'Empowering the Spectator: Ekphrasis as Strategic Response to the Power of Images'. *Symbolism: An International Annual of Critical Aesthetics,* 8: 179–196. New York: AMS Press.

Brown, Alistair (2007) 'Uniting the Two Cultures of Body and Mind in A.S. Byatt's *A Whistling Woman*'. *Journal of Literature and Science* 1.1: 55–72.

Bryson, Norman (1988) 'Intertextuality and Visual Poetics'. *Style* 22.2: 183–193.

Butor, Michel (1970) 'The Imaginary Works of Art in Proust'. Inventory: Essays by Michel Butor. Ed. Richard Howard. London: Cape. 146–184.

Butter, Stella (2007) *Literatur als Medium kultureller Selbstreflextion*. Trier: WVT Wissenschaftlicher Verlag Trier. 214–250.

Buxton, Jackie (1996) '"What's Love Got to Do with It?" Postmodernism and *Possession*'. *English Studies in Canada* 22.2: 199–219.

Calvino, Italo (1980) 'Cibernetica e fantasmi: appunti sulla narrativa come processo combinatorio'. *Una pietra sopra*. Torino: Einaudi. 164–181.

Cambiaghi, Mara (2003a) 'The Invention of Truth and the Paradoxes of Memory in A.S. Byatt's "Sugar" and *The Biographer's Tale*'. *Travelling Concepts III*. Ed. Nancy Pedri. Amsterdam: ASCA Press. 73–86.

Cambiaghi, Mara (2003b) 'The Power of Fiction in A.S. Byatt's *Babel Tower*'. *Symbolism: An International Journal of Critical Aesthetics* 3: 279–304.

Cambiaghi, Mara (2004) 'Verità e finzione nei teatri della memoria di A.S. Byatt'. *Memoria. Poetica, retorica e filologia della memoria*. Eds. Gianfelice Peron, Zeno Verlato and Francesco Zambon. Trento: Università degli Studi di Trento. 427–447.

Cambiaghi, Mara (2005a) 'Unraveling the Past: A.S. Byatt's Theaters of Memory and the Spell of Recall'. *Inventing the Past. Memory Work in Culture and History*. Eds. Otto Heim and Caroline Wiedmer. Basel: Schwabe. 77–93.

Cambiaghi, Mara (2005b) '"Moving Times – New Words" The Sixties on Both Sides of the Channel'. *Time Refigured. Myths, Foundation Texts and Imagined Communities*. Eds. Martin Procházka and Ondřej Pilny. Prague: Litteraria Pragensia. 296–312.

Cambiaghi, Mara (2006) 'The Gendered Memories of Frederica Potter: A.S. Byatt's *A Whistling Woman*'. *Erinnern und Geschlecht: Freiburger FrauenStudien. Zeitschrift für Interdisziplinäre Frauenforschung* 19: 225–244.

Cambiaghi, Mara (2009) 'A.S. Byatt e la circolarità del testo: citazioni, intertestualità e l'epitome della cultura'. *La citazione. Atti del XXXI Convegno Interuniversitario di Bressanone*. Ed. Gianfelice Peron. Padova: Esedra. 609–625.

Cambiaghi, Mara (2010) 'Quegli irriverenti anni Sessanta: la vena polemica di A.S. Byatt tra balbettii della lingua, ribellione genetica e menti incarnate'. *Il discorso polemico. Controversia, Invettiva, Pamphlet. Atti del XXXIII Convegno Interuniversitario del Circolo Filologico Linguistico Padovano*. Ed. Gianfelice Peron e Alvise Andreose. Padova: Esedra. 427–438.

Campbell, Jane (2004) *A.S.Byatt and the Heliotropic Imagination*. Waterloo: Wilfrid Laurier University Press.

Caracciolo, Marco (2014) *The Experientiality of Narrative*. Berlin: De Gruyter.

Carpi, Daniela (2008) 'Ut Pictura Poesis: Literature and Painting'. *Symbolism. An International Annual of Critical Aesthetics*, Vol. 8. 1–15 (New York: AMS Press).

Carroll, Lewis (2005) *The Complete Works*. London: CRW Publishing.

Caute, David (1988) *Sixty-eight: The Year of the Barricades*. London: Hamilton.

Cerezo-Moreno, Marta(2007). 'Female Sacrifice and Gender Violence in A. S. Byatt's Babel Tower. An Ethical Perspective'. The Ethical Component in Experimental British Fiction in the 1960s. Eds. Susana Onega and Jean-Michel Ganteau. Newcastle: Cambridge Scholars Publishing. 91–116.

Childs, Peter (2007) 'The English Heritage Industry and Other Trends in the Novel at the Millennium'. *A Companion to the British and Irish Novel* 1945–2000. Ed. Brian W. Shaffer. Malden: Blackwell. 210–224.

Connor, Steven (1996) *The English Novel in History 1950–1995*. London and New York: Routledge.

Cooper, Tarnya (2003) 'Queen Elizabeth's Public Face'. *History Today* 53.5: 38–41.

Cosslett, Tess (1989) 'Childbirth from the Woman's Point of View in British Women's Fiction: Enid Bagnold's *The Squire* and A.S. Byatt's *Still Life*'. *Tulsa Studies in Women's Literature* 8.2: 263–286.

Cox, Fiona (2013) 'Ovidian Metamorphoses in the Fiction of A.S. Byatt'. *Classics in the Modern World: A 'Democratic Turn'?* Eds. Lorna Hardwick and Stephen Harrison. Oxford: Oxford University Press.

Dällenbach, Lucien (1989) *The Mirror in the Text*. Cambridge: Polity Press.

Damasio, Antonio (1994) *Descartes' Error: Emotion, Reason and the Human Brain*. New York: Putnam.

Damasio, Antonio (1999) *The Feeling of What Happens: Body and Emotion in the Making of Consciousness*. New York: Harcourt Brace.

Damasio, Antonio (2003) *Looking for Spinoza: Joy, Sorrow, and the Feeling Brain*. London: Heinemann.

Davey, G. (1998) '*Still Life* and the Rounding of Consciousness'. *Lancet* 352: 1544–1547.

de Groot, Jerome (2010) *The Historical Novel*. London: Routledge.

Dinnage, Rosemary (1979) 'England in the 50's'. *The New York Times Book Review* 1 April 1979: 20.

Djordjevic, Ivana (1997) 'In the Footsteps of Giambattista Vico'. *Anglia* 115.1: 44–83.

Doran, Susan (2003) 'Elizabeth I, Gender, Power, Politics'. *History Today* 53.5: 29–35.

Draaisma, Douwe (2000) *Metaphors of Memory: A History of Ideas about the Mind*. Cambridge: Cambridge University Press.

Drabble, Margaret Ed. (1985) *The Oxford Companion to English Literature* 5th ed. Oxford: Oxford University Press.

Dusinberre, Juliet (1982) 'Forms of Reality in A.S. Byatt's *The Virgin in the Garden*'. *Critique: Studies in Modern Fiction* 24.1: 55–62.

Dusinberre, Juliet (1983) 'A.S. Byatt'. *Women Writers Talking*. Ed. Janet Todd. New York: Holmes and Meyer. 181–195.

Eagleton, Terry (2005) *The English Novel*. Malden: Blackwell.

Easthope, Antony (1999) *Englishness and National Culture*. London: Routledge.

Ede, Siân (2005) *Art and Science*. London: I.B.Tauris, eBook Collection (EBSCOhost), viewed 1 July 2015.

Ellis, Peter Berresford (1994) *The Druids*. London: Constable & Co.

Erll, Astrid (2005) *Kollektives Gedächtnis und Erinnerungskulturen*. Stuttgart and Weimar: J.B. Metzler.

Erll, Astrid and Ansgar Nünning (2006) 'Concepts and Methods for the Study of Literature and/as Cultural Memory'. *Literature and Memory*. Eds. Ansgar Nünning, Marion Gymnich and Roy Sommer. Tübingen: Francke. 12–28.

Erll, Astrid (2008) 'Cultural Memory Studies: An Introduction'. *Cultural Memory Studies. An International and Interdisciplinary Handbook*. Eds. Erll, Astrid and Ansgar Nünning. Berlin: de Gruyter. 1–15.

Erll, Astrid and Ansgar Nünning Eds. (2008) *Cultural Memory Studies. An International and Interdisciplinary Handbook*. Berlin: de Gruyter.

Fauconnier, Gilles and Mark Turner (2002) *The Way We Think. Conceptual Blending and the Mind's Hidden Complexities*. New York: Basic Books.

Feingold, Ruth P. (2013) 'Every Little Girl Can Grow Up to Be Queen: The Coronation and *The Virgin in the Garden*'. *Literature & History* 22.2: 73–90.

Fiske, John and John Hartley (1978) *Reading Television*. London: Routledge.

Fludernik, Monika (1996) *Towards a 'Natural' Narratology*. London: Routledge.

Fludernik, Monika (2009) *An Introduction to Narratology* [*Einführung in die Erzähltheorie*, 2006]. Abingdon: Routledge.

Fludernik, Monika (2010) 'Narrative and Metaphor'. *Language and Style*. Eds. Dan McIntyre and Beatrix Busse. Basingstoke: Palgrave MacMillan. 347–363.

Fountain, J. Stephen (1994) 'Ashes to Ashes: Kristeva's *Jouissance*, Altizer's *Apocalypse*, Byatt's *Possession* and "The Dream of the Rood"'. *Literature and Theology* 8.2: 193–208.

Fox Keller, Evelyn (1985) *Reflections on Gender and Science*. New Haven: Yale University Press.

Franchi, Barbara (2016) 'Travelling across Worlds and Texts in A. S. Byatt's Sea Narratives'. *Sea Narratives: Interdisciplinary Perspectives on the History, Culture and Geography of the Sea*. Ed. Charlotte Mathieson. Basingstoke: Palgrave MacMillan.

Franchi, Barbara (2018) 'Dangerous Mothers and Their Children: Writing and Other Secrets in *Possession* and *The Children's Book*'. *A. S. Byatt, before and after* Possession: *Recent Critical Approaches*. Eds. Armelle Parey and Isabelle Roblin. Nancy: PUN-Editions Universitaires de Lorraine. 143–160.

Franken, Christien (1997) *Multiple Mythologies. A.S. Byatt and the British Artist-Novel*. Diss. University of Utrecht. Enschede: Print Partners Ipskamp.

Franken, Christien (2001) *Art, Authorship, Creativity*. Basingstoke: Palgrave MacMillan.

Fratucello, Cinzia and Christina Knorr Eds. (1998) *Il cosmo incantato di Schifanoia. Aby Warburg e la storia delle immagini astrologiche*. Ferrara: Palazzo Schifanoia.

Frye, Northrop (1965) *The Anatomy of Criticism* [1957]. Princeton: Princeton University Press.

Genette, Gérard (1976) *Figure III* [*Figures III*, 1972], trans. Lina Zecchi. Torino: Einaudi.

Genette, Gérard (1997) *Palinsesti. La letteratura al secondo grado* [*Palimpsestes. La littérature au second degré*, 1982], trans. Raffaella Novità. Torino: Einaudi.

Gibson, John (2007) 'Introduction: The Prospects of Literary Cognitivism'. *A Sense of the World. Essays on Fiction, Narrative and Knowledge*. Eds. John Gibson, Wolfgang Huemer and Luca Pocci. New York: Routledge. 1–9.

Ginzburg, Carlo (1986) *Miti emblemi spie*. Torino: Einaudi.

Gitzen, Julian (1995) 'A.S. Byatt's Self-Mirroring Art'. *Critique* 36.2: 83–95.

Gombrich, Ernst H. (1970) *Aby Warburg. An Intellectual Biography*. London: The Warburg Institute, University of London.

Gombrich, Ernst H. (1972) *Art and Illusion. A Study in the Psychology of Pictorial Representation* [1960]. London: Phaidon Press.

Goodman, Nelson (1978) *Ways of Worldmaking*. Indianapolis: Hackett Publishing Company.

Gross, Kenneth (2005) 'Satan and the Romantic Satan: A Notebook' [1988]. *Paradise Lost* by John Milton. Ed. Gordon Teskey. New York: Norton. 420–424.

Gutleben, Christian (2001) *Nostalgic Postmodernism: The Victorian Tradition and the Contemporary British Novel*. Amsterdam: Rodopi.

Halbwachs, Maurice (1925) *Les cadres sociaux de la mémoire*. Paris: F. Alcan.

Halbwachs, Maurice (1996) *La memoria collettiva* [1987] [*La mémoire collective*, 1950], ed., trans. and introd. Paolo Jedlowski. Afterword Luisa Passerini. Milano: Unicopli.

Hanson, Clare (2000) *Hysterical Fictions. The 'Woman Novel' in the Twentieth Century*. Basingstoke: MacMillan.

Harf-Lancner, Laurence (1989) *Morgana e Melusina*. Torino: Einaudi.

Harries, Elizabeth Wanning (2001) *Twice Upon a Time. Women Writers and the History of the Fairy Tale*. Princeton: Princeton University Press.

Harries, Elizabeth Wanning (2008) '"Ancient Forms": Myth, Fairy Tale and Narrative in A.S. Byatt's Fiction'. *Contemporary Fiction and the Fairy Tale*. Ed. Stephen Benson. Detroit: Wayne State University Press. 74–97.

Harth, Dietrich (2008) 'The Invention of Cultural Memory'. *Cultural Memory Studies*. Eds. Astrid Erll and Ansgar Nünning. Berlin: de Gruyter. 85–96.

Heinz, Sarah (2007) *Die Einheit in der Differenz: Metapher, Romance und Identität in A.S. Byatts Romanen*. Tübingen: Gunter Narr.

Heinz, Sarah (2008) 'Freiheit ohne Grenzen? Das Freiheitsdilemma und seine Konsequenzen in A.S. Byatt's *Babel Tower* und *A Whistling Woman*'. *Literatur und Lebenskunst*. Eds. Anna-Margaretha Horatschek, Susanne Bach, Stefan Glomb and Stefan Horlacher. Trier: WVT Wissenschaftlicher Verlag. 267–286.

Hekman, Susan J. (1990) *Gender and Knowledge. Elements of Postmodern Feminism*. Cambridge: Polity Press.

Hemenway, Priya (2008) *The Secret Code. The Mysterious Formula that Rules Art, Nature and Science*. Köln: Evergreen.

Hewison, Robert (1986) *Too Much: Art and Society in the Sixties*. London: Methuen.

Hicks, Elizabeth (2010) *The Still Life in the Fiction of A.S. Byatt*. Newcastle upon Tyne: Cambridge Scholars Publishing.

Hicks, Elizabeth (2011) 'Public and Private Collections in A.S. Byatt's *The Children's Book*'. *Mosaic* 44/2: 171–185.

Hidalgo, Pilar (2005) 'From Natural History to Neuroscience: Memory and Perception in A.S. Byatt's Fiction'. *Revista Canaria de Estudios Ingleses* 50: 145–60.

Holmes, Frederick M. (1994) 'The Historical Imagination and the Victorian Past: A.S. Byatt's *Possession*'. *English Studies in Canada* 20.3: 319–34.

Hulbert, Ann (1993) 'The Great Ventriloquist: A.S. Byatt's *Possession: A Romance*'. *Contemporary British Women Writers*. Ed. Robert E. Hosmer. Basingstoke: MacMillan. 55–61.

Humpherys, Anne (2007) 'The Afterlife of the Victorian Novel: Novels about Novels'. *A Companion to the Victorian Novel*. Eds. Patrick Brantlinger and William B. Thesing. Malden: Blackwell. 442–456.

Hutcheon, Linda (1985) *A Theory of Parody*. New York: Methuen.

Irigaray, Luce (1985) *Speculum of the Other Woman*, trans. Gillian C. Gill. Ithaca, New York: Cornell University Press.

Irigaray, Luce (1993) *Sexes and Genealogies*. New York: Columbia University Press. 55–72.

Iser, Wolfgang (1997) 'Intertextuality: The Epitome of Culture'. Foreword. *Memory and Literature: Intertextuality in Russian Modernism*. By Renate Lachmann. Minneapolis: University of Minnesota Press. vii–xviii.

Iser, Wolfgang (2007) 'Culture: A Recursive Process'. *A Sense of the World. Essays on Fiction, Narrative and Knowledge*. Eds. John Gibson, Wolfgang Huemer and Luca Pocci. New York: Routledge. 318–331.

Jansen, Odile (2000) 'Women as Storekeepers of Memory: Christa Wolf's Cassandra Project'. *Gendered Memories*. Eds. John Neubauer and Helga Geyer-Ryan. Amsterdam: Rodopi. 35–43.

Johnson, Jennifer Anne (2010) 'Soothsaying Song Thrushes and Life- Giving Snails: Motifs in A.S. Byatt's *Babel Tower* and *A Whistling Woman*'. *Journal of English Studies* 8: 57–71.

Jordan, Constance (1990) 'Representing Political Androgyny: More on the Siena Portrait of Queen Elizabeth I'. *The Renaissance Englishwoman in Print: Counterbalancing the Canon*. Eds. Anne M. Haselkorn and Betty S. Travitsky. Amherst: University of Massachusetts Press. 157–176.

Kansteiner, Wulf and Harald Weilnböck (2008) 'Against the Concept of Cultural Trauma'. *Cultural Memory Studies. An International and Interdisciplinary Handbook*. Eds. Astrid Erll and Ansgar Nünning in collaboration with Sara B. Young. Berlin: de Gruyter. 229–240.

Keen, Suzanne (2006) 'The Historical Turn in British Fiction'. *A Concise Companion to Contemporary British Fiction*. Ed. James F. English. Malden: Blackwell. 167–187.

Kelly, Kathleen Coyne (1996) *A.S. Byatt*. New York: Twayne.

Kenyon, Olga (1988) *Women Novelists Today: A Survey of English Writing in the Seventies and Eighties*. Brighton: Harvester.

Kermode, Frank (1980) 'The Argument of "The Garden"'. *Andrew Marvell Poems*. Ed. Arthur Pollard. London: MacMillan. 198–215.

Klein, Kerwin L. (2000) 'On the Emergence of "Memory" in Historical Discourse'. *Representations* 69: 127–150.

Kristeva, Julia (1980) *Desire in Language: A Semiotic Approach to Literture and Art*. Ed. Léon S. Roudiez. New York: Columbia University Press.

Kuzniar, Magdalena (2012) 'Living on Texts: Intertextuality in *The Virgin in the Garden* by A.S. Byatt'. *The Lives of Texts: Exploring the Metaphor*. Eds. Katarzyna Pisarska and Andrzey Slawomir Kowaleyzk. Newcastle upon Tyne: Cambridge Scholars Publishing.

Lachmann, Renate (1997) *Memory and Literature. Intertextuality in Russian Modernism*, trans. Roy Sellars and Anthony Wall. Minneapolis: University of Minnesota Press. Trans. of *Gedächtnis und Literatur: Intertextualität in der russischen Moderne*. Frankfurt am Main: Suhrkamp, 1990.

Lachmann, Renate (2004) 'Cultural Memory and the Role of Literature'. *European Review* 12.2: 165–178.

Lachmann, Renate (2008) 'Mnemonic and Intertextual Aspects of Literature'. *Cultural Memory Studies. An International and Interdisciplinary Handbook*. Eds. Erll, Astrid and Ansgar Nünning. Berlin: de Gruyter. 301–310.

Laing, Stuart (1997) 'The Television Revolution in Britain in the Sixties'. *The Sixties*. Eds. David Alan Mellor and Laurent Gerverau. London: Philip Wilson Publishers. 168–177.

Lakoff, George and Mark Johnson (2003) *Metaphors We Live By* [1980]. Chicago: University of Chicago Press.

Lara-Rallo, Carmen (2009a) 'Museums, Collections and Cabinet: "Shelf after Shelf after Shelf"'. *The Exhibit in the Text: The Museological Practices of Literature*. Eds. Caroline Patey and Laura Scuriatti. Oxford: Peter Lang. 219–239.

Lara-Rallo, Carmen (2009b) 'Pictures Worth a Thousand Words: Metaphorical Images of Textual Interdependence'. *Nordic Journal of English Studies* 8.2: 91–110.

Lara-Rallo, Carmen (2010) '"The Metamorphosis of Freedom": Utopia and Dystopia in A.S. Byatt's Quartet'. *Topic: The Washington and Jefferson College Review* 56: 81–93.

Lara-Rallo, Carmen (2011) '"She Thought Human Thoughts and Stone Thoughts": Geology and the Mineral World in A.S. Byatt's Fiction'. *Restoring the Mystery of the Rainbow. Literature's Refraction of Science*. Eds. Cedric Barfoot and Valeria Tinkler-Villani. Amsterdam and New York: Rodopi. 487–506.

Lindholm, Charles (1990) *Charisma*. Oxford: Basil Blackwell.

Longoni, Anna M. (2000) *La Memoria*. Bologna: Il Mulino.

Lowes, John Livingston (1933) *The Road to Xanadu: A Study in the Ways of the Imagination* [1927]. London: Constable.

Lüthi, Max (1970) *Once Upon a Time: On the Nature of Fairy Tales*. New York: Frederick Ungar.

Mack, John (2003) *The Museum of the Mind*. London: The British Museum Press.

Maltz, Diana (2012) 'The Newer Life. A.S. Byatt, E. Nesbit and Socialist Subculture'. *Journal of Victorian Culture* 17.1: 79–84.

Manier, David and William Hirst (2008) 'A Cognitive Taxonomy of Collective Memories'. *Cultural Memory Studies. An International and Interdisciplinary Handbook*. Eds. Astrid Erll and Ansgar Nünning in collaboration with Sara B. Young. Berlin: de Gruyter. 253–262.

Markowitsch, Hans J. (2008) 'Cultural Memory and the Neurosciences'. *Cultural Memory Studies. An International and Interdisciplinary Handbook*. Eds. Astrid Erll and Ansgar Nünning in collaboration with Sara B. Young. Berlin: de Gruyter. 275–283.

Marsh, Kelly A. (1995) 'The Neo-Sensation Novel: A Contemporary Genre in the Victorian Tradition'. *Philological Quarterly* 74.1: 99–123.

Martin, Bernice (1981) *A Sociology of Contemporary Cultural Change*. Oxford: Blackwell.

Marwick, Arthur (1998) *The Sixties*. Oxford: Oxford University Press.

Matussek, Peter (2001) 'The Renaissance of the Theater of Memory'. *Janus* 8: 4–8.

McLuhan, Marshall (1964) *Understanding Media: The Extensions of Man*. London: Routledge.

Mendelson, Edward (2017) *Early Auden, Later Auden: A Critical Biography*. Princeton: Princeton University Press.

Merkin, Daphne (2003) 'The Novel as Information Superhighway'. Rev. of *A Whistling Woman* by A.S. Byatt. New *York Times*, 19 Jan., Section 7: 10. <http://www.nytimes.com/2003/01/19/books/the-novel-as-information-superhighway.html>

Merleau-Ponty, Maurice (2002) *Phenomenology of Perception*, trans. Colin Smith. London: Routledge.

Meyer, Michael (2012) 'Antonia S. Byatt's Intermedial "Art Work": The Empire Knits Back'. *Anglistik* 23.2: 139–147.

Mitchell, Kate (2009) '(Feeling It) As It Actually Happened: History as Sensation in A.S. Byatt's *Possession. A Romance*'. *Literature and Sensation*. Eds. Anthony Uhlmann, Helen Groth, Paul Sheehan and Stephen McLaren. Newcastle upon Tyne: Cambridge Scholars Publishing. 266–279.

Mitchell, Kate (2010) *History and Cultural Memory in Neo-Victorian Fiction*. Basingstoke: Palgrave MacMillan.

Mitchell, W.J. Thomas (1995) *Picture Theory*. Chicago/London: Chicago University Press.

Müller, Wolfgang G. (1991) 'Interfigurality'. *Intertextuality*. Ed. Heinrich F. Plett. Berlin: de Gruyter. 101–121.

Murdoch, Iris (1985) 'Still Life with Sunflowers: Iris Murdoch talks to A.S. Byatt at the ICA'. *Books and Bookmen* (July): 28–29.

Murphet, Julian (2004) 'Fiction and Postmodernity'. *The Cambridge History of Twentieth-Century English Literature*. Eds. Laura Marcus and Peter Nicholls. Cambridge: Cambridge University Press. 716–735.

Nalbantian, Suzanne (2003) *Memory in Literature: From Rousseau to Neuroscience*. Basingstoke: Palgrave.

Noble, Michael J. (2001) 'A Tower of Tongues: *Babel Tower* and the Art of Memory'. *Essays on the Fiction of A.S. Byatt: Imagining the Real*. Eds. Alexa Alfer and Michael J. Noble. Westport: Greenwood. 61–74.

Nora, Pierre Ed. (1984–1992) *Les Lieux de Mémoire*, 3 Vols. Paris: Gallimard.

Nora, Pierre (1989) 'Between Memory and History: *Les Lieux de Mémoire*'. *Representations* 26: 7–25.

Nowak, Helge (1997) 'A.S. Byatt's *Possession* for British and American Readers'. *Erfurt Electronic Studies in English* 8: 1–24. <http://webdoc.sub.gwdg.de/edoc/ia/eese/rahmen22.html> [accessed 20 July 2015]

Onega, Susana (2007) 'The Ethics of Narrative Form in A.S. Byatt's *Babel Tower*'. *On the Turn: The Ethics of Fiction in Contemporary Narrative in English*. Eds. Bárbara Arizti and Silvia Martínez-Falquina. Newcastle upon Tyne: Cambridge Scholars Publishing. 53–76.

Otis, Laura (2001) *Networking: Communicating with Bodies and Machines in the Nineteenth Century*. Ann Arbor: University of Michigan Press.

Panagiotidou, Maria-Eirini (2012) 'An Introduction to the Semantics of Intertextuality'. *Journal of Literary Semantics* 41.1: 47–65.

Passerini, Luisa (1996) 'Afterword'. *La memoria collettiva*. By Maurice Halbwachs. Milano: Unicopli. 189–195.

Patey, Caroline and Laura Scuriatti Eds. (2009) *The Exhibit in the Text. The Museological Practices of Literature*. Bern: Peter Lang.

Pereira, Margarida Esteves (2004) 'Refracting the Past in Praise of the Dead Poets'. *Refracting the Canon in Contemporary British Literature*. Eds. Susana Onega and Christian Gutleben. Amsterdam: Rodopi. 149–164.

Pfister, Manfred (1985) 'Konzepte der Intertextualität'. *Intertextualität. Formen, Funktionen, anglistische Fallstudien*. Eds. Ulrich Broich and Manfred Pfister. Tübingen: Niemeyer. 1–30.

Phelps, Gilbert (1990) 'The Post-War English Novel'. *The New Pelican Guide to English Literature. The Present*, Vol. 8 [1983]. Ed. Boris Ford. Harmondsworth: Penguin. 417–449.

Plett, Heinrich F. Ed. (1991) *Intertextuality*. Berlin: de Gruyter.

Plotz, Judith (2001) 'A Modern "Seer Blest": The Visionary Child in *The Virgin in the Garden*'. *Essays on the Fiction of A.S. Byatt: Imagining the Real*. Eds. Alexa Alfer and Michael J. Noble. Westport: Greenwood. 31–45.

Popova, Yanna (2014) 'Figurative Language and Cognition'. *The Encyclopedia of the Novel*. Ed. Peter Melville Logan. Malden: Wiley Blackwell. 244–251.

Preston, Peter (2012) '"Myths of Desire": D.H. Lawrence, Language and Ethics in A.S. Byatt's Fiction'. *The Legacies of Modernism: Historicising Postwar and Contemporary Fiction*. Ed. David James. Cambridge: Cambridge University Press.

Reynolds, Margaret and Jonathan Noakes (2004) 'An Interview with A.S. Byatt'. *A.S. Byatt. The Essential Guide*. London: Vintage. 11–32.

Ricoeur, Paul (1977) *The Rule of Metaphor*: Multi-Disciplinary Studies of the Creation of Meaning in Language, trans. Robert Czerny with Kathleen McLaughlin and John Costello. Toronto: University of Toronto Press.

Rippl, Gabriele (2000) 'Visuality and Ekphrasis in A.S. Byatt's *Still Life* and "Art Work"'. *Anglistentag 1999. Proceedings*. Eds. Bernhard Reitz and Sigrid Rieuwerts. Trier: W VT. 519–534.

Rippl, Gabriele (2001) 'Vom Abfall zur Kunst: Antonia Byatt's Arbeit am Kulturellen Gedächtnis'. Sammeln – Ausstellen – Wegwerfen. Ed. GiselaEcker, MartinaStangeand UlrikeVedder. Königstein (Ts): Helmer. 240–253.

Rippl, Gabriele (2005) *Beschreibungs-kunst: Zur Intermedialen Poetik Angloamerikanischer Ikontexte (1880–2000)*. München: Wilhelm Fink.

Rossi, Paolo (2000) *Logic and the Art of Memory. The Quest for a Universal Knowledge* [*Clavis Universalis. Arti della memoria e logica combinatoria da Lullo a Leibniz* 1960] [1983], trans. Stephen Clucas. London: The Athlone Press.

Samuel, Raphael (1989) *Patriotism: The Making and Unmaking of British National Identity*. Vol. 1. London: Routledge.

Samuel, Raphael (1994) *Theatres of Memory*. London: Verso.

Sanchez, Victoria (1995) 'A.S. Byatt's *Possession*: A Fairytale Romance'. *Southern Folklore* 52.1: 33–52.

Schacter, Daniel L. Ed. (1995) *Memory Distortion. How Minds, Brains and Societies Reconstruct the Past*. Cambridge, MA: Harvard University Press.

Schirato, Tony and Jen Webb (2007) *Understanding the Visual* [2004]. London: Sage.

Schmidt, Katharina (2001) 'Cosmos and Star Paintings 1995–2001'. *Anselm Kiefer: The Seven Heavenly Palaces 1973–2001*. Basel: Fondation Beyeler. 75–77.

Schumann, Kuno (1983) 'The Concept of Culture in Some Recent English Novels'. *Anglistentag 1981: Vorträge*. Ed. Jörg Hasler. Trierer Studien zur Literatur 7. Frankfurt: Lang. 111–127.

Seligardi, Beatrice (2012a) 'Solo connettere'. Il frammento come dispositivo eccentrico in *Babel Tower* di A.S. Byatt. *Elephant & Castle*, 7 - *Il frammento* <http://cav.unibg.it/elephant_castle>

Seligardi, Beatrice (2012a) ' "A snake of black language": il processo come struttura narrativa in *Babel Tower* di A.S. Byatt'. *Between*, II.3 <http://www.Between-journal.it>

Sorensen, Susan D. (2004) 'Something of the Eternal: A.S. Byatt and Vincent Van Gogh'. *Mosaic: A Journal for the Interdisciplinary Study of Literature* 37.1: 63–81.

Spinozzi, Paola (2006) 'Ekphrasis as Portrait: A.S. Byatt's Fictional and Visual *Doppelgänger*'. *Writing and Seeing: Essays on Word and Image*. Eds. Rui Carvalho Homem and Maria de Fátima Lambert. Amsterdam: Rodopi. 223–231.

Splendore, Paola (1991) *Il ritorno del narratore. Voci e strategie del romanzo inglese contemporaneo*. Parma: Pratiche Editrice.

Steiner, George (1967) Language and Silence. London: Faber and Faber.

Stetz, Margaret D. (2012) 'Enrobed and Encased: Dying for Art in A.S. Byatt's *The Children's Book*'. *Journal of Victorian Culture* 17.1: 89–95.

Steveker, Lena (2009) *Identity and Cultural Memory in the Fiction of A.S. Byatt: Knitting the Net of Culture*. Basingstoke: Palgrave MacMillan.

Stewart, Jack (2008) 'Still Life in Byatt's *Still Life*'. *Symbolism: An International Annual of Critical Aesthetics* 8: 43–68.

Stewart, Jack (2009) 'Ekphrasis and Lamination in Byatt's *Babel Tower*'. *Style* 43.4: 494–516.

Stewart, Jack (2011) '"Living Metaphor" in *Still Life*'. *Symbolism: An International Annual of Critical Aesthetics* 11: 169–192.

Stuby, Anna Maria (1992) *Liebe, Tod und Wasserfrau: Mythen des Weiblichen in der Literatur*. Wiesbaden: Westdeutscher Verlag.

Taylor, David John (1993) 'Reading the 1950s: A.S. Byatt's *The Virgin in the Garden* and *Still Life*'. *After the War. The Novel and English Society since 1945*. London: Chatto and Windus. 90–102.

Todd, Richard (1997) *A.S. Byatt*. Plymouth: Northcote House.

Tredell, Nicolas (1994) 'A.S. Byatt'. *Conversations with Critics*. Manchester: Carcanet. 58–74.

Tripp, Ronja (2013) *Mirroring the Lamp*. Trier: WVT.

Turner, Mark (1996) *The Literary Mind*. New York: Oxford University Press.

Turner, Mark (2006) 'The Art of Compression'. *The Artful Mind*. Ed. Mark Turner. New York: Oxford University Press.

Turner, Victor (1986) *The Anthropology of Performance*. New York: PAJ Publications.

Uhsadel, Katharina (2005) *Antonia Byatts Quartet in der Tradition des englischen Bildungsroman*. Heidelberg: Winter.

Uhsadel, Katharina (2012) 'The Continuity of Victorian Traces: A.S. Byatt's *The Children's Book*'. *Journal of Victorian Culture* 17.1: 72–79.

Wachtel, Eleanor (1994) *Writers & Company in Conversation with Eleanor Wachtel*. San Diego: Harcourt Brace & Co. 77–89.

Walezak, Emilie (2018) 'A. S. Byatt, Science, and the Mind/Body Dilemma'. *Journal of Literature and Science* 11.1: 106–119. Available at <http://www.literatureandscience.org/> Accessed 6 August 2018.

Wallhead, Celia M. (1999) *The Old, the New and the Metaphor: A Critical Study of the Novels of A.S. Byatt*. London: Minerva Press.

Warburg, Aby (1998) *Il rituale del serpente*. Afterword Ulrich Raulff. Milano: Adelphi. Trans. of *Schlangenritual. Ein Reisebericht* [1988]. London/Berlin: The Warburg Institute/Wagenbach.

Wasserman, Jason Adam and Stevenson, Shannon Lindsey. (2014) 'Bioethics'. *The Wiley Blackwell Encyclopedia of Health, Illness, Behavior, and Society*, 1st ed. Eds. William C. Cockerham, Robert Dingwall and Stella R. Quah. Hoboken, NJ: John Wiley & Sons. 116–124. Published Online: 21 FEB 2014. 1–9.

Waugh, Patricia (1995) *The Harvest of the Sixties*. Oxford: Oxford University Press.

Waugh, Patricia (2006) 'The Woman Writer and the Continuities of Feminism'. *A Concise Companion to Contemporary British Fiction*. Ed. James F. English. Malden: Blackwell. 188–208.

Waugh, Patricia (2007) 'Postmodern Fiction and the Rise of Critical Theory'. *A Companion to the British and Irish Novel 1945–2000*. Ed. Brian W. Shaffer. Malden: Blackwell. 65–82.

Webb, Ruth (1999) '*Ekphrasis* Ancient and Modern: The Invention of a Genre'. *Word and Image. A Journal of Verbal/Visual Enquiry* 15.1–4: 7–18.

Wells, Lynn (2003) *Allegories of Telling*. Amsterdam: Rodopi. 103–138.

Wells, Lynn (2007) 'A. S. Byatt's *Possession: A Romance*'. A Companion to the British and Irish Novel 1945–2000 [2005]. Ed. Brian W. Shaffer. Malden: Blackwell. 538–549.

Westlake, Michael (1989) 'The Hard Idea of Truth'. *PN Review* 15.4: 33–37.

Wheeler, Wendy (2006) '"The Loom of the Inordinate": A.S. Byatt's Woven Realism.' *British Fiction Today*. Eds. Philip Tew and Rod Mengham. London: Continuum. 165–176.

Whitehead, Anne (2009) *Memory*. London and New York: Routledge.

Wilson, David L. and Zack Bowen (2001) *Science and Literature: Bridging the Two Cultures*. Gainesville: University Press of Florida.

Worton, Michael (2001) 'Of Prisms and Prose: Reading Paintings in A.S.Byatt's Work'. *Essays on the Fiction of A.S. Byatt*. Eds. Alexa Alfer and Michael J. Noble. Westport: Greenwood. 15–30.

Yates, Frances A. (1964) *Giordano Bruno and the Hermetic Tradition*. London: Routledge.

Yates, Frances A. (1966) *The Art of Memory*. London: Routledge.

Yates, Frances A. (1969) *Theatre of the World*. Chicago: University of Chicago Press.

Yates, Frances A. (1977) *Astraea* [1975]. Harmondsworth: Penguin Books.

Yelin, Louise (1992) 'Cultural Cartography: A.S. Byatt's *Possession* and the Politics of Victorian Studies'. *Victorian Newsletter* 81 (Spring): 38–41.

List of Artworks

Literary and Cultural Studies, Theory and the (New) Media

Edited by Monika Fludernik and Sieglinde Lemke

Vol. 1 Zuzana Fonioková: Kazuo Ishiguro and Max Frisch: Bending Facts in Unreliable and Unnatural Narration. 2015.

Vol. 2 Michael Weber: Die Chronologie von Emily Brontës *Wuthering Heights*. 2017.

Vol. 3 Monika Fludernik / Henrik Skov Nielsen (eds.): Travelling Concepts: New Fictionality Studies. 2020.

Vol. 4 Golnaz Shams: Social Minds in Drama: The Delineation of Mentalities and Collectives. 2020.

Vol. 5 Mara Cambiaghi: A.S. Byatt's Art of Memory. 2020.

Vol. 6 Michael Weber: Timelines in Emily Brontë's *Wuthering Heights*. 2020.

www.peterlang.com/view/serial/LICUS